Chasing Dragons:
An Introduction to the
Martial Arts Film

CHASING DRAGONS: AN INTRODUCTION TO THE MARTIAL ARTS FILM

David West

I.B. TAURIS

LONDON · NEW YORK

Published in 2006 by I.B.Tauris & Co Ltd
6 Salem Road, London W2 4BU
175 Fifth Avenue, New York NY 10010
www.ibtauris.com

In the United States of America and Canada
distributed by Palgrave Macmillan a division of St Martin's Press
175 Fifth Avenue, New York NY 10010

ISBN-10: 1 85043 982 6
ISBN-13: 978 1 85043 982 0

A full CIP record for this book is available from the British Library
A full CIP record is available from the Library of Congress

Library of Congress Catalog Card Number: available

Typeset in Palatino by JCS Publishing Services
Printed and bound in India by Replika Press Pvt. Ltd.

Contents

Illustrations

Acknowledgements

Thanks to Patrick Evans at Artsmagic (www.artsmagic.co.uk), David at Darwall Smith Associates, Paul Smith at Metro-Tartan Video (www.tartanvideo.com), Simon and the Ronald Grant Archive, Lisa DeBell at the Associates, Rachel Dengiz and Carter Logan at Plywood Productions, Dee and Sambrooke at Momentum Pictures. I am also grateful to Philippa Brewster at I.B.Tauris, Jessica Cuthbert-Smith, Lyn and Morley West and special thanks go to Danielle and Marielle.

Introduction

There have been systems of combat, both armed and empty-handed, in countless different cultures throughout history, from the Ancient Greek arts of wrestling and *pankration*, through to the development of boxing in England in the eighteenth century, to the Eastern martial arts like *Shotokan* karate and *Wing Chun* kung fu. There is one offspring of all these that was a singular phenomenon of the twentieth century – the art of screenfighting. With the advent of motion pictures, performers have trained to fight not for honour or revenge, but for the camera. In any given film, screenfighting may include elements from a number of distinct schools of combat, or may showcase the techniques of one particular style. There does not seem to be a direct correlation between real fighting ability and screenfighting skills – some very talented kickboxers have made poor screen combatants – so it seems that fighting for the movies is an art related to, but yet peculiar from, the traditional martial arts themselves. This book is about those performers who fight at twenty-four frames per second and the filmmakers who bring their highly specialised and physically demanding craft to the screen.

The book is divided geographically, covering the cinemas of Japan, Hong Kong and the United States, and tackles the films in a roughly chronological manner. Rather than try to offer an encyclopedia of martial arts cinema, the focus is on particular filmmakers and performers whose contributions to the genre have been substantial. The film titles I have used are from the English-language releases where possible; where there was no English-language release I have followed the transliteration of the title that has been used in other publications. There is a glossary for those unfamiliar with the terminology of martial arts movies.

Japan

Japan – A Selective History

This introduction covers the periods of history commonly referenced in Japanese martial arts movies and the origins of the social
hierarchy that pervades Japan to this day. All dates are measured by
the Western calendar.

The origins of the line of the Japanese imperial family have been
lost to history, but the Emperor Temmu, who reigned from AD 673
to 686, fostered the belief that the royal line was descended from a
god named Jimmu, the great-great-grandson of Amaterasu, the Sun
Goddess. The divinity of the emperor has been important to the survival of the imperial household. The geographical nature of Japan, a
series of mountainous islands, meant that several centuries of civil
war passed before Japan approached unification. From AD 1180 to
1185, Japan saw civil war between the powerful Minamoto and
Taira clans. The Taira were defeated and Minamoto Yoritomo
became the de facto ruler of the country. To legitimise his authority,
he had Emperor Go-Toba give him the title *seii tai-shogun*, meaning
'barbarian-subduing great general', commonly abbreviated to shogun, relegating the emperor to a powerless figurehead. In 1333 the
Ashikaga clan took over the shogunate and the country remained
relatively quiet until 1441, when the sixth Ashikaga shogun was
assassinated. The title passed to his eight-year-old son, who died in
1443. Control then passed from the shogun to the local military leaders, the *shugo*, and civil war broke out once more.

This period of conflict, the Onin War, began in 1467. The *shugo*
families battled each other into extinction and other families rushed
to fill the power vacuum. In 1491 Hojo Soun, a sixty-year-old

samurai, called himself *daimyo*, meaning 'big name' and set out to seize as much territory as possible. Others followed his example and the age of the *daimyo* began.

The Portuguese introduced firearms to Japan in 1542 as the fighting raged on. In 1570 Oda Nobunaga became shogun and began to pacify the country. In 1582 Nobunaga was assassinated and replaced by Toyotomi Hideyoshi, who continued to subjugate the warring factions. Hideyoshi passed a law that forbade anyone who was not a samurai from carrying a long sword, thus elevating the warrior class and disarming the general populace. In 1600 at the Battle of Sekigahara, Hideyoshi's son, Toyotomi Hideyori, was defeated by Tokugawa Ieyasu, marking the start of the Tokugawa dynasty, which would last for over three centuries.

In 1603 Tokugawa Ieyasu formally became shogun, the first time the title had been used since 1588, marginalising Emperor Go-Yozei. Ieyasu and his heirs brought peace to Japan through absolute control, building upon the foundations laid by Nobunaga and Toyotomi. They established a complex bureaucracy called the *bakufu* to run the country. Under this system the *daimyo* became regional governors and the samurai became bureaucrats. To prevent insurgency, the *daimyo* were relocated away from their traditional provinces, cutting off local support. They were required to spend half of every year in the capital Edo and many were ordered to leave their families there permanently, where they would be executed at the first hint of rebellion. The system was ruthless and all pervasive, covering numerous details of everyday life, from forbidding peasants to leave their fields in search of new jobs, to dictating the appropriate clothing for each social class, and governing where households were allowed to construct toilets. During the 1630s, fearing that the influence of the West – particularly Christianity – would undermine the shogun's authority, Japan went into *sekoku* – national seclusion. From 1635 the Japanese were forbidden from travelling overseas, while those Japanese residing outside their homeland were banned from returning under penalty of execution. The country was frozen in time, with little access to foreign developments in technology. It preserved peace but the cost was stagnation.

The Tokugawa dynasty is the most popular period for samurai films because it presented the warrior class with a dilemma. During the years of civil war the samurai had been in constant demand, but with peace there was a sudden surplus of fighting men. Samurai with permanent posts in wealthier households were guaranteed an income and employment, but the *ronin*, masterless samurai, had to make a living in a world where their fighting skills were no longer required. Some became bandits, gamblers (*yakuza*), or joined sword-fighting schools.

The feudal system was dismantled in 1868 when the Emperor Matsuhito was restored to power by an alliance of anti-shogunate clans in the Meiji Restoration. This was the beginning of the end for the samurai class. The wearing of swords was banned and the stipends paid to samurai were phased out. Japan opened up to foreign trade and the shogunate disappeared. There followed a brief period of relative intellectual and social growth during the time surrounding the reign of the Emperor Taisho (1912–26), until the militaristic nature of the Japanese state re-asserted itself. Fearful of foreign invasion, Japan poured its resources into the military and set about building an empire, bringing to an abrupt end the promise of the Taisho period. The invasions of China and Korea followed, accompanied by horrific human rights abuses committed by the Japanese forces. Japan entered the Second World War allied to the Axis powers and made the catastrophic mistake of bombing Pearl Harbor, bringing the United States into the war.

In the final days of the Second World War, when an American invasion of Japan seemed inevitable, there was the real possibility that the emperor would order the entire nation to commit ritual suicide rather than face the humiliation of defeat. Mercifully, the emperor did not make this order, called the Honourable Death of the Hundred Million (*ichioku gyokusai*), and the American occupation lasted seven years. Democracy was introduced to Japan with universal suffrage and the emperor was once more reduced to the role of figurehead. Unfortunately for Japanese cinema the Allied firebombing destroyed much of the country's film heritage. The handful of prints that survived were still not safe after the war, as the American administration set up the Civil and Education Section to review scripts for both new films and those movies still extant. Many films deemed counter-productive to the occupation were burnt, further depleting the number of pre-war films that survived.

After the war the prodigious energy of the Japanese was directed at manufacturing, leading to rapid industrialisation and the code of loyalty that had bound samurai to *daimyo* transformed into the loyalty between worker and employer.

Key Terms

There are several terms and ideas that are central to any discussion of Japanese martial arts cinema. The most obvious of these is samurai, meaning 'retainer'. *Ronin* refers to a masterless samurai, one with no fixed job or position. During the Tokugawa period the class system, *shi-no-ko-sho*, comprised four major groups, samurai, peasants, artisans and merchants. The peasants had the worst deal: they grew the rice upon which everyone relied, yet they were powerless and had virtually no rights. They shouldered the burden of paying taxes, calculated in rice, which was measured in units of *koku*, each *koku* being the amount of rice necessary to feed one man for one year. By contrast, the samurai, who accounted for roughly six per cent of the population, effectively produced nothing, but because they were at the top of the hierarchy, they reaped the benefits of the peasants' labour.

It was a deeply unjust system and in part it owed its survival to the notion of *shushigaku*. This is the concept of pre-determinism – that the circumstances of a person's life are decided before birth and are unalterable. There was very little movement up or down the class system. Born a samurai, die a samurai. Born a peasant, die a peasant. *Shushigaku* is a driving force in many movies.

Two other important terms are *giri* and *ninjo*. *Giri* means duty, the allegiance and obedience owed to a feudal lord, to one's clan. In contrast, *ninjo* means personal desire and is frequently at odds with *giri*. There is a long tradition of stories dealing with the conflict between these two opposing forces, going back at least as far as the plays written for the puppet theatre by Chikamatsu Monzaemon (1653–1725).

Bushido was the code of conduct that governed the lives of the samurai. The best distillation of the ideology of *bushido* is in the book

Hagakure (meaning 'hidden by leaves' or 'hidden leaves'). The book is a collection of the thoughts of a retired samurai called Yamamoto Tsunetomo recorded by a young clerk Tashiro Tsuramoto between 1710 and 1716. Yamamoto was born in 1659 and worked as a bureaucrat under Nabeshima Mitsushige (1632–1700). When his master died, he retired from public life, shaved his head and became a Buddhist priest. Yamamoto's *bushido* was intensely nihilistic: 'The Way of the Samurai is found in death. When it comes to either/or, there is only the quick choice of death' (Yamamoto, 2000, p. 17).

Hagakure was much beloved by Mishima Yukio, the writer who committed *hara-kiri* (ritual suicide) in November 1970. The book was popular during the Second World War, when it was given to soldiers to fill them with the spirit of *bushido*, although its popularity plunged after the war, when it was seen as part of Japan's unsuccessful imperial doctrine. Mishima embraced the nihilism in Yamamoto's work, writing: '… [Yamamoto] is concerned with death as a decision, not with natural death. He spoke not of resignation to death from illness, but of resolution to self-destruction' (Mishima, 1977, p. 46). William Scott Wilson, who translated an English language edition of *Hagakure*, had this to say about Yamamoto:

> In his twenty years of service he did nothing for which he is noted in Japanese history, and today his name is virtually unknown to the Japanese public. It is a fact that he never once participated in a battle, and the values that he advocated belonged to a period almost one hundred years before his time. (Yamamoto, 2000, p. 15)

Considering that Yamamoto did not take part in one single battle, such macho posturing and virulent nihilism must be taken with a pinch of salt:

> A certain person was brought to shame because he did not take revenge. The way of revenge lies in simply forcing one's way into a place and being cut down. There is no shame in this … No matter if the enemy has thousands of men, there is fulfilment in simply standing them off and being determined to cut them all down, starting from one end. You will finish the greater part of it. (Yamamoto, 2000, p. 29)

Yamamoto died quietly in his bed at the age of sixty-one. The famous Japanese story, 'The Vendetta of the Loyal Forty-Seven Ronin' (*Kanadehon Chushingura*) by Seika Mayama, offers a perfect example of Yamamoto's interpretation of *bushido*. The story was first performed as a puppet play in 1746 and subsequently as *kabuki* theatre and has been adapted for the cinema many times. The tale concerns forty-seven *ronin* who take revenge for the death of their master, then commit suicide. The story was banned by the Allied occupation forces after the Second World War as it was deemed too militaristic and a hindrance to the modernisation and pacification of Japan.

Kurosawa Akira

Many people have suggested that I write an autobiography, but I have never felt favourably disposed toward the idea. This is partly because I believe that what pertains only to myself is not interesting enough to record and leave behind me. More important is my conviction that if I were to write anything at all, it would turn out to be nothing but talk about movies. In other words, take 'myself', subtract 'movies' and the result is 'zero'. (Kurosawa, 1983, p. xi)

Kurosawa's *Rashomon* won first prize at the 1951 Venice Film Festival and was pivotal in opening the doors to the West for Japanese filmmakers. Kurosawa Akira was born in 1910 and his father, Kurosawa Yutaka, was a member of the last generation of samurai. Yutaka took his son on regular trips to the cinema to see both Japanese and foreign movies, sowing the seeds of his interest in film. As a young man Kurosawa was a struggling painter, he joined the Proletarian Artists' League and was involved with the radical underground left for a short time. In 1935 he answered a newspaper advertisement announcing that PCL (the Photo Chemical Laboratory, one of the smaller Japanese filmmaking studios) was hiring assistant directors. Kurosawa served much of his apprenticeship at PCL with director Yamamoto Kajiro, whose influence on him was profound. Yamamoto insisted that his assistant directors learnt every aspect of filmmaking, so Kurosawa's training encompassed everything from editing to set construction and acting as an extra. Yamamoto told Kurosawa that if he wanted to direct he had to be a scriptwriter first, so Kurosawa applied himself to writing with vigour. Many of his early screenplays were published in film journals, won awards or were produced by other directors.

On *Horses* (1941), Kurosawa served as second unit director to Yamamoto, who had such confidence in his protégé that Kurosawa was given responsibility for directing a large part of the film. When the movie was completed, he set about trying to find a project for his official directorial debut.

Sugata Sanshiro (1943)

... I was reading the newspaper one day when an advertisement for a new book caught my eye. It was for a novel called *Sugata Sanshiro*, and for some reason my interest was terrifically aroused. The advertisement described the content only as the story of a rowdy young judo expert, but I just had a gut feeling that 'This is it.' There was no logical explanation for my reaction, but I believed wholeheartedly in my instinct and did not doubt for an instant. (Kurosawa, 1983, p. 121)

Kurosawa's screenplay was adapted from Tomita Tsuneo's novel and the movie contains numerous elements that became intrinsic to the martial arts film: the clash of rival martial arts styles, the climactic duel, the relationship between master and student, the connection between victory over oneself and victory over one's opponent. It is a blueprint for the 1970s kung fu cinema of Hong Kong.

The movie tells the story of Sugata Sanshiro (Fujita Susumu) and his evolution as a *judoka* (see Glossary). After watching a gang of jiu-jitsu men meet defeat at the hands of judo master Shogoro Yano (Denjiro Okochi), Sanshiro becomes his disciple. The robust Sanshiro is an able student but gets into trouble for picking fights. Scolded by his master he spends the night in a pond. With the dawn, Sanshiro sees a lotus flower opening and he experiences a moment of revelation. Meanwhile, a dangerous jiu-jitsu master, Gennosuke Higaki (Ryunosuke Tsukigata), is beating up judo students and desires a match with Sanshiro. They fight on a windswept mountainside and Sanshiro emerges victorious.

The rivalry between different martial arts schools is apparent in the conflict between jiu-jitsu and judo. Historically, Jigoro Kano developed judo from his study of jiu-jitsu and in the film judo is spiritually progressive, concerned with developing its students into complete human beings, as Jigoro Kano wrote:

Judo is the way to the most effective use of both physical and spiritual strength. By training you in attacks and defenses it refines your body and your soul and helps you make the spiritual essence of judo a part of your very being. In this way you are able to perfect yourself and contribute something of value to the world. (Kazuzo, 1967, p. 9)

The conflict is framed as the battle between progressive (judo) and regressive (jiu-jitsu). The jiu-jitsu men challenge the judo master because they fear change; they are unenlightened. At the start of the story Sanshiro is in need of spiritual growth too. After brawling with the locals, he has to face his *sensei*, Shogoro, who rebukes his errant pupil:

Shogoro:	I rather wanted to see you in action. You're very strong, really very strong indeed. Maybe you are even stronger than I am now. But you know, there is very little similarity between your kind of judo and my kind of judo. Do you know what I mean? You do not know how to use it, you do not know the way of life. And to teach judo to someone who does not know that is like giving a knife to a madman.
Sanshiro:	But I know it.
Shogoro:	That is a lie. To act as you do, without meaning or purpose, to hate and attack – is that the way of life? No, the way is loyalty and love. This is the natural truth of heaven and earth. It is the ultimate truth and only through it can a man face death.

Sanshiro leaps into the garden pond and spends the night clinging to a post. He could climb out but is attempting to impress his master with this willingness to face death, presumably by freezing or drowning. This reflects the samurai spirit and nihilism found in *bushido*, but Kurosawa rejects this mindset. When the lotus petals open at dawn, Sanshiro is spiritually reborn; this scene is indebted to Yoshikawa Eiji's novel *Miyamoto Musashi*, about the famous swordsman. Both stories see the development of a martial artist's technique as inseparable from his development as a human being.

Thereafter the film concerns itself with the rivalry between judo (whose power to enlighten has now been demonstrated) and jiu-jitsu. Sanshiro fights jiu-jitsu master Hansuke Murai (Shimura Takashi, one of Kurosawa's regulars throughout his career) at a demonstration for the local police. This fight contains little in terms of detailing martial arts techniques. The best sequences are in the first half of the film, when Shogoro throws the jiu-jitsu men into the river and when Sanshiro throws the locals around at the fair. In these scenes the throws are clearly demonstrated for the audience. In the match with Hansuke, one of the combatants will move in for a throw, often with the camera in a medium close-up. The image then cuts to an empty frame into which a body tumbles. The throws themselves occur off-screen. Kurosawa is less interested in the physical techniques than in the philosophical bearing of his characters.

Reflecting the wartime sensibilities under which the film was made, the villainous Gennosuke dresses in Western fashions, while everyone else wears Japanese clothes. Gennosuke's lack of enlightenment is linked with his adoption of Western manners. It is difficult to attach any anti-Western sentiment to Kurosawa, who was an avid consumer of all cinema, foreign or not, and whose work was criticised in Japan as being too Western. It is likely that this element exists to satisfy the censors from the Ministry of the Interior, who were on the lookout for anything they could label 'too Anglo-American'.

The final duel takes place on a mountainside in a gale and it is a visually impressive sequence, but Kurosawa is not interested in the martial arts techniques themselves. Gennosuke strangles Sanshiro with a technique called *gyaku-juji-shime*, whereby he uses the lapels of Sanshiro's *judogi* jacket to cut off the blood supply to the brain. The image cuts to the clouds racing by overhead, then to the flower opening in the pond, the moment of Sanshiro's enlightenment. The image cuts back to Sanshiro, no longer grimacing, and he brushes off Gennosuke's strangle. Sanshiro throws Gennosuke and the fight is over. Kurosawa skips over the technical question of how Sanshiro breaks free from Gennosuke's stranglehold because the scene is about judo, not as technique, but as a path to enlightenment. It is not a naturalistic expression of combat, but an expressionistic one, revealing the central theme of the story – defeating one's opponent means defeating oneself, an idea that permeates the martial arts genre.

Sanshiro Sugata, Part Two (1945)

Kurosawa followed *Sanshiro Sugata* with *The Most Beautiful* (1944), about young women working in a factory to support the war effort. Kurosawa married the leading actress, Yaguchi Yoko, in 1945. After

The Most Beautiful, he was instructed by Toho Studios (the renamed PCL) to make a sequel to *Sanshiro Sugata*. In the director's autobiography, he comments: '*Sugata Sanshiro, Part Two* was not a remake, so the situation could have been worse, but it was still a question of refrying to a certain extent. I had to force myself to arouse the desire to go back to it and continue it' (Kurosawa, 1983, p. 135).

Like *Sanshiro Sugata*, the plot contains many elements central to the genre. Set in 1887, Sanshiro saves a young Japanese boy from being beaten by an American sailor. Consequently the American ambassador invites Sanshiro to a boxing exhibition, where he is horrified to see a down-on-his-luck jiu-jitsu man take a thrashing from an American boxer. The two younger brothers of Gennosuke, the villain from the first film, challenge Sanshiro. His *sensei* forbids him to fight, but Sanshiro fights the American boxer to demonstrate the superiority of Japanese martial arts. He accepts the challenge from Tesshin, Gennosuke's brother, who is a *karateka*. Sanshiro wins the battle and all is well with the world. This is probably the least well regarded of Kurosawa's films. Donald Richie has described it as: '... so very bad ... The first *Sugata* managed to avoid all of the clichés of the wartime Japanese film; the second subscribes to most of them' (Richie, 1984, p. 24).

Sanshiro Sugata, Part Two was released three months before the Japanese surrendered at the end of the Second World War. Made in Japan's darkest hour, it is a blatant piece of anti-US propaganda. This is forgivable given the circumstances in which it was made and the director was under pressure from the Ministry of the Interior to support their anti-American agenda. More problematic is the handling of the action sequences in which Kurosawa displays scant regard for either historical accuracy or cinematic technique.

The film begins in 1887 when the heavyweight boxing champion of the world was John L. Sullivan, who won the title under the rules of the London prize ring, fighting with bare knuckles, rounds ending with knockdowns, in a squared-off ring usually in a field or on a barge to evade the attention of the authorities. The Marquis of Queensbury rules, which forbade grappling and introduced padded gloves and three-minute rounds, would not be used in a title fight until 1892. In his prime, Sullivan was a fearsome fighter, weighing at least 190 pounds with an aggressive, brawling style. Kurosawa gives the audience William Lister, who the ring announcer in the film claims is America's finest and weighs 176 pounds. Lister fights with padded gloves, in a canvas-floored ring, using Queensbury rules. The actor who plays Lister is a terrible boxer and all the boxing scenes are poorly handled. The worst is the confrontation between Sanshiro and the American sailor, who performs a parody of boxing, moving his hands in circles with his palms facing upwards. He would only need to say 'C'mon, put 'em up, put 'em up' and he'd be the Lion from *The Wizard of Oz*. Whilst it is clear that the intention is to show the superiority of Japanese martial arts to Western fighting forms, the direction of these sequences is so weak as to render such a message impotent. The 'boxers' can't fight, so Sanshiro's victories are meaningless. What Sanshiro needs is an opponent who is his equal, as Gennosuke was in *Sanshiro Sugata*. Sadly, Tesshin does not measure up. The script goes to some lengths to build him up as a serious menace, but the brothers are caricatures, Tesshin is bad and Genzaburo is mad – literally.

> We put him in a tousled long black wig like those used in the Noh drama. He wore white make-up all over his face, and bright red lipstick. We put him in a white costume and had him carry the 'bamboo grass of madness' that crazed characters in Noh plays hold. (Kurosawa, 1983, p. 136)

There is no depth to either of the two brothers. The duel between Tesshin and Sanshiro takes place on a snow-covered mountain, referencing the climax of the first film and mostly consists of Tesshin grimacing and shouting. Tesshin's strikes lack conviction and are unconvincing. At one point he swings at Sanshiro and misses and a moment later a small tree next to him breaks in half, causing the audience to burst out laughing, when I saw the film. After being shouted at for a long time, perhaps fed up with all the noise, Sanshiro throws Tesshin down the mountainside.

In the next scene Tesshin is badly injured and bedridden. Why rolling down a mountainside covered in thick, soft snow would have been so traumatic is not explained. As in the first movie, Kurosawa is not concerned with the practical applications of judo; Sanshiro triumphs because he is the more enlightened person. This idea is not expressed with the same eloquence as in the earlier film, but is still present. Sanshiro tends to the injured Tesshin, enunciating his nobility and kindness. This is comparable to the Wong Fey Hung series made in Hong Kong, where the man of virtue always triumphs precisely because he is virtuous (for more about Wong Fey Hung, see the Hong Kong section).

Three people are credited with contributions to the choreography – Sato Kinnosuke and Takamura Norikazu for the judo and Konishi Yasuhiro for the karate – but there is no one listed for boxing. The film's lack of historical accuracy is disappointing in a director usually meticulous in his re-creations of period settings, but when the film is viewed in the light of Japan's wartime predicament, it is a little more understandable.

A key element that Kurosawa introduced to the martial arts movie with *Sanshiro Sugata, Part Two* was the spirit of national pride. Sanshiro's decision to fight William Lister springs from his desire to restore the good name of Japanese martial arts after the defeat of the jiu-jitsu man. This became a vital component of 1970s kung fu cinema and in such films more is at stake than the hero's personal status; the pride of his whole country is on the line. If the American boxer had knocked out Sanshiro, it would have meant that Japanese martial arts, Japanese culture and the Japanese themselves were inferior to their foreign counterparts. It is not a sophisticated polemic, but is easily communicated to an audience and satisfies a nation's vanity.

Seven Samurai (1954)

Mifune Toshiro was an aerial photographer in the Japanese air force during the war and joined Toho Studios hoping to become a cameraman. When there were no openings in the camera department he auditioned for the 'New Faces' programme, a scheme intended to create a roster of fresh acting talent. In his autobiography, Kurosawa remembers Mifune's audition:

> A young man was reeling around the room in a violent frenzy. It was as frightening as watching a wounded or trapped savage beast trying to break loose. I stood transfixed. But it turned out that the young man was not really in a rage, but had drawn 'anger' as the emotion he had to express in his screen test. He was acting. When he finished his performance, he regained his chair with an exhausted demeanor, flopped

down and began to glare menacingly at the judges. (Kurosawa, 1983, p. 160)

The untrained Mifune had a raw energy that impressed Kurosawsa sufficiently that he intervened to ensure Mifune was accepted. Mifune's first leading role was in *Snow Trail* (1947), directed by Taniguchi Senkichi, from a screenplay by Taniguchi and Kurosawa. Taniguchi cast Mifune, despite the latter telling him that he had no interest in acting. Kurosawa and Mifune made their first film together with *Drunken Angel* (1948) and thereafter they collaborated repeatedly, making a total of fifteen movies before they parted ways following *Red Beard* (1965). Of these, the most celebrated is 1954's *Seven Samurai*, concerning a group of farmers who learn that a gang of bandits are planning to ransack their village after the barley harvest. Facing starvation, the villagers hire seven samurai to defend them, led by Kambei (Shimura Takashi), along with Katsushiro,

1. Kikuchiyo (Mifune Toshiro) and the other six *ronin* from *Seven Samurai*. Kambei (Shimura Takashi) is second from the right.

Kyuzo, Gorobei, Heihachi, Sichiroji and Kikuchiyo (Mifune Toshiro). The samurai fortify the village, rally the farmers and defeat the bandits, losing four of their number in the process.

In pure genre terms this is better described as a *jidai-geki* (period drama), than as a *chambara* (swordplay film). There is no universally accepted way to distinguish between the two genres, since both feature period settings and may concern samurai and contain sword duels. However, the essence of the *chambara* is the isolated protagonist who lives by his sword. *Seven Samurai* is an ensemble piece, with no central, alienated hero, so – despite the many battle scenes – it fits more easily under the *jidai-geki* heading.

The script is an adventure story about heroic samurai, yet Kurosawa does not celebrate *bushido*, but examines it as a way of life and finds it wanting. Kurosawa was by nature anti-militaristic and he is not interested in these samurai because they embody the warrior code. He finds the characters attractive because they defy the conventions of *bushido*. Samurai wore their hair in topknots, the loss of which was so humiliating that most samurai would commit suicide should they lose theirs (as in Kobayashi's *Harakiri*). When the farmers meet Kambei, the samurai is shaving off his hair to disguise himself as a monk and rescue a baby held hostage by a thief. Kambei's willingness to sacrifice his status immediately marks him out as an exceptional samurai. This articulates the film's central theme: these *ronin* are willing to make sacrifices to protect the helpless. It is a motif repeated throughout the story, when Heihachi dies rescuing Rikichi the farmer during the raid on the bandit camp, or when three of the samurai die defending the village.

Ever the humanist, Kurosawa is just as interested in the farmers as in the samurai. Farmers Rikichi, Manzo, Yohei and Gisaku are all developed characters, with strengths and failings of their own. Manzo is petty and fatalistic. Possessed by a spirit of *shushigaku*, he is inclined to give up when he learns of the bandits' plan to ransack the village. When Rikichi suggests that they make bamboo spears and fight, Manzo argues with him.

Manzo: They'd kill us all if we lost, even pregnant women and babies.
Rikichi: Anything's better than this. Either we kill them, or they kill us.
Manzo: We were born to suffer; it's our fate. If they come, let's give them the crop without a struggle.

Manzo is resigned to a life of misery, believing that he is trapped by the feudal system and powerless to resist fate, although Kurosawa saves his most powerful condemnation of the feudal system for the *ronin* Kikuchiyo to enunciate. After Kikuchiyo finds a cache of weapons and armour that Manzo has stolen from murdered samurai, Kambei and the others are horrified. Heihachi comments 'I'd like to kill every single farmer in the village.' Kikuchiyo, enraged by the sanctimonious attitude of his comrades, makes an intensely passionate speech that is delivered almost direct to camera:

> Farmers are deceitful, miserly, cowardly, mean, stupid, murderous! You make me laugh! But who made animals of them? You did! You damned samurai! Whenever you fight you burn villages, destroy crops, take away food, rape women, enslave men, kill them if they resist! Do you hear, you damned samurai!?

Kurosawa's admiration for the bravery of the samurai is tempered by his awareness of the injustice of the times in which they lived. At the end, when four of the seven *ronin* have been killed, the farmers are seen working in the fields with Manzo and Rikichi singing happily. In sombre contrast, the three surviving samurai are shown against the backdrop of the graves of their comrades. Kambei comments 'We've lost yet again'. When Shochiroji looks at him, confused, Kambei continues 'The farmers are the victors ... not us'. To drive the point home, as the camera lingers on the four graves, the happy sound of the farmers singing is replaced by a dirge-like score and the image fades to black. Kurosawa mourns the nihilism inherent in *bushido* and he does not let the audience forget the ultimate fate of all warriors; sooner or later their path ends in death.

A major development from *Sanshiro Sugata* to *Seven Samurai* lies in Kurosawa's direction of the action scenes. The battles in *Seven Samurai* possess the essential quality of appearing to be out of control, unlike the stiffness of his earlier fight sequences. The final battle with the bandits takes place in a downpour, filling the screen with motion and chaos. The combat is furiously fast and Kurosawa's use of multiple cameras with long lenses has been copied ever since. The long lenses throw the viewer into the thick of the battle, heightening the emotional intensity of the scene as the cameras pick up the performers' every expression. When Kambei shoots a bandit off his horse, the bandit falls into a frame that is frantic with the legs of the horse, the farmers stabbing with their spears, and the incessant rain. The battle scenes in *Seven Samurai* mark a high point in the director's career.

Another key genre element found in *Seven Samurai* is the concept of a warrior undergoing a series of rites of passage, a journey to manhood, in this case performed by the youngest samurai Katsushiro (Kimura Ko). He falls in love, loses his virginity and kills his first man, but Kurosawa does not offer an endorsement of the warrior code. Katsushiro may have completed his rites of passage but after the bandits are dead, after Kyuzo and Kikuchiyo lie slain, Katsushiro falls to his knees and weeps. The naivety that he possessed when he first met Kambei is gone. He has tasted battle and followed the path of a samurai and instead of finding himself filled with bravery and potency, he cries. Kurosawa admires the samurai not for their martial skill, but for their humanity and compassion.

After *Seven Samurai*, Kurosawa made films in a variety of genres. *Record of a Living Being* (1955) was a contemporary drama about a man obsessed with the atomic bomb; *Throne of Blood* (1975) was a brilliant adaptation of *Macbeth*; *The Lower Depths* was a character-study piece. Then in 1958, Kurosawa returned to the *jidai-geki* with *Hidden Fortress*.

Hidden Fortress (1958)

Hidden Fortress is a straightforward adventure movie about a princess and the general who protects her on the run in enemy territory, although the two main characters are farmers, Tahei (Chiaki Minoru) and Matashichi (Fujiwara Kamatori). Kurosawa's humanism is hard at work, evinced by his choice of making the two farmers, who are petty, treacherous and vulgar, the focus of the story. Tahei and Matashichi constantly bicker and squabble, then swear loyalty to each other under duress, only to resume arguing when the danger has passed.

Kurosawa finds a connection between all members of society. Princess Yuki (Uehara Misa) orders her protector, Makabe Rokurota (Mifune Toshiro) to buy a slave girl from her abusive owner when they stop at an inn. Makabe does so with reluctance, but just as the princess saves the girl from a life of slavery, the girl in turn saves the princess from being raped by the farmers. This is replayed with Makabe and his rival Tadakoro Hyoei (Fujita Susumu from *Sanshiro Sugata*). When Makabe enters an enemy camp, in pursuit of a patrol, he is confronted by Hyoei and they agree to a duel. It is all conducted with classic samurai honour – they decide to battle, choose to fight with lances, and Hyoei patiently waits while Makabe selects a suitable lance. The duel is a highlight of the movie and demonstrates Kurosawa's continuing development in directing action sequences. The fight is performed with vigour and commitment from both performers. The choreography is excellent and the combatants interact with their environment, tearing through the encampment, which is shredded in the process. The duel ends when Makabe breaks Hyoei's lance and at this point Kurosawa reaffirms his rejection of *bushido*. Defeated, Hyoei waits for Makabe to kill him, but the victor drops his lance and walks away, telling Hyoei that they will meet again. Much later, after the princess, Makabe and the slave girl have been captured, Hyoei is sent to identify them. His face is heavily scarred and he tells Makabe that he should have killed him, rather than leave him alive to face his lord's wrath. The princess scolds Hyoei, 'What you make of another's kindness is up to you!' Subsequently Hyoei defects and frees the prisoners. As she turns to flee, the princess calls out 'Hyoei! Don't die a dog's death! Come with us!' He leaps onto a horse and follows Makabe and Yuki back to her clan's territory. The message here is to choose life, not death, however glorious self-destruction may be considered under the samurai code. As he escapes, Makabe takes the time to scoop up the slave girl; everyone is worth saving, regardless of social status.

Hidden Fortress has been criticised as being too lightweight, lacking any great philosophical depth or social commentary, but Kurosawa was not trying to be profound. After the darkness of *Throne of Blood* and *The Lower Depths*, the director wanted a change of mood with 'No heavy themes ... I want to make a 100% entertainment film, full of thrills and fun' (Galbraith, 2001, p. 253).

Nevertheless, Kurosawa's humanism is elegantly articulated by the princess. After their capture, she tells Makabe 'I saw people as they really are. I saw their beauty and ugliness with my own eyes. I thank you, Rokurota! I have no regrets in dying now.' This is a tidy encapsulation of Kurosawa's goal as a filmmaker – to show people in all their beauty and ugliness.

Miyamoto Musashi – Zen and Sword

Miyamoto Musashi, Japan's most famous swordsman, was born in the village of Miyamoto in the province of Mimasaka in 1584. After his mother died he was raised by a priest who was unable to restrain Musashi's violent temperament. In the introduction to his translation of Musashi's *A Book of Five Rings*, Victor Harris recounts Musashi's first recorded fight:

> Whether he was urged to pursue Kendo by his uncle, or whether his aggressive nature led him to it, we do not know, but it is recorded that he slew a man in single combat when he was just thirteen. The opponent was Arima Kihei, a samurai of the Shinto Ryu School of military arts, skilled with sword and spear. The boy threw the man to the ground, and beat him about the head with a stick when he tried to rise. Kihei died vomiting blood. (Miyamoto, 1989, p. 13)

Musashi's life was one of contrasts. He was capable of extraordinary violence and won over sixty duels, yet was interested in the arts, studied painting, and several of his ink-brush paintings survive. He mingled with priests, craftsmen and artisans and his most enduring legacy is the book he wrote when he was sixty years old. *A Book of Five Rings*, or *Go Rin No Sho*, contains Musashi's guide to strategy and is divided into five sections, Ground, Water, Fire, Wind and Void. Musashi devoted his life to mastering swordsmanship and self-improvement. It is strange now to think of this quest for perfection in terms of hacking people down with a sword, but for Musashi the constant fights and training were the best method for piercing the veil of dreams that hide enlightenment. Musashi's personal sword-style favoured using both the long and short swords simultaneously, although later in life he limited himself to using a wooden sword, having become unbeatable.

There have been several filmed versions of Musashi's life, based upon a mixture of historical facts and the serialised novel by Yoshikawa Eiji, originally published between 1935 and 1939. The two versions to be discussed here are the three-part series directed by Inagaki Hiroshi and starring Mifune Toshiro, and the five films directed by Uchida Tomu, starring Nakamura Kinnosuke. Other adaptations include Naruse Mikio's 1929 film and Mizoguchi Kenji's 1944 production, both titled *Miyamoto Musashi*.

Inagaki's three films, made between 1954 and 1956, offer a distinctly sanitised account of Musashi's life. The first film has had various titles depending on where and when it was released. In Japan it was simply *Miyamoto Musashi*, but in the West at one time or another it has been *The Legend of Musashi, Samurai,* and *Samurai I – Miyamoto Musashi*. It enjoyed considerable success in the West for a Japanese film, drawing critical praise for its use of colour (still a novelty in 1954) and winning an Honorary Oscar in 1955. Mifune Toshiro played the central role in Inagaki's films. Musashi was originally called Takezo and the first film begins with Takezo and his pal Matahachi joining the Ashikaga army for the Battle of Sekigahara (fought in 1600 between the forces of Toyotomi Hideyori and Tokugawa Ieyasu. Takezo and Matahachi joined Toyotomi's side. Toyotomi lost and his troops were routed). In the aftermath, Matahachi absconds with two women who sheltered the pair after the battle, while Takezo goes on the run. He is captured by the priest Takuan and locked in a room full of books for three years. When Takezo emerges, having begun his quest for enlightenment, Takuan gives him his new name and he sets out to follow the way of the samurai, leaving the lovesick girl Otsu behind. The story is action packed, featuring an impressive battle at Sekigahara and equally ferocious fights between Takezo and bandits and border guards. There is virtually no bloodshed or any post-dubbed sound effects in the fight sequences. Inagaki relies upon the skill of the performers to carry the action and this works well in the first film, where the battles feature Takezo fighting several opponents simultaneously. Inagaki uses long takes in wide shots to cover these fights. The distance between camera and subject helps to create the illusion of impact in the sword blows.

Duel at Ichijoji Temple (1955)

In the second film in the series, *Duel at Ichijoji Temple,* Inagaki stages a series of duels. The opening portrays Musashi's match with a sickle-and-chain fighter called Baiken. The direction of the one-on-one confrontations is not as convincing as that of the larger-scale battles. In the duel Baiken steps out of the frame and Musashi slashes at the point off-screen where it is implied Baiken is standing.

Baiken staggers back into view and falls to the ground. On first sight it is not very clear what has happened, for the viewer does not see Musashi's sword connect with Baiken. Inagaki never overcomes this problem; when Musashi duels with Denshichiro of the Yoshioka clan, the pair square off, exchange strikes and then Inagaki cuts to a different scene altogether. Musashi's technique is hidden from the audience and it is unsatisfying to be denied watching him win. Inagaki is a director of delicate sensibility regarding scenes of sex or violence. It is implied that Akemi, the second girl to follow Musashi around declaring her undying love, is raped by Yoshioka Seijuro, but it all happens off-screen and is only hinted at. This is preferable to the exploitative graphic nature of the *chambara* films made by Toho Studios in the 1970s, which featured innumerable violent rape scenes, but in the direction of the duels it is frustrating.

Duel at Ichijoji Temple suffers from a weak narrative, relying upon numerous coincidences to propel the plot. Musashi constantly bumps into both Akemi and Otsu, who continue to pine for him. Matahachi runs into his mother in the street; Akemi runs into Kojiro, the only swordsman whose ability rivals that of Musashi. Kojiro then runs into Otsu and Matahachi. Everybody keeps running into everyone else and the film becomes almost farcical. The melodramatic handling of the scenes in which different women – not just Akemi and Otsu, but also the famous courtesan Lady Yoshino (Kogure Michiyo) – swoon over Musashi does not help matters. Musashi rejects so many beautiful women that it makes one wonder about his sexual orientation. This was not Inagaki's intention, rather he was hoping to show that Musashi's dedication to self-improvement and swordsmanship was all consuming, but his handling of the romantic scenes is clumsy.

Lady Yoshino plays her part in Musashi's progress towards enlightenment, telling him that he lacks affection. In the film's climactic battle, when Musashi comes face-to-face with Seijuro, he easily overpowers the Yoshioka samurai, but spares his life. This is the first instance of Musashi showing compassion rather than destroying an enemy. Inagaki expands on this concept in the third film, *Duel at Ganryu Island* (1956), when Musashi refuses to be provoked into a fight with the spear master Agon, despite Agon's goading him. Inagaki portrays Musashi's emotional maturation as vital to his mastery of the sword, exploring the genre theme of the importance of self-mastery.

The culmination of the series is the duel between Musashi and Sasaki Kojiro, master of the 'swallow turn' technique, who employs a particularly long sword in combat. Again, the strike that wins the match and slays Kojiro is not shown to the audience. In a series of rapid and confusing shots the two men slash at each other and then leap apart. Kojiro smiles to see a small cut on Musashi's forehead, before falling to the ground dead. Inagaki used the same technique in the duel with Baiken in *Duel at Ichijoji Temple*, hiding the moment of impact. It doesn't work here either.

The five films about Musashi directed by Uchida Tomu were made between 1961 and 1965 and featured Nakamura Kinnosuke in the central role. *The Swordsman* and *Zen and Sword* are two of the English titles given to the first instalment, which was called *Miyamoto Musashi* in Japan. Uchida's film covers the same period as the first part of Inagaki's trilogy, although Uchida does not show the Battle of Sekigahara, opening his account in the bloody aftermath as Takezo and Matahachi go on the run. There is little action in the first movie, which instead concentrates on Takezo's volatile nature. Where Mifune played Takezo as a man with an explosive temper, Nakamura plays him as a raving maniac. It's a wild performance, intended to portray how far Takezo had to progress before reaching enlightenment. Unlike Inagaki, who leaves the moment of Takezo's spiritual awakening to happen off-screen, Uchida lets the audience share in his transformation. Locked in the room full of books, Takezo is surrounded by darkness. As he reads and begins to consider the spiritual dimension of life, dawn breaks and sunlight pours in through the shutters, illuminating Takezo's face amidst the shadows, and he experiences enlightenment. That's the end of the first film, and the second, *Showdown at Hannyazaka Height* (1962), delivers much more swordplay. It features Musashi fighting Agon, the spear-wielding priest, and has a spectacular battle against a gang of bandits. Uchida's action sequences are more ambitious than those of Inagaki and considerably less sanitised. In this version Musashi kills Agon in their confrontation and the battle with the bandits sees blood flowing freely. Musashi beheads one bandit with a single stroke, resulting in a huge spurt of blood. Unlike Inagaki, Uchida does not protect the audience from the brutality that was part of Musashi's nature. The best example of this is in their differing portrayals of Musashi's conflict with the Yoshioka clan.

In Inagaki's trilogy, Musashi acts with the greatest honour, despite the Yoshioka clan's attempts to murder him. Inagaki does not show Musashi slay Denshichiro onscreen and he spares Seijuro in their duel. This was artistic licence, for in reality Musashi battered the fallen Seijuro with a wooden sword until he had to be carried away. The only person left to challenge Musashi from the Yoshioka clan was Seijuro's young son, Hanshichiro, so the clan arranged a duel in his name and sent seventy swordsmen to ambush Musashi at Ichijoji Temple. This is absent from Inagaki's account of Musashi's life, which substitutes the adult Seijuro for the boy at Ichijoji, due to the ruthless manner in which the swordsman met this challenge. Uchida, by contrast, approaches the subject with relish in his fourth film *The Duel of Ichijoji* (1964). Musashi arrives at the site before dawn and cinematographer Yoshida Sadaji shot this sequence with a coloured filter, rendering the scene in shades of green and black. The Yoshioka clansmen arrive with Hanshichiro and Musashi runs screaming into their midst. He kills Hanshichiro with a single stroke and then cuts his way through the Yoshioka samurai. To avoid being surrounded, Musashi moves into the rice fields where thick mud prevents anyone from leaving the narrow paths. Unable to attack in numbers, the Yoshioka clansmen have to face Musashi individually and he slaughters them. In Inagaki's account, Musashi flees through the forest, rather than face the entire clan, but Uchida has his hero stay and fight to the bloody end. When all his enemies are dead – over seventy men – an exhausted Musashi collapses in a field of ferns. As the sun rises, the image slowly shifts from monochrome to colour and it becomes clear that the ground itself has turned red with the blood of the Yoshioka. It is a very powerful sequence, assisted by Nakamura's performance, which captures the savagery at the heart of the swordsman. Inagaki would never have depicted such brutality on the part of a man presented as the noble embodiment of the samurai spirit. Uchida's interpretation is more daring and reflects an approach to the subject that is not content with mere hero worship.

Both directors close their series with the duel between Musashi and Kojiro. Inagaki's staging of the duel emphasises the honour and nobility of all concerned. The two swordsmen approach each other with respect, their duel a perfect expression of *bushido* itself. Uchida is not so restrained. Where Mifune Toshiro portrayed Musashi as a little rough around the edges, in Uchida's *Musashi vs. Kojiro* (1965), Nakamura brings out the brutality for which the fighter was notorious. Having considered how to counter the extra length of Kojiro's blade, Musashi carves a wooden sword from an oar as he is en route to Ganryu Island. In Inagaki's film, Musashi advances up the beach and squares off with his opponent. In Uchida's version, he leaps out of the boat and hurls himself at Kojiro, screaming with murderous intent. There is no great respect evident between the combatants and the duel seems devoid of the chivalry found in the earlier film. Nakamura's Musashi clearly wants to kill his opponent, played on this occasion by the excellent Takakura Ken, where in Inagaki's film Musashi wins but his victory is tinged with remorse. The later version of the character has more in common with the sort of man idealised by Yamamoto Tsunetomo in *Hagakure*: 'Lord Naoshige said, "The Way of the Samurai is a mania for death. Sometimes ten men cannot topple a man with such conviction." One cannot accomplish feats of greatness in a normal frame of mind. One must turn frantic and develop a mania for dying' (Mishima, 1977, p. 134).

Uchida and Nakamura's version of the famous warrior may be a better approximation of the real man, whose savagery was well documented. The bloodiness of the action sequences reflects Uchida's choice to avoid shielding the audience from the horrific nature of combat as Inagaki had done. Nakamura is excellent throughout the series and his battles are staged with bravura. Uchida goes into more detail regarding Musashi's creation of his two-sword style in the third film *Duel Against Yagyu* (1963), and his decision to use the wooden oar in his duel with Kojiro. The numerous *chambara* films of the 1970s picked up where Uchida left off, with fight sequences drenched in blood and gore, but those films would have none of the redeeming qualities found in Uchida's work. Where the later films simply present action for the sake of entertainment, Uchida, like Inagaki, detailed Musashi's spiritual growth alongside his mastery of *kendo*.

The *Chambara* Film and the Hero as Stray Dog

Where the films based upon the life of Miyamoto Musashi reflect an interest in self-advancement and spirituality, the anti-heroes of the subsequent *chambara* films are unconcerned with notions of enlightenment. They are outsiders, alienated from polite society, hence the reference to stray dogs. The hero as outcast who wanders into town and stirs up trouble is an idea that finds resonance in many genres. It is present in the Western, in films like *Shane* (1953), in film noir including *Red Rock West* (1992), and in post-apocalyptic visions of the future, notably the Australian 'Mad Max' trilogy (1979, 1981, 1985).

Yojimbo (1961)

Yojimbo, meaning bodyguard, is one of the most popular collaborations between Kurosawa Akira and Mifune Toshiro. The film is invariably included in retrospectives of the director's career and has been much imitated, with American remakes including *A Fistful of Dollars* (1964) and *Last Man Standing* (1996).

Mifune plays a nameless *ronin* who wanders into a small town where two rival gangs are at war. The gangs are led by Ushitora – backed by Tazaemon the silk merchant – and Seibei, supported by Tokuemon the saké merchant. Sensing an opportunity to make some money, the *ronin*, calling himself Sanjuro, plays a game of hiring himself out to first one side, then to the other, for constantly increasing fees. He is exposed when he helps a farmer and his wife escape the clutches of Tokuemon and Sanjuro is captured and beaten. He escapes and recuperates while Ushitora wipes out Seibei's gang. Sanjuro returns for a final showdown in which he single-handedly decimates Ushitora's thugs. His work complete, Sanjuro turns and walks out of town.

This film eloquently enunciates the notion of the *chambara* hero as stray dog. At the start when the *ronin* stops for a drink at a farm, the farmer sneers, 'The scent of the blood attracts the hungry dogs'. As the *ronin* enters the town, a dog runs past him, carrying a severed hand in its mouth. The link between the *ronin* and the animal is reinforced when one of Ushitora's *yazuka* mocks him, 'Come on, it's a public road, even for dogs'. This is an essential trait of the *chambara* protagonist – he is a wandering outcast, a stray dog. His skills are only in demand where there is violence and unrest. In peace his deadly sword arm is of no value so he must follow the scent of blood. When Sanjuro first arrives in town, he cannot afford to pay the innkeeper for the food and saké he orders. Peace was a curse for many samurai under the feudal system. The *ronin* lived by his sword, for that was the only role society permitted him, in keeping with the belief in pre-determined fate. Kurosawa further comments on this through the minor character of the farmer's son. As the *ronin* stops for a drink, the farmer's son is planning to head into town to join one of the gangs:

Farmer: You'll be killed. Who wants to be a gambler? Stay at home and farm.

Son: Who wants a long life eating mush? A short, exciting life for me!

At the climax, the farmer's son is part of Ushitora's gang, but Sanjuro spares the young man, telling him to 'Go home! A long life eating mush is best'. The farmer's son runs off, back to his appointed place in life on the farm. Sanjuro does not kill the young man because he knows he is not supposed to be there – born a farmer, die a farmer. The class system offers no alternative.

Chambara are often compared to Westerns and Kurosawa has some fun with this idea through the character of Unosuke (Nakadai Tatsuya, another Kurosawa regular). Unosuke is a dandy with a pistol, the only gun in town, which he brandishes at every opportunity. Kurosawa makes fun of Unosuke's posturing and his obsession with his six-shooter. After being mortally wounded, Unosuke, bleeding on the ground, asks Sanjuro to hand him his gun, 'Without my pistol, I feel incomplete. I can't die without it. Let me hold it.' Sanjuro gives him the gun and Unosuke tries to shoot him, but collapses. His dying words are 'At the gate of hell ... I'll be waiting for you', making empty threats to the end; Sanjuro replies, 'He died as he lived'. Kurosawa does not consider the gun-wielding Unosuke to be the equal of a master swordsman like Sanjuro. Kurosawa himself was a student of *kendo* throughout high school and he is implying that any fool can pull a trigger, but using a sword takes talent.

The film is very funny as Kurosawa dismantles many *chambara* conventions. The *yakuza* in both gangs are cowards at heart. When

2. Sanjuro (Mifune Toshiro), the sword for hire from Kurosawa's much-imitated *chambara* classic, *Yojimbo*.

tricked into a face-to-face confrontation, the gangsters are terrified and hold their swords in trembling hands. When Seibei announces the attack to his men and exhorts them to be brave, he can't stop his hands from shaking as Sanjuro pours him a drink. They are completely lacking in the nihilistic spirit of *bushido*, which Yamamoto described as: '... a mania for death ...' (Mishima, 1977, p. 34). The *yakuza* are not resigned to death, but are petrified of getting hurt. This is why both Ushitora and Seibei are so keen to hire Sanjuro – here at last is someone not scared of combat. Seibei's resident swordmaster runs away rather than take part in a battle, disgraceful behaviour for even the lowliest samurai.

Unlike some of the later *chambara* characters, Sanjuro is not totally alienated from society. By intervening to save Kohei and his wife Nui from Tokueon's clutches, Sanjuro displays his compassionate side. This costs him when Unosuke finds the thank-you letter the farmer sends Sanjuro. It is at this point that Sanjuro finally becomes emotionally involved in the *yakuza* conflict, leading to the violent showdown at the film's climax. This sequence is brilliantly executed as Sanjuro faces ten members of Ushitora's gang. As Sanjuro and the *yakuza* advance on each other, the music is tense and ominous, building suspense by keeping time with their steps. Unosuke says 'Stay where you are!' Sanjuro shrugs, smiles, and his sword leaps into action. Nine men are cut down in moments, in a brilliant display of *iaido* and *kendo* (see Glossary); Mifune is a gifted screen swordsman. Unlike Uchida's Musashi series, or any of Toho Studios *chambara* films from the 1970s, *Yojimbo* is relatively bloodless. There are no arterial spurts of blood, no gaping wounds. The actions are convincing because of the performance, reflecting a tremendous improvement from *Sanshiro Sugata, Part Two*. Kurosawa would push this boundary back in the sequel to *Yojimbo*, simply titled *Sanjuro*.

Sanjuro (1962)

Made the following year, *Sanjuro* is not as popular as *Yojimbo* and is not revived as regularly in retrospectives, but it is more morally complicated than its predecessor. Once again the *ronin*, played by Mifune Toshiro, wanders into a town full of trouble. A group of nine young samurai believe they have uncovered evidence of corruption in the local government. Iori, their leader, reports their findings to his uncle Mutsuta, the chamberlain, who warns them to stay out of it. Iori goes to the local superintendent, Kikui, who agrees to meet the young samurai. Alas, Kikui is involved in the corruption and is setting the young men up. Sanjuro saves them from capture and the nine men reluctantly follow Sanjuro's lead to rescue the chamberlain's wife and daughter from Kikui's men. After the chamberlain is freed and order restored, Muroto, Kikui's right-hand man and a master swordsman, confronts Sanjuro, who reluctantly kills him, then leaves town.

Like *Yojimbo*, this is a comedy and may be described as a comedy of manners. Kurosawa relishes the opportunity to contrast the well-bred, immaculately dressed young samurai with the rough, scruffy and ill-mannered Sanjuro. The youngsters kneel with perfect posture whenever they sit, whilst Sanjuro slouches lazily, scratching himself like a dog, even when addressing the chamberlain's high-class wife. After he rescues them from Kikui's ambush, the samurai all bow to Sanjuro, saying, 'We don't know how to thank you.' He replies, 'You needn't. Just give me some money. I've not eaten for days.' This appalling lack of manners stuns the young men, who can't believe Sanjuro is so blunt about money, but Sanjuro is not interested in formality. He is practical and pragmatic and uses these traits to fullest advantage in handling Kikui and Muroto. To learn Kikui's plans, Sanjuro pretends to want to join his clan. Loyalty to one's master is a vital part of *bushido*, taken to extremes in the notion that loyal samurai should commit *hara-kiri* upon the death of their master. This particular form of *hara-kiri* was known as *tsuifuku*. Sanjuro feels no loyalty at all to Kikui and his behaviour is beyond the boundaries of *bushido*. When the young samurai hear that Sanjuro plans to offer his services to Kikui, they can't agree on his motives for doing so. The idea of tricking someone in that manner is so alien that half of them believe Sanjuro sincerely desires to join Kikui's clan. When Sanjuro's trickery is exposed, Muroto is so offended that he seeks out Sanjuro and challenges him. Sanjuro tries to talk him out of fighting, but Muroto is furious:

Sanjuro: Must you?
Muroto: Yes. You made fools of us. You're the most treacherous man I've ever met!
Sanjuro: Don't be angry. I couldn't help it. I respect you and ...

Muroto: It's too late now. Fight!

Clan loyalty is further diminished in the character of the guard taken prisoner by Iori and his companions. They lock him in a closet, but the chamberlain's wife lets him out, gives him clean clothes and food. When the samurai return, the guard quietly puts himself back in the closet. As he learns more about Kikui's activities, his loyalty shifts until he is supporting Iori's side. When the ruse to have Kikui dispatch his men to look for Iori at an old temple is successful, the young samurai and the guard all leap about in celebration, until the guard remembers that he is supposed to be their prisoner and meekly shuts himself back in the closet. It's ridiculous but then, for Kurosawa, so is *bushido*.

The greatest difference between *Sanjuro* and its predecessor is that in the second film Kurosawa is never willing to condone Sanjuro's violence. When the hapless guard is first captured, there is an exchange between Sanjuro and the chamberlain's wife about what to do with him:

Sanjuro:	Kill him. He saw us.
Chamberlain's Wife:	Don't do that. Did you kill the other guards?
Sanjuro:	Had to. To save you.
Chamberlain's Wife:	Forgive me, since you killed them to rescue us, but killing people on the slightest pretext is a bad habit. You glitter too much.
Sanjuro:	Glitter?
Chamberlain's Wife:	Like a drawn sword.
Sanjuro:	A drawn sword?
Chamberlain's Wife:	Like an unsheathed sword. You cut well, but a really good sword remains in its scabbard.

Sanjuro comes to endorse her opinion. When four of Iori's group are captured, Sanjuro kills their guards in a dazzling display of swordsmanship. Afterwards he is furious, 'You forced me to kill them!' he shouts before slapping the samurai. It is interesting to compare this to *Yojimbo*, where there was an undeniable glee in watching Sanjuro cut down the villainous *yakuza*. Ushitora's gang included the monstrous giant, the ugly, boar-like Inokichi and the posturing Unosuke. Their deaths are well deserved and Sanjuro's vengeance upon them is satisfying and uncomplicated. In the climactic duel of *Sanjuro*, there is sadness and a sense of futility. Sanjuro tries to talk Muroto out of fighting, the polar opposite to the eagerness with which he confronts the *yakuza* in *Yojimbo*, where he smiles immediately before drawing his sword. In the second film, Sanjuro is forced to fight and kills Muroto with a brilliant use of *iaido*, drawing his sword and striking in the same movement. The nine young samurai are impressed. 'Splendid!' says Iori. 'Fool! Don't be impertinent!' barks Sanjuro, 'Watch out! I'm in a bad mood. He was just like me, an unsheathed sword. We're not in our scabbards. But the lady is right, a really good sword remains in its scabbard. You'd do well to stay in yours. Don't follow me or I'll kill you!' The samurai kneel and bow. 'Goodbye' says Sanjuro, who turns and walks away, rejecting the hero worship of the young men just as Kurosawa rejects the self-destruction of *bushido*. This is a more complex and ambiguous ending than the climax of *Yojimbo*. Here, Kurosawa celebrates Sanjuro's skill while simultaneously condemning the loss of life that accompanies the application of that skill. Muroto may consider himself to be a villain, but Kurosawa sees him as another victim of *bushido*. It is this dynamic that distinguishes *Sanjuro* as Kurosawa commented: 'Personally, I think this film is very different from *Yojimbo*. In Japan the audience does too. The youngsters loved *Yojimbo*, but it was the adults who liked *Sanjuro*' (Richie, 1984, p. 162).

A second point of comparison is with the end of *Duel at Ganryu Island*, where Miyamoto Musashi, played by Mifune, is congratulated after slaying his rival Kojiro, with the words, 'That was splendid', the same compliment paid to Sanjuro. Musashi accepts the compliment and his victory is the ultimate expression of the character's quest for self-improvement, but Kurosawa cannot accept such a proposition. Sanjuro rejects the compliment, just as Kurosawa spurns the simple adulation of Inagaki's films about Musashi.

At the close Sanjuro heads out of town; this is the essence of the stray dog hero, who lives by his sword and his wits and must always move on to the next adventure. Sadly, most of the later *chambara* films lack the humanity and humour that Kurosawa and Mifune brought to the character of Sanjuro.

The Adventures of Zatoichi

That said, one long-running *chambara* series contained touches of humanism and an interest in the lower castes of Japanese feudal society that Kurosawa was so fond of. The star of the series was Katsu Shintaro who played Zatoichi (Ichi for short), a blind masseur who wanders from town to town in Tokugawa-era Japan. Katsu was born in 1931, the son of a musician, and started his career as a singer. He came to prominence as an actor in *Hakuoki* (1959), called *Samurai Vendetta* in the West, but became a household name in Japan with the success of the Zatoichi series. Zatoichi first appeared in a story by Kan Shimozawa, but it was on screen that the character became a staple of Japanese popular culture.

Being blind, Ichi is at the very bottom of the class system, looked down upon by everyone. He is a master swordsman and is feared as much as loathed by the *yakuza* he comes into conflict with. Katsu appeared in twenty-six movies about the blind swordsman, beginning in 1962 with *Zato Ichi Monogatari*, known in the West as either *The Life and Opinion of Masseur Ichi* or *The Tale of Zatoichi*. The series started at Daiei Studios, but after Daiei ceased movie production Toho took over. Following 1973's *Zatoichi in Desperation*, the character made the transition to a television series, lasting over 100 episodes, before making a final cinematic outing with the original star in 1989. Numerous directors worked on the films, including Misume Kenji, Okamoto Kihachi and Ikehiro Kazuo, but they all follow a basic formula. Ichi wanders into a town where trouble is about to boil over; he slays a lot of *yakuza* or corrupt samurai and typically saves either a young girl or orphan in the process.

The first film laid the groundwork; the story mixes fact and fiction, concerning the historical battle between two rival *yakuza* groups, those of Shigezo Sasagawa and Sukegoro Iioka. The narrative features the real-life figure of Hirate Miki, a famous *ronin*, but is centred on the fictional figure of Zatoichi. The first scene to establish Ichi's screen persona sees him tricking a group of *yakuza* playing dice, exposing their greed and dishonesty, while supplementing his own income. Ichi is an excellent example of the stray dog hero. A true outcast, despised by polite society, feared by the *yakuza*, he is only able to mix with prostitutes and gamblers. His job as a travelling masseur means that he is a man without a home, like the wandering *ronin* in *Yojimbo*. Whilst staying with Sukegoro, one of the *yakuza* bosses, Ichi saves a young woman called Otane from her brutish ex-husband, displaying one of his defining characteristics as defender of the powerless. Otane falls for Ichi and at the end of the film wants to leave town with him, but he won't let her lower herself by being associated with a blind gambler, so he sneaks away, confirming his stray dog credentials.

There is a climactic duel between Ichi and Hirate, where, as in the closing of *Sanjuro*, victory is touched with remorse. Hirate is dying of consumption and insists on fighting Ichi to have an honourable death by combat. Director Misume Kenji employs fluid camerawork to link the swordsmen. The shot begins in a medium close-up on Ichi, on the right of the frame, facing left; the camera moves forwards, pans around in a circle and comes to rest on Hirate, placing him in exactly the same position – right of the frame, facing left, in a medium close-up. This reveals the conceit that these two men are linked; both are outcasts, forced to live by their swords. After Ichi has cut him, Hirate says, 'Magnificent! Rather than getting killed by scoundrels, I wanted to die at your hands.' Hirate follows *bushido* to the end, choosing a death in combat and displaying the nihilism at the centre of the warrior code.

Following the battle Ichi is furious with the triumphant gang boss Sukegoro, who spent the entire battle hiding. Sukegoro says, 'What a happy and wonderful occasion. Join me for a drink.' Ichi replies,

> Fool! Your men are lying dead in the boats. They died for no reason. What's so happy and wonderful about that? We gangsters are outlaws, shunned by society. That's why we have to honour our own code. But you act like you have the right to raise your face to the sun without shame. You fool!

This speech, drawn from Kan Shimozawa's short story, defined Ichi's philosophy and was repeated, with slight variations, throughout the series. In *Zatoichi at the Fire Festival* (1970) Ichi takes on the local *oyabun*, Yamikubo, who is extorting protection money from the peasants, intensifying their poverty. When Ichi fights Yamikubo's gang he scolds their leader even as he is killing his men, 'Yakuzas like us must always keep to the backstreets, men like you walk the highway and force aside the locals, you kill them without so much as a thought. And you call that making amends for your ancestors' sins? People like you shouldn't be allowed to live.' Ichi is the voice of the oppressed in a fashion unimaginable for characters as alienated as Ogami Itto, from the 'Lone Wolf and Cub' series, whose mission of vengeance is purely personal. Like Sanjuro, Ichi can't ignore the plight of the helpless, displaying the series' humanistic streak.

The Zatoichi movies are less bleak than the later nihilistic films about stray dog heroes from the 1970s. Ichi has a ribald and bawdy sense of humour. In *Zatoichi Meets the One-Armed Swordsman* (1971) Ichi farts out of a window to drive away the men spying on him with a prostitute. In *Zatoichi at the Fire Festival*, when Ichi stops at an inn to rest, there is a comical scene of the husband and wife who run the place squabbling and fighting. It's pure slapstick and lightens the mood.

Redemption is a common plot element, although not for Ichi, who considers himself irredeemable. In *Zatoichi at the Fire Festival*, Ichi reforms Umeji, a young man who, at the start, is working as a pimp and wants to join Yamikubo's *yakuza* gang. In the same story Ichi reforms Okiyo (Ohara Reiko), who is sent by the *yakuza* to break Ichi's spirit by making him fall in love with her. Of course Okiyo is won over by Ichi's selflessness and she ends up falling for him. In the end, true to the essence of the stray dog, Ichi rejects her. This is both an expectation of the genre – stray dogs can't settle down – and an expression of Ichi's self-loathing. Ichi strikes the classic *chambara* pose, walking alone out of town, isolated in the frame, reflecting his social alienation.

Ichi is a much more emotional character than many of his *chambara* counterparts. He falls in love, is hurt when wronged and vengeful when roused. He is often smitten by attractive women, unlike a great many of the more aloof heroes like Miyamoto Musashi. Ichi keeps the company of prostitutes, reflecting his earthy, vulgar nature. In *The Legend of Zatoichi* (1989) he has sex with Ohan, the beautiful head of the Bosatsu *yakuza* gang. He is not someone in search of enlightenment and self-perfection; he is far too pragmatic for that. Ichi faces life head-on and this drives his desire to protect the powerless and punish the guilty. Whilst unpretentious and rowdy, the character has a strong moral centre that is the source of his heroism.

The action scenes throughout the series are performed with style, no mean feat given that Katsu has to pretend to be blind even when he's fighting. He usually keeps his eyes closed, or rolls his pupils up so only the whites of his eyes are visible. Ichi's abilities are fantastic, even for a sighted character, never mind a blind one. He is a lethal combatant, capable of taking on dozens of men with his cane sword. The plots often include set-ups for fights in environments that favour blind Ichi over his adversaries – in darkened rooms, in the shadows of forests, under murky water. Ichi's skills require a considerable suspension of disbelief from the viewer, but his abilities remain largely consistent throughout the series and quickly become an accepted facet of the character. Katsu performs the swordplay using a reverse grip, Ichi's signature style, and is a very fast screen swordsman.

An interesting addition to the series was the already-mentioned *Zatoichi Meets the One-Armed Swordsman*, an early crossover between the cinemas of Hong Kong and Japan. *The One-Armed Swordsman* had been a big hit in 1967 for Hong Kong director Chang Cheh and actor Wang Yu. The Hong Kong film industry was experiencing international success for the first time with the popularity of the kung fu genre and production standards were improving. By contrast, the golden age of Japanese cinema was some twenty years past, so this collaboration marked a point at which the fortunes of the two industries intercepted. The plot concerns a Chinese swordsman, Wong Kang (Wang Yu), who is visiting Japan. He befriends a family of Chinese street performers, only to see them killed by samurai from the Nambu clan when their son accidentally blocks the path of an official procession. Wong kills several of the samurai before fleeing, while Ichi finds the orphaned boy and soon runs into Wong, but they are unable to communicate because of the language barrier. Believing that Ichi has betrayed him, Wong fights the blind swordsman and Ichi has to kill Wong to save himself.

The action scenes are an odd mixture of Japanese and Hong Kong techniques. Ichi fights with his usual speed and ferocity, whereas Wong's fights, performed by Wang Yu, are typical of the Hong Kong movies of the period. He makes frequent leaps that cover impossible distances, performed with the assistance of off-screen trampolines and some creative editing, a staple of Hong Kong films in the late

1960s and early 1970s. His action sequences lack any sense of realism; Wang Yu was never the most gifted screenfighter and his shortcomings are highlighted by the contrast with Katsu's skilful execution of his sword techniques. Wang Yu clearly benefited from his experience on the Japanese set and some of his later works, notably *Beach of the War Gods* (1973) and *Blood of the Dragon* (1978) displayed the influence of Japanese *chambara*, both in the nature of their protagonists and in the direction of the combat sequences.

In 1989, when Katsu was nearly sixty years old, he made one final cinematic outing as the blind swordsman with *The Legend of Zatoichi*, sometimes referred to as *Zatoichi 26* or *Shintaro Katsu's Zatoichi*. Katsu directed, produced and starred in the film and there is a sense of coming full circle. He replays the gambling sequence from the very first Zatoichi film, wherein Ichi tricks a group of *yakuza* playing dice, and in the scene with Ichi and Ohan, the female *yakuza* boss, she references his speech to Sukegoro Iioka, again from the first film. Otherwise, the movie is a straightforward Ichi adventure, in which villainous *yakuza* are slain and Ichi is forced to duel a *ronin* whom he has befriended. The movie explicitly addresses the notion of *shushigaku* through the phrase 'A falling leaf does not hate the wind', which is repeated throughout the narrative. Ichi, when forced to slay the *ronin* in the finale, concludes that a falling leaf does hate the wind – he may be trapped by fate into living by the sword, but he does not address life with a sense of fatalism. Ichi struggles tirelessly with the injustices of the feudal system and is a figure of hope, not one of resignation.

Oichi, the Blind Swordswoman

The success of Zatoichi inspired Shochiku Studios to try their luck with a blind hero. They chose Oichi, the blind swordswoman, a character who first appeared in a *manga* by Tanashita Teruo. In the West the films were known as the 'Crimson Bat' series, of which there were four entries, released in Japan in 1969 and 1970. *Crimson Bat, the Blind Swordswoman* (1969) introduced Oichi, played by television actress Matsuyama Yoko and established her stray dog status. The movie opens with Oichi rescuing an old man from a gang of thugs, immediately confirming the character's role as defender of the helpless. Like Zatoichi, Oichi is a master swordfighter, an expert gambler and enemy of the *yakuza*. In the third film, *Watch Out, Crimson Bat*, she befriends two orphans, another staple motif from the Zatoichi films.

Oichi is prone to falling in love with the various *ronin* she encounters and there is a strong melodramatic streak running through the stories. Oichi's stray dog status demands that her romantic inclinations must always be unsatisfied and her tendency to fall for men she frequently has to fight is analogous to Zatoichi's tendency to befriend *ronin* whom he invariably has to slay. A handful of qualities separate Oichi from her male counterparts. Being a woman, Oichi is not bound by *bushido*, for she is not a samurai, although the stories make little use of this facet. In *Watch Out, Crimson Bat* Oichi criticises the *ronin* Gennosuke for his stubborn adherence to *bushido*, but it is not a subject given much consideration. The filmmakers instead focus on keeping the plot moving and delivering regular doses of swordplay, rather than exploring philosophy.

Oichi is not an outcast to the same degree as Zatoichi or many of her male *chambara* counterparts. The social stigma attached to her blindness is softened by the character's physical attractiveness and Oichi does not suffer the same degree of alienation experienced by many of the genre's protagonists. At the close of the first film, she is seen in the classic stray dog pose, isolated in a long shot, the outcast hero. By contrast, at the end of *Watch Out, Crimson Bat*, the camera remains in a close-up on Oichi's face as she walks out of town, denying her the status of true stray dog by failing to frame her as a solitary figure against a wider landscape. The audience stays with Oichi, rather than watching her leave, suggesting a greater sense of social inclusion than that typically associated with *chambara* heroes.

The series did not achieve the same longevity as the Zatoichi franchise and Matsuyama Yoko retired from the film industry to raise a family after the fourth film, *Crimson Bat – Oichi: Wanted Dead or Alive* (1970).

Kobayashi Masaki and the Family under *Bushido*

Kobayashi Masaki was a Second World War combat veteran and, like his contemporary Okamoto Kihachi, the war left Kobayashi with a hatred for Japan's militarism. Kobayashi was drafted into the imperial army in 1941, but throughout the war he remained at the rank of private, refusing promotion. He was captured by the Americans and spent the final days of the war in a POW camp. He emerged a committed pacifist and in 1946 returned to the film industry as an assistant director at Shochiku Studios, under director Kinoshita Keisuke. Kobayashi directed the mammoth project *The Human Condition*, a nine-hour trilogy adapted from the series of anti-war novels by Gomikawa Junpei. The series made a star of Nakadai Tatsuya, who took on a role in Kobayashi's work comparable to that of Mifune in Kurosawa's films.

Harakiri (1962)

Kobayashi directed two martial arts films, *Harakiri*, released in Japan as *Seppuku*, and *Samurai Rebellion* (1967), originally titled *Rebellion*. *Harakiri* won the Special Jury Prize at the Cannes Film Festival and tells the story of Tsugumo Hanshiro (Nakadai Tatsuya), a destitute *ronin* who presents himself at the house of the Iyi clan, requesting permission to use their grounds to commit suicide. Seeking to dissuade him, clan elder Saito Kageyu tells Tsugumo the story of the last *ronin* to make such a request – Chijiiwa Motome. Concerned that Chijiiwa might be threatening suicide to extort money from the clan, a tactic employed by unscrupulous *ronin*, Saito and the senior Iyi samurai compelled Chijiiwa to go through with the suicide, forcing him to use his own blunt bamboo sword to cut his stomach open. Tsugumo reveals that Chijiiwa was his son-in-law and he came to the Iyi clan out of desperation when he needed money for a doctor for his sick wife and baby son, both of whom died shortly afterwards. Tsugumo explains that in the weeks preceding his arrival at the Iyi mansion he has taken the topknots from three of the samurai responsible for forcing Chijiiwa to kill himself. Outraged, Saito orders his men to kill Tsugumo, who fights his way through the mansion until he reaches the room containing the clan's ancestral armour. He smashes the armour to the ground and cuts open his own stomach before being shot by the rifles of the Iyi clansmen.

Kobayashi's concern is the impact of *bushido* on the family. The formalities that filled the lives of the samurai and the rituals surrounding *hara-kiri* are demonstrated in great detail. Just as the Iyi clansmen used tradition and formality to trap Chijiiwa into performing *hara-kiri*, Kobayashi uses these conventions to expose the inhumanity and lack of compassion at the heart of *bushido*. Mishima Yukio, who performed ritual suicide to end his own life, considered the nature of *hara-kiri* in his writings on *Hagakure*:

> [Yamamoto] is concerned with death as a decision, not with natural death. He spoke not of resignation to death from illness, but of resolution to self-destruction ... Here is the typical Japanese view that being cut down in battle and committing ritual suicide are equally honorable; the positive form of suicide called *hara-kiri* is not a sign of defeat, as it is in the West, but the ultimate expression of free will, in order to protect one's honour. (Mishima, 1977, p. 46)

However, in *Harakiri*, the ritual is monstrous. Kobayashi makes Chijiiwa's disembowelment, performed with a bamboo sword, dreadful to behold. Acting as *kaishaku* (the second who decapitates the person performing suicide once they have disembowelled themselves), Omadaka refuses to behead Chijiiwa, to end his suffering, until Chijiiwa has completely cut his stomach open. Chijiiwa resorts to biting his own tongue off to force Omadaka's hand. Chijiiwa does not perform *hara-kiri* of his own free will – he is forced to do so by the Iyi clan who are determined to make an example of him. It is no glorious act of honour, not even a nihilistic demonstration of free will. The performance of Ishihama Akira, as Chijiiwa, is exceptional and the suicide sequence is intensely disturbing.

Under the *bushido* code, the loss of a samurai's topknot was a grave matter as Tsugumo points out to Saito as he recounts his duels with the Iyi swordsmen:

> Taking a man's head is not easy. But to take only his top-knot was harder still! Irrespective of skill, to lose one's top-knot is equivalent to losing one's head. A laxity and dishonour which even death cannot wipe away! Yet they claim illness and hide until their top-knots grow back, Honourable Elder! You boast of traditions of bravery, but even the code of the House of Iyi seems to be only a false front!

3. Tsugumo (Nakadai Tatsuya) in the third of his duels against the swordsmen of the Iyi clan from *Harakiri*.

Here Kobayashi uses Tsugumo to highlight the hypocrisy of those in power. For all Saito's claims that forcing Chijiiwa to kill himself was part of the proud *bushido* tradition, his own clansmen fail to live up to the same standards. The film is full of attacks upon the feudal system, including the dissolution of the Geishu clan for repairing Hiroshima Castle, an act interpreted as a precursor to rebellion by the shogunate. As Tsugumo tells Saito, 12,000 innocent retainers lost their livelihoods as a result. There is a parallel with the actions of the Japanese government during the Second World War, sending countless innocents to their deaths in pursuit of imperial expansion. It is interesting to compare the virulence of the attacks on the feudal system by Kobayashi and Okamoto with Kurosawa's work. Kobayashi and Okamoto were combat veterans whose anger with the Japanese authorities pervades their work. Kurosawa does not address *bushido* and the feudal system with the same vehemence. The ending of *Seven Samurai* is mournful and *Yojimbo* and *Sanjuro* satirise the warrior code, but there is none of the raw anger present in *Harakiri* or *Samurai Assassin* (1965).

Kobayashi never misses an opportunity to attack *bushido*. When Tsugumo learns that his son-in-law had pawned his sword blades for money, he is angry with himself and apologises to Chijiiwa's corpse: 'Forgive me! It was I who was so thoughtless! You sold those blades. You sold them for Miho's sake. And still, I never realized … Yet I never parted with mine. I would never have dared! In my ignorance, I clung to these worthless symbols!' As Omadaka tells Chijiiwa, a samurai's sword is his soul, but Kobayashi rejects this fundamental concept, calling swords 'worthless symbols'. The sword may be the symbol of *bushido*, but *bushido* destroys human beings, it cares nothing for the men whose lives it dominates. Substitute imperial Japan for the word *bushido* and Kobayashi's intentions are clear.

There is a futility to *Harakiri* as elder Saito clings to the *bushido* code and resolves to hide Tsugumo's actions from history. He orders the clan scribe to record that all the samurai slain by Tsugumo died of illness. With great irony, he instructs his subordinates to care for the injured, 'See that no others die of illness! The injured must be given treatment immediately!' Regarding Yazaki and Kawabe, who unlike Omadaka have failed to commit suicide following their duels with Tsugumo, Saito orders their deaths to hide their dishonourable conduct: 'Go immediately! Order them to die by *hara-kiri*! And take some skilled men with you. Should they refuse, they are to be slain on the spot! Understand? Also, these men, Omadaka too, are victims of illness, not *hara-kiri*!'

Elder Saito knows that *bushido* has its limitations, ordering his assistant to take 'some skilled men' along. He clings to a system that he knows is flawed, just as human beings are flawed. Saito is not defending *bushido* so much as hiding behind it, unable to confront reality on its own chaotic terms. Kobayashi is a realist; Tsugumo's attack on the system fails because he is just one man, dwarfed by the colossal feudal system that has driven him to desperation.

Samurai Rebellion (1967)

Samurai Rebellion takes this as its central theme, dealing with the impact of *bushido* upon another family. Sasahara Isaburo (Mifune Toshiro) is a minor official in the Matsudaira clan, responsible for maintaining the armoury, but as the country is at peace he has little to do and occupies his time perfecting his swordsmanship. Isaburo is unhappily married to Suga, a harpy who never has a kind word for anyone. Lord Matsudaira, the regional *daimyo*, wants to get rid of his troublesome mistress Ichi and orders Isaburo's eldest son, Yogoro, to marry her. Ichi has already borne a son for Matsudaira and the baby is second in line to inherit his estate. Unable to refuse, Yogoro accepts the arrangement and Isaburo is delighted to discover that Ichi is a wonderful woman. She and Yogoro have a baby girl called Tomi. Matsudaira's first son dies, making Ichi's boy the heir apparent. She is instructed to leave Yogoro because the mother of the clan's heir cannot be married to a lowly vassal. Yogoro, Ichi and Isaburo defy Matsudaira and she refuses to leave, incurring the wrath of the clan. Ichi is taken hostage but kills herself rather than allow Isaburo and Yogoro to surrender. Yogoro is slain and Isaburo sets out for Edo, intending to report Matsudaira's tyranny to the shogun. At the border he is forced to kill his friend Tatewaki, but is attacked by a large number of Matsudaira samurai, who shoot him. He dies calling out to the baby Tomi, telling her to grow up to be just like her mother.

Thematically, the film has much in common with *Harakiri*. The central character is a retired warrior trying to care for his family. The feudal system is still the target for Kobayashi's ire and the director again goes into great detail regarding all the formalities of Isaburo's life as a samurai during peacetime. The film reiterates his sense of despair at being faced with the enormity of trying to topple an unjust system. What separates Tsugumo in *Harakiri* from Isaburo in *Samurai Rebellion* is that where Tsugumo was happy before *bushido* destroyed his family, Isaburo starts the narrative deeply unhappy. It is apparent that Isaburo loathes his overbearing wife. When discussing the proposed union of Yogoro and Ichi, he tells Tatewaki: 'Yogoro is silent, but he wouldn't be happy marrying a mistress who's borne a child. Marrying unwillingly due to pressure. Different circumstances, but like my own marriage. I don't want him to repeat my mistake.'

Mifune's performance as the hen-pecked husband is expertly under-played; Isaburo can scarcely look at his wife. When he refuses to acquiesce to Matsudaira's demands, Isaburo experiences liberation for the first time. He defies not just his *daimyo*, but also his wife, her extended family and the rest of the clan. As the revolt comes into the open, Isaburo seems pleased. When his youngest son Bunzo makes a final plea for Isaburo and Yogoro to accede to Matsudaira, Isaburo tells him: 'Tell everyone for me, for the first time in my life I feel really alive'. By casting off the smothering weight of duty and obedience, the burden of *giri*, Isaburo becomes a free human being.

The duel between Isaburo and Tatewaki offers a deconstruction of the genre's icons. Tatewaki is played by Nakadai Tatsuya, an actor with a great deal of experience in the *chambara* genre. Carrying the baby Tomi, Isaburo reaches the clan's border, where Tatewaki is waiting for him. With great solemnity, the men perform every formality demanded of samurai – Tatewaki asks for Isaburo's travel permit, knowing full well that he doesn't have one. When the formalities are over and they have agreed to a duel, Tatewaki drops his formal manner and asks if Tomi is cold. The image cuts to Tatewaki cradling the baby while Isaburo prepares her food. The sight of the two master swordsmen who are about to face each other in mortal combat tending to the baby is not presented as cute. It highlights the tragic nature of their circumstances. They may be friends but they are trapped under the full weight of *bushido* and compelled to fight. It is inconceivable to Tatewaki to abandon his responsibility as head of the border guard and to let Isaburo pass; his duty takes precedence over his friendship. Tatewaki chooses an honourable death in combat rather than the disgrace of letting Isaburo pass. This is central to Kobayashi's theme – death is the only release for samurai. In life the constraints of *bushido* are inescapable.

After the duel, the clan's samurai attack Isaburo. The identity of the samurai whose shot kills Isaburo is never revealed, which is precisely the point. It is not an individual that kills Isaburo; it is the system itself. Kobayashi takes a moment in the battle to linger on the samurai slain by Isaburo. The camera shows their faces to make clear that all these men are victims of *bushido*, their violent deaths the product of an intransigent society. They are not the anonymous minions who fall before Ogami Itto in the 'Lone Wolf and Cub' series. Kobayashi is not willing to trivialise the deaths of anyone in his story.

In the end, Isaburo's rebellion fails; it dies with him in the field. This is a powerful rejection of the nihilism central to the samurai code. In *Hagakure*, Yamamoto Tsunetomo wrote: 'To say that dying without reaching one's aim is to die a dog's death is the frivolous way of sophisticates. When pressed with the choice of life or death, it is not necessary to gain one's aim' (Yamamoto, 2000, p. 17). This very nihilism was what attracted Mishima Yukio to the book, and in his writings on *Hagakure*, Mishima commented:

> Hagakure is simply expressing the relativistic position that rather than to live on as a coward having failed in one's mission, having failed in one's mission it is better to die. Here is the nihilism of Yamamoto, and here, too, is the ultimate idealism, born of his nihilism … If we value so highly the dignity of life, how can we not also value the dignity of death? No death may be called futile. (Mishima, 1977, p. 105)

This potent nihilism enabled the Japanese to send *kamikaze* pilots to crash their planes into American ships during the Second World War. It was vital to the existence of the feudal system, which demanded that the samurai hold his lord's life in higher esteem than his own. Kobayashi's rejection of this philosophy is absolute. He refuses to grant Isaburo's death any dignity and Isaburo does not die defending his lord, his honour or his nation. He dies rebelling against all of them and his anonymous death marks the futility of his actions. It is not noble, it is dreadful and in this manner Kobayashi damns the *bushido* code for dehumanising and destroying the very people whose lives it governed.

Okamoto Kihachi

The careers of Nakadai Tatsuya and Mifune Toshiro continued to interweave. They appeared together in Kurosawa's *High and Low* (1963) and when Mifune parted ways with Kurosawa, Nakadai became the most prominent member of Kurosawa's troupe, taking lead roles in *Kagemusha* and *Ran*. Another director to exploit the considerable talents of the pair was Okamoto Kihachi. Born in 1924, Okamoto was drafted into the Japanese army in 1943 after graduating from university. He saw active duty during the fighting in the Pacific, where there were horrific numbers of casualties and many of Okamoto's fellow graduates were killed in action. The influence of this experience upon Okamoto's work was profound. Whilst Kurosawa was a humanist who rejected *bushido*, the great director never saw combat first hand. As a war veteran, Okamoto displays in his work an abiding disgust with the path of the warrior that possesses an intensity Kurosawa could not match. Where *Yojimbo* and *Sanjuro* are comedies, Okamoto's films, *Samurai Assassin*, *The Sword of Doom* (1966) and *Red Lion* (1969), are tragic.

Samurai Assassin (1965)

This is an outstanding example. Based on the book *Samurai Nippon* by Gunji Jiromasa, it concerns a *ronin*, Tsurichiyo Niiro (Mifune Toshiro) who wants to be a man of status. The story is set in 1860 as the Tokugawa shogunate was crumbling before the Meiji Restoration. Niiro is the son of a concubine and does not know the identity of his father. This lack of respectability cost Niiro the love of Kikuhime, the daughter of a high-ranking *daimyo*. To improve his social standing, Niiro joins a group of samurai from the Mito clan who plan to assassinate Lord Ii Naoshige, a senior *bakufu* official.

Niiro kills his best friend Einosuke to keep his place in the conspiracy, but the leader of the group decides to remove him anyway. Niiro survives the attempt on his life and joins the Mito clansmen in their assault upon Lord Ii, unaware that Ii is his father and that the Mito conspirators have removed all mention of him from their records so that he will not receive the advancement in status he believes will be his reward.

There is a strong sense of predeterminism underlying the script. Niiro's desire for advancement is doomed from the start – the son of a concubine has no chance of improving his status under the rigid Tokugawa class system. Niiro's inability to let go of his desire is his downfall. When he meets Okiku, an inn owner who is the spitting image of his lost love Kikuhime, she asks him to live with her and to abandon his dreams of status. His inability to accept her offer, to lay down his sword, is an excellent example of the dilemma faced by the *ronin* under the Tokugawa. To lay down their swords was to lose their identity, to lose their souls. Niiro is acutely aware of his status as an outsider and this is what drives him. He tells Kenmotsu, the leader of the conspiracy, 'A true *ronin*, a starving dog, nobody can predict what he might do'. This reiterates the notion of *ronin* as stray dog, the perpetual outcast.

The film explores the conflict between *giri* and *ninjo*, between duty and desire. Einosuke is Niiro's only real friend, despite being his opposite. Where Niiro has embraced the irresponsibility of the *ronin*'s lifestyle, drinking and gambling as he pleases, his friend is married with a son and a stable home life. Einosuke is the man Niiro wants to be; when he kills Einosuke to maintain the good graces of the Mito conspirators, he is killing his dream. Okamoto is emphatic in his contention that following orders (*giri*) can be disastrous, a reflection of his personal disillusionment from his wartime experiences, when the blind obedience of the Japanese almost led to the destruction of the country.

Kuze Ryu, who coordinated the swordplay in *Yojimbo* and *Sanjuro*, is credited with the fight choreography and his work is excellent. The final battle, the attack upon Lord Ii and his retainers, is reminiscent of the climax of *Seven Samurai*. The conspirators attack in thick falling snow, which adds to the sense of chaos and desperation. Niiro beheads Lord Ii, but it is a dreadful hollow victory as he walks up and down in the snow brandishing his father's head. Niiro is seen in a wide shot, alone and gradually becoming obscured by the snow – fading from view even as he will fade from history having been removed from the Mito clan's account of their conspiracy. The message is clear; violence leads nowhere, with the implied critique of Japan's wartime imperial dreams. While *Samurai Assassin*, *The Sword of Doom* and *Red Lion* are all set at the end of the Tokugawa dynasty, Okamoto uses the films to condemn Japan's involvement in the Second World War and the self-destructive nature of ruthless ambition.

The Sword of Doom (1966)

Okamoto returned to the same themes in *The Sword of Doom*, one of the darkest *chambara* ever made. Ryunosuke, (Nakadai Tatsuya) is the apotheosis of the anti-hero, a merciless killer with no conscience. The story begins in 1860, the same year that *Samurai Assassin* takes place. On a mountain pass an old man and his granddaughter Omatsu stop to rest. While Omatsu looks for a stream, the old man prays to Buddha, asking that he may die soon so he won't be a burden on Omatsu. Ryunosuke overhears this and kills the old man. Ryunosuke then kills a samurai called Bunnojo in a *kendo* match and leaves town with the man's widow, Hama, whom he had previously raped. They move to Edo where Ryunosuke – living under an assumed name to avoid Bunnojo's vengeful brother Hyoma – works as an assassin for Serizawa, the leader of a group of conservative samurai opposed to reform of the shogunate. Serizawa and his gang move to Kyoto in 1863, where they join the Shinsen group. Hyoma is hot on Ryunosuke's trail and meets Omatsu and her guardian Shichibei. Omatsu is training to be a courtesan in the establishment where the Shinsen Group is partying. She is discovered eavesdropping on Serizawa and Ryunosuke and when he realises that she is the girl whose grandfather he killed, Ryunosuke's mind snaps. He is attacked by members of the Shinsen group loyal to Kondo, Serizawa's rival. The film ends abruptly with Ryunosuke slashing at the camera with his sword, insane with rage.

The film is Okamoto's most powerful attack on the futility of violence and a demonstration of his distrust of the power-hungry.

Ryunosuke is an exceptional swordsman. When attacked by Bunnojo's comrades following the fatal *kendo* match, he slays them all without anyone so much as touching him. Okamoto does not celebrate this loss of life, despite the visceral thrill of watching Ryunosuke in action. He articulates this through the fencing instructor Shimada (Mifune Toshiro), who considers swordsmanship as the path to enlightenment and is the antithesis of the merciless Ryunosuke. When the Sincho gang attacks Shimada he is forced to kill in self-defence. After capturing their leader, Shimada is furious, 'You hot-headed men made me kill against my will! The men lying here were good swordsmen! Dying like dogs! How can you atone for this? ... The sword is the soul. Study the soul to study the sword. An evil mind, an evil sword.'

This aptly illustrates the difference between the two. Shimada kills only when left with no choice and is so distressed about having killed, even in self-defence, that the following day he avoids the subject when talking to Hyoma. By contrast, Ryunosuke kills for money and he is tormented, trying to drown his sorrows in saké.

The climax defies genre conventions. Okamoto sets up the expectation of a final duel between Ryunosuke and Hyoma. He shows Hyoma training under Shimada's guidance and practising the thrust attack that Shimada believes is his best chance for victory. By bringing together Omatsu, her guardian Shichibei who found her on the mountain pass, and Hyoma, the stage is set for a showdown. Hyoma and Shichibei wait outside for Ryunosuke so Hyoma can kill him. Inside, when Ryunosuke realises Omatsu's identity, he becomes deranged. He hears a howling wind and the voices of those he has slain – the old man, Hama, her baby, and shadows of each person appear on the blinds in the room. Ryunosuke slashes at them, tearing the blinds apart. He hears Shimada's words: 'An evil mind, an evil sword'. Then the Shinsen men appear and attack him. Ryunosuke fights like a demon, killing countless samurai. The building catches fire and fills with smoke. Ryunosuke fights on, calling for Serizawa, unaware that Kondo's men have murdered his accomplice. No matter how many he slays, more men attack him. Ryunosuke keeps on killing, staggering through the building like a wounded animal until the image freezes on Ryunosuke slashing at the camera. It is an incredibly violent ending and offers no closure.

Hyoma is left waiting, his quest for vengeance unresolved. The number of men who attack Ryunosuke makes no sense; there are far more than could be accounted for at the Shinsen group's party. This is deliberate, for Okamoto will not grant the audience the release of watching Ryunosuke die. His intention is to make clear that violence offers no satisfaction. Ryunosuke is doomed to keep fighting without respite, for he has entered a hell of his own making, trapped by his bloodthirsty nature. There is no release, not for Ryunosuke, nor for the audience. This is a masterstroke by Okamoto, who defies the conventions of a genre that celebrates the violent nature of its protagonists, particularly in the later *chambara*. Ryunosuke is a monster and Okamoto leaves him where monsters belong, in hell.

The cinematography by Murai Hiroshi surrounds Ryunosuke with dark shadows, pressing in upon him, reflecting and intensifying the darkness at the heart of the swordsman. The unscrupulous character of the power hungry is seen in Serizawa and Kondo's rivalry: even as Serizawa is bribing Ryunosuke to eliminate Kondo, his intended target is planning Serizawa's death in another part of the building. This reveals Okamoto's deep distrust of all ambitious men, an attack upon the imperial aspirations of the Japanese government in the 1930s and 1940s.

Red Lion (1969)

Mifune and Okamoto were reunited on two more occasions, for *Red Lion* and *Zatoichi Meets Yojimbo* (1970). The latter is an entertaining but unexceptional entry in the long-running Zatoichi series, but *Red Lion* merits further consideration. The story begins during the Meiji Restoration, as the emperor and his troops are on their way to Edo to claim power. The opening shows people celebrating in the streets, chanting 'It's okay! It's okay! Never mind!' in anticipation of a new world where the peasants will have better lives. Mifune plays the illiterate Gonzo, a peasant's son with a stutter. He is an expert fighter and has joined the imperial forces, where the commanders have announced that with the restoration, taxes will be halved and outstanding debts cancelled. The Sekiko troops, Gonzo's unit, led by Sozo Sagara (Tamura Takahiro), are assigned to spread the news ahead of the imperial procession. En route is Gonzo's hometown,

Sawando, and he convinces Sozo to let him travel ahead. In Sawando, Komatora (Hanazawa Tokue), the local moneylender and constable, has rounded up families with outstanding debts. He is not pleased when Gonzo arrives and liberates Komatora's hostages, including the girls he has forced to work as prostitutes to repay debts. The ex-prostitutes become Gonzo's most ardent supporters as he tries to convince everyone that the imperial restoration heralds a new world order. Gonzo is reunited with his old love Tomi (Iwashita Shima), but learns that the imperial commanders have executed the entire Sekiko troop. The emperor never intended to cut taxes or debts. Sozo's unit was used to pacify the population and ensure a trouble-free passage to Edo, and were then executed as traitors, to alleviate the emperor from having to deliver on such promises. The imperial forces enter Sawando looking for Gonzo. Tomi kills Komatora but is shot by the imperial troops. Gonzo charges at the imperial forces, but is shot and killed. Oharu, one of the ex-prostitutes, starts singing 'It's okay! It's okay! Never mind!' and the other villagers join in until the entire village is chanting. They sing and dance and en masse push the imperial troops out of the village. For one glorious moment, the world is really turned on its head, just as Gonzo had promised.

At the outset, the tone is light-hearted and satirical, until it gradually becomes darker and more tragic. Okamoto treats film and time as flexible, rather than rigid and linear, in contrast to both *Samurai Assassin* and *The Sword of Doom*. There are flashbacks to establish the relationships between characters in Sawando. Further, there are humorous fantasy sequences as the villagers imagine their new world under the emperor. They visualise the local deputy Kintayuu pulling a plough; Kisoya, another figure of oppression, is a street performer; and the hated Komatora is a dog. In his fantasy, Gonzo is a senior government official in a fancy Western outfit. The sequence demonstrates Okamoto playing with genre, departing from a narrative form, the *jidai-geki*, that is typically linear and naturalistic.

Okamoto dismisses all symbols of authority. When Gonzo arrives in town, Komatora tries to impress him with his *jitte*, the symbol of his position under the shogunate, comparable to a sheriff's badge in the American Western. Gonzo sneers at Komatora, 'You are always behind the times! Showing off something like that won't do you any good!' The symbols of the shogun have lost their potency, as society is in a state of chaos. In turn, the symbol of Gonzo's position is a headpiece of bright red hair, the mark of an officer in the imperial forces. When the townspeople drive the imperial troops out of Sawando, the red mane is trampled under foot. Okamoto does not spare the emperor's icons from his scornful gaze. They are as impotent as those of the shogun. This is one of two key themes in the movie – that those in power, whether shogunate or imperial, are only interested in themselves. This is enunciated by the cynical Hanzo, a swordsman that Komatora hires to kill Gonzo, who believes the imperial restoration will do nothing to improve the peasants' lives: 'The only thing that'll change is the flower on the official crest.' Okamoto endorses Hanzo's cynicism in his presentation of the treacherous imperial commanders who sacrifice the loyal Sozo and the Sekiko troop. This reflects an undercurrent that exists throughout Okamoto's work, expressing his sense of betrayal with the Japanese government that sacrificed so many men during the Second World War.

The second theme, one that was present in *Samurai Assassin* and *The Sword of Doom* is the rejection of violence as a solution to problems. Gonzo and Hanzo are outstanding swordsmen, but both die by the bullets of the imperial soldiers. When Mobile Unit One, a band loyal to the shogunate, attack the imperial troops, they do so in true *bushido* fashion. They announce their names as they charge, as all samurai were meant to do when entering battle. It is a futile gesture, for the imperial soldiers do not call out their names as they pick off Mobile Unit One with their rifles. *Bushido*, according to Okamoto, is rapidly approaching extinction. In a wonderful subversion of the genre, the imperial troops are driven out of Sawando not by violence, but by a group of commoners singing and dancing. It is a more hopeful ending than the savagery of *The Sword of Doom*, or the acerbic irony of *Samurai Assassin*. The swordsmen are dead, but the villagers experience the power of mass peaceful action. There is no precedent for this scene in the genre. It reflects a modern sensibility, demonstrating Okamoto's flexible approach to history. In *Red Lion* he projects modern methods of peaceful protest back in time to the 1860s. Whilst there was a sense of resignation to the closing sequence of *Seven Samurai*, where the *ronin* were acutely aware of the price of their warrior lifestyle, both films share an optimism that the life of the farmers and the poor can be improved if they do something extraordinary, whether that is the hiring of samurai or mass peaceful protest. Okamoto may not share Kurosawa's lofty reputation, but he was a dynamic filmmaker whose career deserves wider exposure.

Gosha Hideo

Like Okamoto, Gosha Hideo is relatively unknown in the West, despite his tremendous success in Japan. Born in 1929, Gosha served in the Japanese navy after high school, before studying business at Meiji University. He joined Nippon Television in 1953, working as a reporter, then producer, before directing. His biggest hit was the popular *chambara* television series *Three Outlaw Samurai* and in 1964 he adapted the concept for his feature film debut. Gosha stayed with the *chambara* genre until 1979's *Hunter in the Dark*, switching to quasi-pornography in 1982 with films about prostitutes and *yakuza*.

Gosha was unusual in moving from television to cinema, when it was more common for directors and stars to go from film to the small screen. His work provides a bridge between the revered classics of Japan's golden age and the violent, nihilistic *chambara* of the 1970s. Unlike his early contemporaries, Gosha lacked a humanistic ideology, but was more interested in genre as an end in itself.

Three Outlaw Samurai (1964)

The feature film *Three Outlaw Samurai* displays the director's propensity for employing intertextual genre shorthand, using established archetypes and situations to bypass the need for in-depth characterisation. His primary concerns are always plot and action. The story here concerns three *ronin* who protect a group of farmers, led by Jimbei, when they take the local magistrate's daughter hostage to force him to accept their petition for lower taxes. Shiba (Tamba Tetsuro) is the first character to appear on screen and is introduced as a solitary figure wandering along a dirt road in the countryside. His scruffy attire and isolation in the frame reference the opening of Kurosawa's *Yojimbo* and this is just one example of Gosha's use of intertextuality. Shiba steps into the film with no individual characteristics, but as a generic *chambara* stray dog protagonist. As the story unfolds, Gosha fills in virtually no background details for Shiba, or any of the other *ronin*, relying on the audience's familiarity with the genre archetype to fill in the blanks. Asked why he has chosen to aid the farmers, Shiba replies, 'Why? Perhaps because I spent a night under the same roof.' That is the sum total of his motivation – he has to become involved in the conflict or there would be no film. The second *ronin* to join the farmers' cause is Sakura (Nagato Isamu) and his explanation is no more than 'I'm originally from a farm myself'. For Gosha, that is sufficient to move the plot onwards.

The third and final *ronin*, Kikyo (Hira Mikijiro) is the most interesting of the three in genre terms, because he displays qualities of the anti-hero type that would become prevalent in the 1970s. He is self-serving, working for the corrupt magistrate because he wants a comfortable lifestyle. He is sexually attracted to the morally bankrupt woman who makes a living selling peasant girls to brothels. He is not completely alienated, for Kikyo joins Shiba's side when the magistrate breaks an oath sworn as a samurai. Kikyo respects the *bushido* code and risks his life to help the farmers, but he marks a step in the transformation of the *chambara* protagonist.

The ending displays Gosha's cynicism and the absence of the humanistic streak found in the films of Kurosawa, Kobayashi and others. The three farmers who started the uprising have been slain and those who still survive are too afraid to present Jimbei's petition to the clan's lord when he passes through their village. Despite the sacrifices of Jimbei and his friends and the dangers faced by the three *ronin*, the villagers do nothing to change their fate – the notion of predeterminism underpins this scene. This provides a counterpoint to Kurosawa's *Seven Samurai*. Both movies deal with *ronin* coming to the aid of oppressed farmers, but where *Seven Samurai* sees the farmers participating in their salvation, *Three Outlaw Samurai* ends with the peasants passively accepting their miserable place in the feudal system. Shiba, Sakura and Kikyo head out of town leaving the feudal system undented, the peasants still oppressed by heavy taxes, the world unchanged. All the genre elements are in place, there are corrupt officials, poor farmers, brave *ronin*, a climactic battle and duel, but the film never aspires to be more than an exercise in genre. It is a well-executed work, with beautiful black-and-white cinematography, decent performances and exciting fight scenes. The film opens and closes with Gosha displaying his fluency in the language of the genre: at the end, Shiba throws a hairpin into the air and the *ronin* walk off in the direction it points towards when it lands, another motif from *Yojimbo*.

Sword of the Beast (1965)

Gosha's second film, *Sword of the Beast* continued the exploration of the anti-hero, again in the form of actor Hira Mikijiro. Here he plays a *ronin* called Gennosuke who is on the run from his former clan, having been duped into assassinating the clan's first minister in the belief that doing so would open the way for reform and promotion. The first minister's daughter Misa and her fiancé Daizaburo are on Gennosuke's trail. Trying to lose his pursuers in the mountains, he meets Yamane (Kato Goh) and his wife Taka (Iwashita Shima), who are illegally gathering gold for the chamberlain of their clan.

Gennosuke is barely a hero, he is lustful, desperate and ambitious. He fits the mould of the stray dog outcast, having been sentenced to death by his former clan, and he asserts his rejection of feudal loyalty by refusing to die. What links and dooms both Yamane and Gennosuke is their ambition. Gennosuke participates in the minister's assassination readily and Gosha leaves room for the viewer to doubt the purity of his motives – whether he is sincere in his support for reform or simply greedy for self-advancement. Yamane is similarly consumed by the desire to climb up the ranks of samurai and his devotion to his clan is revealed when a gang of bandits take his wife Taka hostage and threaten to rape and kill her if Yamane does not hand over his gold. He refuses and only the intervention of Gennosuke saves Taka. She is horrified that Yamane puts the mission and the clan above her life, telling Gennosuke, 'I wish I could be a beast. I can't stand living for a mission. I'd rather be a beast and roam about freely.' Gennosuke has experienced this freedom by fleeing his clan, but has not found happiness either. Gosha's characters are trapped by the feudal system and thereby doomed. A distrust of authority pervades Gosha's work. The chamberlain of Yamane's clan has him and Taka killed to cover up their illegal gold mining, despite the fact that the gold will guarantee the clan's financial security.

At the close, after Gennosuke has saved Misa from bandits and exacted retribution upon the corrupt chamberlain, Misa and Daizaburo allow Gennosuke to leave unharmed, their vendetta unsatisfied. He walks off alone into the darkness, fading into black. As in *Three Outlaw Samurai*, Gosha offers no happy ending, for while Gennosuke may have survived, he is an outcast with nowhere to go. It is appropriate that he walks off into the dark, for he is man without a future, analogous to the samurai class that is similarly destined to vanish.

Tenchu (1969)

The theme of the futureless anti-hero is central to *Tenchu* (1969), originally called *Hitokiri* in Japan. Okada Izo (Zatoichi star Katsu Shintaro) is a destitute samurai who joins the pro-emperor Tosa clan in the closing days of the Tokugawa dynasty. A group of Tosa loyalists, led by Takechi Hanpei (Nakadai Tatsuya), are eliminating their political rivals. Okada proves to be their most capable assassin and his fame grows with each killing until his success threatens to expose the activities of Takechi and his group to the authorities.

The title *Tenchu* means 'heaven's punishment' and is the Tosa loyalists' motto. They call out '*tenchu*' when conducting an assassination, declaring that they are empowered by the divine authority of the emperor, although it becomes clear that no one in the Tosa gang is acting out of noble idealism. Okada desires individual acclaim and during a raid in Ishibe starts shouting out his name and clan membership instead of crying '*tenchu*'. He wants everyone to know of his participation in the battle to further his fame. Takechi orders Okada to kill not just pro-shogunate officials, but figures loyal to the emperor who threaten Takechi's influence. The Tosa loyalists talk about reform, but are motivated by greed and lust for power. This being a film by Gosha, they are destined to fail. Only one character, the thoughtful and reflective Sakamoto, understands that the imperial reformation will mean the end of the samurai class. All the rest are blinded by ambition and plunge towards their own annihilation.

A recurring visual device revealing the weight of *shushigaku* on Okada is the use of frames within the image. He is frequently enclosed by frames that make him appear trapped – an easel, the legs of chairs, prison bars. He does not know it, but Okada is caught by fate and, try as he may to free himself, he will never succeed; for example when he tries to leave the Tosa loyalists only to find no other clan will hire him for fear of Takechi. His only release is death, but Gosha does not end with the expected climactic duel. Okada confesses the many murders he has committed on Takechi's orders to the seniors of the Tosa clan and is crucified. Despite the many lengthy and bloody sword battles, Gosha closes with Okada dying on the cross, executed as a criminal without honour and denied the right to commit suicide. His mighty sword arm has brought him nothing but a painful death in disgrace. In this regard,*Tenchu* shares some thematic common ground with Okamoto's work; violence is ultimately self-destructive.

This theme is enunciated the first time the audience sees Okada. Living in a hovel, he goes outside, draws his sword and slashes angrily at anything within arm's reach, before cutting furiously at the air itself. This is a metaphor for the entire film: no matter how much Okada slashes with his sword, he accomplishes nothing. Despite the huge number of men he slays in Takechi's service, his reward from his leader is to be left in jail as a liability and tortured by the prison guards. This expresses the same sentiment as *Sword of the Beast*, in which Yamane's loyalty to his clan ends in betrayal and death.

Mishima Yukio appears in *Tenchu* as Tanaka Shinbei, a member of the Satsuma clan who, like the Tosa, support the imperial cause. Tanaka is the best swordsman in the Satsuma group, but unlike the wild and brutish Okada, he is sober and composed in battle. The two become friends, but Okada is ordered to frame Tanaka for murder to discredit the Satsuma group. When arrested, Tanaka commits suicide rather than face dishonour and it is undeniably eerie watching Mishima perform this sequence in the knowledge that he actually commited *hara-kiri* in November 1970, the year after the film's release. Tanaka's suicide confirms Gosha's message – the only ending for violent, ambitious men is death.

Goyokin (1969)

Where *Tenchu* and *Sword of the Beast* feature anti-heroes as protagonists, in *Goyokin* Gosha allows for the possibility of heroism. Sometimes known as *Steel Edge of Revenge*, *Goyokin* means 'official gold', that is, gold belonging to the shogun. The Sabai clan, short of money, steal a shipment of shogunate gold from a shipwreck and kill a village of fishermen to cover up the crime. One of the Sabai samurai, Magobei (Nakadai Tatsuya) is disgusted but leaves the clan rather than cross his brother-in-law Tatewaki (Tamba Tetsuro), the chamberlain. Magobei makes Tatewaki give his word that the crime will never be repeated, but three years later the Sabai clan is still in financial trouble and Tatewaki plans to steal another shipment. Magobei learns of the scheme and heads back to Sabai. On the way, he meets Samon (Nakamura Kinnosuke), a shogunate agent posing as a *ronin*, and Oriha (Asaoka Ruriko), the only survivor from the village that was wiped out three years earlier. The three of them head for Sabai to prevent another massacre.

The essential premise – a corrupt clan stealing shogunate gold – is the same as *Sword of the Beast*, but the melancholy Magobei is the opposite of the fiery Gennosuke from the earlier film. Nakadai plays Magobei as a haunted man, full of regret, who returns to Sabai to cleanse himself of the guilt he has been carrying. He tells Shino, the wife he left behind when he became a *ronin*, 'I have a duty to carry out. I must stop the slaughter, so I can regain my worth as a human being. I have decided to return to Sabai to save the fishermen so that I, also, might have a new life.' Where Gennosuke sought to escape his clan's vendetta, Magobei seeks personal redemption through thwarting his clan's ruthless chamberlain and thus Magobei is the more heroic of the two characters; he seeks not survival, but salvation and justice.

In *Goyokin* Gosha is even less interested in personalising the villagers than he was in *Three Outlaw Samurai*. The fishermen are always seen in a large, faceless mass and, like the farmers in *Three*

Outlaw Samurai, they do not participate in the struggle to save their lives. This is another example of Gosha's use of established genre motifs. He doesn't care to characterise the helpless villagers, they serve as a plot device to propel the action. When Samon and Magobei attack the Sabai samurai in the fishing village, the locals cower in their huts. There is no humanistic desire to view all of society as being equal and inter-connected.

In true Gosha fashion, he closes not with a scene of peasants singing happily after they have been saved, (compare with *Seven Samurai*), but he rounds off the film with a group of drummers. Samon asks Magobei if the drummers are for a festival. 'No, it's a funeral', he replies, 'Our funeral. The end of the samurai.' Magobei then strikes a variation of the classic stray dog pose, walking out of town, a black figure against the white snow, but with his wife Shino following him. The comment about 'the end of the samurai' is another nod to genre requirements, which demand that *chambara* address the plight of the samurai class at the close of the Tokugawa period. Gosha includes this somewhat belatedly, but he ensures he has his bases covered.

Goyokin is the last of Gosha's most interesting works. The rot that infected the Japanese film industry set in with a vengeance in the 1970s and Gosha was not immune to it. *Bandits versus Samurai Squadron* (1978) was his next *chambara* film after the *yakuza* drama *The Wolves* (1972). *Bandits versus Samurai Squadron* sees the director delivering a functional genre movie intended to draw back Japan's lost audiences with a mixture of sex and violence. The movie begins with a battle scene and thus guarantees the viewer instant gratification, rather than waiting to introduce characters or build suspense. The film is over-long at nearly three hours, with a muddled plot and Gosha displays little imagination in his direction, introducing characters with onscreen titles to save him the bother of establishing their relationships. There is a good deal of gratuitous sex and female nudity, providing titillation to accompany the bloody action scenes.

The movie is poorly shot by cinematographer Masao Kosugi, with flat compositions and murky lighting. This marks a considerable decline from the outstanding photography of Tadashi Sakai in *Three Outlaw Samurai*, with his crisp lighting and excellent use of depth of field in composition. Toshitada Tsuchiyu filled *Sword of the Beast* with noir-inflected shadows to heighten mood and tension, and *Goyokin* saw beautiful use of widescreen framing and the juxtaposition of white snow with bursts of colour from cinematographer Kozo Okazaki. *Bandits versus Samurai Squadron* compares very poorly, as does Gosha's last *chambara* film, *Hunter in the Dark* (1979), which is marred by an excessive propensity for under-exposure, resulting in muddy colours and turbid photography.

Hunter in the Dark contains Gosha's customary warning about the futility of ambition, ending with a duel between corrupt police officer Okitsugu (Tamba Tetsuro) and underworld boss Gomyo (Nakadai Tatsuya) in which they succeed only in mutual destruction. Otherwise it is an unremarkable *chambara* and thereafter Gosha moved into exploitation filmmaking.

Gosha's films lack the passion of the best of his contemporaries, but his early works provide a case study of a director in full command of the iconography and language of a genre, and one for whom creating pure genre works seems to have been a worthy end in itself. It may be noted that it is possible to trace much of John Woo's aesthetic to the later Gosha films. *Hunter in the Dark* and *Tenchu* address the concept of identity and their violent, nihilistic protagonists would not seem out of place in any of Woo's Hong Kong gangster movies.

The Decline of the *Chambara* Genre

The decline of the Japanese film industry began in the 1960s, initially brought about by the introduction of television and consequent dwindling cinema revenues. During the 1950s the Japanese studios had capitalised on the breakthrough success of *Rashomon* and had successfully attracted Western audiences to their films. The works of Ozu, Inagaki, Kobayashi, Kurosawa, Mizoguchi and Honda all found their way to Western theatres, whether on the art-house circuit or dubbed for US drive-ins. The monster movies featuring Godzilla, Gamera and the rest were a reliable source of income for

Toho, but in the 1960s the studios failed to consolidate their international position.

The impact of television on the Japanese film industry was profound and saw the mass audience abandon domestic cinema in favour of staying at home watching television. Film production peaked in 1960, when 537 Japanese films were made, whilst in 2000 just 282 domestic films were released. With the passing of the general audience Kurosawa Akira was unable to raise funds for his expensive projects inside the studio system after *Red Beard*. The great director formed a venture with three of his contemporaries, Kobayashi Masaki, Kinoshita Keisuke and Ichikawa Kon, under the name The Club of the Four Knights. The group made just one project, Kurosawa's *Dodesukaden* (1970), but it was a flop and a despondent Kurosawa attempted suicide in December 1971. For the rest of his career he had to raise funds with help from outside Japan. *Dersu Uzala* (1975) was produced and shot in Russia, and thereafter his works, including *Kagemusha* (1980), were made with the financial backing of admiring American filmmakers, notably George Lucas and Francis Ford Coppola. It is extraordinary to think that the man who is regarded as Japan's greatest filmmaker was unable to raise funds in his home country. So, if the Japanese studios weren't financing Kurosawa, what kind of movies were they making?

The studios' goal was to produce cheap, commercially dependable product, whether this meant monster movies, salaryman comedies, or martial arts films. The new films did not follow the precedents established by the previous generation of filmmakers, either ideologically or artistically. There was a shift away from films that drew upon historical source material and a naturalistic conceptualisation of feudal Japan. The primary fount of ideas became *manga*, the comic books that account for roughly half of Japan's publishing output. Their popularity, which transcends gender, age and class boundaries, far exceeds that of their American counterparts; 1.9 billion *manga* were sold in 1995. *Manga* come in many genres, from romances to sports stories, and in the martial arts arena *manga* has become the principal point of reference for contemporary Japanese filmmakers. In the wake of the collapse of the mass domestic movie audience in the 1960s, the practice of adapting *manga* for the cinema displays the industry's desire to bring back viewers by offering them characters and stories already successfully established in Japanese popular culture.

Aside from the loss of the general audience, there is another dimension to the decline of Japanese cinema, that of the artistic deterioration of the films themselves. Unlike Kurosawa, Kobayashi and their contemporaries, the younger filmmakers had not experienced either combat or the deprivations of wartime. They grew up during the economic boom of the 1950s and 1960s and were products of the repressive education system that replaced the more open-minded schooling of the Taisho period. Kurosawa wrote in his autobiography:

> In my day there were many ... teachers who harboured a libertarian spirit and a wealth of individual qualities. By comparison with them, among today's schoolteachers there are too many plain 'salaryman' drudges. Or perhaps even more than salarymen, there are too many bureaucrat types among those who become teachers. The kind of education these dispense isn't worth a damn. (Kurosawa, 1983, p. 56)

Alex Kerr devotes an entire chapter of his book *Dogs and Demons – The Fall of Modern Japan* to exploring and condemning the ideology that drives the Japanese education system, with its emphasis on learning by rote: 'Facts memorized for exams are only a by-product, for the real purpose of education in Japan is not education but the habit of obedience to a group ...' (Kerr, 2001, p. 285). He argues persuasively that the goal of the Japanese school system is to produce loyal, diligent companymen to feed the economic machine, not to foster individuality or personal growth. The importance of subservience to the group is paramount:

> Students may not change out of their winter uniforms even if the weather is hot – everyone must sweat until the appointed day comes for the change into spring clothes ... In 1996, Habakino City, near Osaka, introduced uniforms for teachers as well ... From hair and dress, the rules extend in the hundreds to issues that go beyond the schoolyard. Many schools require children to wear uniforms on weekends ... (Kerr, 2001, pp. 289, 290)

The end result is students who: '... have not been taught analytical thinking, the ability to ask unusual or creative questions, a sense of brotherhood with the rest of mankind, or curiosity about and love for the natural world' (Kerr, 2001, pp. 302, 303).

This opinion finds support from Asano Kenichi, Professor of Communication Studies at Doshisha University, whose article 'Why Japan Remains a Threat to Peace and Democracy in Asia' appeared in *Censored 2004*. On the Japanese press, Asano wrote, 'Those who work in Japanese media circles do not use their constitutional right to carry out investigative reporting. The Japanese press, as a whole, lacks any scepticism toward authority' (Phillips, 2003, p. 314). The impact all this had on the cinema of Japan was evident in the loss of the humanism and anti-militarism that shaped the works of Kurosawa, Kobayashi and Okamoto. The martial arts films of the 1970s were radically different in character to those they succeeded.

The 'Lone Wolf and Cub' Series

Adapted from the *manga* written by Kazuo Koike and set during the Tokugawa dynasty, the 'Lone Wolf and Cub' series chronicles the adventures of Ogami Itto and his son Daigoro as they wander Japan pursued by the agents of the Yagyu clan. The first film *Sword of Vengeance* (1972), directed by Misumi Kenji, sets up the premise. Ogami is the official executioner of the shogun, acting as *kaishaku* for anyone the shogun has ordered to commit suicide. The Yagyu clan want one of their members to be official executioner and their leader Retsudo frames Ogami for treason and murders his wife. Refusing a shogunate order to commit suicide, Ogami sets out on the road of vengeance, taking his infant son with him in a pram or baby carriage filled with weapons.

What separates this series from the work of more ambitious directors like Kobayashi or Kurosawa is that, where the older generation used the *chambara* genre to criticise the *bushido* code and to condemn the nihilism of the samurai, 'Lone Wolf and Cub' offers an unconditional endorsement of *bushido*. Ogami frequently talks of being 'at the crossroads to hell' and he has no hopes of ever laying down his sword. He isn't a stray dog so much as a rabid one; he exists only to keep killing and he certainly has the 'mania for death' admired by Yamamoto Tsunetomo in *Hagakure*. He battles hundreds of men at a time, with the weapons in the baby carriage becoming more outlandish as the series progresses. In *Sword of Vengeance* the baby cart has handles that detach to become a halberd. By the third film, *Baby-*

cart to Hades (1972), directed by Misumi Kenji, the front of the carriage opens to reveal what appear to be machine guns. The carriage is waterproof, arrowproof, bulletproof, fireproof; like Ogami himself it's indestructible. In the sixth film, *White Heaven in Hell* (1974), directed by Kuroda Yoshiyuki, the carriage is fitted with skis and Ogami rides it like a sled down a snow-covered mountain while pursued by an army of skiing ninja and samurai. The mind boggles.

The films display none of the compassion of Japan's great filmmakers. In *White Heaven in Hell*, a trio of ninja try to unnerve Ogami by killing everyone he comes into contact with. They kill a lady who passes Ogami and Daigoro on a road, a candy vendor and an innkeeper. There is no sense of injustice about these murders. The victims are never given personalities; neither Ogami nor the audience feels their deaths. They are merely part of a plot device and the absence of any emotion reflects the growing cynicism and superficiality of Japanese cinema in the 1970s. The extraordinary numbers of samurai who fall to Ogami's sword are not personified; they are faceless bodies cut down to reconfirm continually his status as superman. The few opponents who are afforded any screen time before meeting their grisly demise are caricatures. In *Babycart in Peril* (1972), directed by Saito Buichi, Ogami kills a swordswoman who defeats her male opponents by flashing her tattooed breasts to distract them. In *White Heaven in Hell* he fights Kaori, a knife-throwing expert and daughter of Retsudo who scarcely has any personality at all. She is introduced practising knife-throwing, then is sent to challenge Ogami, who kills her. Each movie invariably climaxes with a massive battle in which Ogami mows down scores of ninja and samurai and there's always another villain waiting in the wings, swearing to kill Ogami when next they meet.

The treatment of women in the series is deplorable. In *Sword of Vengeance*, Ogami is hired to kill a group of mercenaries hiding out at a hot-spring resort. Ogami allows himself and Daigoro to be taken prisoner. His sword is taken away, he is beaten and forced to have sex with a prostitute while the thugs watch. The following morning, he kills all the mercenaries without breaking a sweat. It is apparent that he could have killed them all at any moment. Why he chooses to be humiliated and forced to perform sex acts is never explained. The prostitute is impressed by both Ogami's sexual prowess and his martial skills. She claims that he had sex with her to save her from the mercenaries, but it's clear that they are no match for Ogami. He doesn't interfere with a violent rape that he witnesses upon arriving at the hot springs, so it's difficult to argue that he saves the prostitute out of compassion. The violence against women can only be considered to be gratuitous and exploitative.

Kusumoto Eiichi supervised the action choreography on the series and his work is a far cry from the best of Kuze Ryu, who worked with Kurosawa and Okamoto. Kusumoto's choreography is wildly over the top. The series is exceptionally bloody, with countless limbs severed, bodies decapitated, and huge spurts of blood accompanying every sword stroke. Ogami leaps impossibly high in the air and slays opponents by hurling his sword at them. The knife-thrower Kaori from *White Heaven in Hell* doesn't throw her knives directly at her opponents. She juggles them and throws one high into the air so it falls straight down, piercing the top of her victims' skulls. The juggling looks ridiculous; perhaps the device was more convincing in the comic books. To be fair, Wakayama Tomisaburo has talent as a screenfighter. He is quick on the draw and performs his fights with focus and conviction. It is a shame that much of what happens is so preposterous. Ninja burrow through the ground and leap out of every shadow. *Babycart in Peril* features a samurai whose sword bursts into flame on command and many characters display superhuman endurance. In *Babycart to Hades*, Ogami has a long chat about *bushido* with a samurai he has impaled with his sword. At the climax of *Babycart in Peril*, Ogami is stabbed in the gut, then in the back. He collapses, but Daigoro removes the sword from his father's back, Ogami gets to his feet and pushes the baby carriage off again. How he can do this is never explained; he's simply indestructible. Ogami is a male fantasy, an invincible warrior. He is not on a journey to enlightenment, as Sanshiro Sugata and Miyamoto Musashi were. None of the films deliberately attempts to satirise the genre. The violence is presented purely as entertainment. The films have no social agenda and no conscience, a far cry from the Japanese films of the 1950s and 1960s.

The stories are humourless and unrelentingly grim. Ogami never smiles or makes a joke. The only human dimension to his character is provided by the presence of his son, Daigoro. Remove the little boy and Ogami would become completely inhuman. Daigoro himself has very little emotional range, like his father he is stoical and dour. It is only in the sixth film, *White Heaven in Hell*, that director Kuroda Yoshiyuki allows Daigoro to react to the endless slaughter around him. Instead of mute stoicism, Daigoro gasps and covers his mouth. Neither of the other directors on the series – Misumi Kenji and Saito Buiichi – even allowed Daigoro to do that. He watches silently, expressionless as his father sends limbs and heads flying left and right. Alas, this is the only appropriate reaction to the continuous carnage. Ogami is unsympathetic and scarcely human, and since his opponents are either underdeveloped or featureless, there is no reason to care about all the fighting. There is no one to care about.

When the American television series *Shogun* was a massive hit in 1980, the first two films in the 'Lone Wolf' series were edited into one and released in the West as *Shogun Assassin*. The finished product is even more action-heavy than the Japanese originals, since *Shogun Assassin* is essentially a collection of fight scenes. The plot is somewhat simplified, with Yagyu Retsudo recast as the shogun who, consumed by paranoia, turns against Ogami. In the United Kingdom, the film was considered so gruesome that it was banned as a 'video nasty' and only officially released to home video twenty years later.

Lady Snowblood

The two films featuring the Lady Snowblood character were based upon the *manga* by writer Koike Kazuo, who penned 'Lone Wolf and Cub', and artist Kamimura Kazuo. Toshiya Fujita began directing at Nikkatsu Studios, in their Pinku Eiga section, making pornography. At Nikkatsu he worked with actress Kaji Meiko – famous for their 'Women in Prison' series – who played the lead in the 'Snowblood' films. Their first collaboration was the 'Alleycat Rock' series about girl bikers, and when Toho Studios attached Meiko to 'Lady Snowblood', she recommended Toshiya as director.

The series is thematically similar to 'Lone Wolf and Cub', featuring an alienated protagonist consumed by a mission of vengeance. *Lady Snowblood – Blizzard from the Netherworld* (1973), introduces

Yuki, the daughter of Sayo, whose husband and son were murdered by a gang of three men and one woman, who raped her. Sayo kills one of the men and is sent to prison, where Yuki is born. She dies moments after Yuki's birth and the girl is raised to be the instrument of her mother's revenge. This is a good example of *shushigaku*, for the path of Yuki's life is set out before she enters the world. Her quest for vengeance is not of her own choosing, but it defines her life. There is no conflict between *giri* and *ninjo*. Yuki is devoted to the hunt for retribution and does not display any doubt or regret about her role. She is like Ogami Itto, cut off from all emotions except the desire for vengeance. Yuki meets a writer, Ashio Ryurei, who becomes sympathetic to her quest, yet she never seems to form any connection to Ryurei; he is merely another instrument in her mission. When he is kidnapped by men working for Kitahama Okono, the woman that Yuki is hunting, it is not clear if Yuki rescues him because she cares for him, or because she's on Okono's trail. Yuki's adventures are humourless and suffer the same shortcomings as the 'Lone Wolf' series. Yuki is so detached and remote that it is impossible to identify with her. The villains are completely evil, with no depth of characterization, so that it is hard to care about their fates either.

Lady Snowblood – Blizzard from the Underworld does contain some stylistic elements that separate it from 'Lone Wolf and Cub'. It is set after the imperial restoration in 1874 and the end of national seclusion, which is unusual for a *chambara* film. The music contains several Western pieces: a jazz score accompanies one sequence of Ryurei at work, while *The Waltz on the Blue Danube* plays over the masquerade ball. Furthermore, Toshiya does not maintain the illusion of naturalism. In two sequences he includes drawings from the 'Lady Snowblood' comic book to fill in the back-story. Secondly, after Okono's death, a curtain descends from the top of the frame, suggesting the end of an act in a play. This is reminiscent of Ichikawa Kon's film *An Actor's Revenge* (1962), which employed deliberately theatrical sets and lighting techniques, plus a soundtrack that offered a wild mixture of traditional Japanese music, a Hollywood-style score and jazz. Toshiya is by no means the equal of Ichikawa and in his hands the techniques are applied in a haphazard and inconsistent manner. Ichikawa overplayed the melodramatic nature of *An Actor's Revenge* because it was impossible to underplay the ridiculous story. Toshiya's film lacks the same melodramatic qualities and his use of comic book images, chapter headings and the theatrical curtain do not present a fully realised aesthetic approach to the material.

Hayashi Kunishiro choreographed the action and he has Yuki fight with the same reverse-grip style as Zatoichi. Meiko handles her fight scenes well, although the impossibly high leaps and somersaults that she performs are artificial and unconvincing. The training sequences of young Yuki learning to fight are bizarre. Her tutor is the priest Dokai and one of his methods involves rolling Yuki down a steep hill in a barrel. Aside from developing an extraordinary resistance to motion sickness, the purpose of this exercise remains a mystery. Clumsy and distracting handheld camerawork spoils the scenes in which Dokai teaches Yuki to wield a sword. All the battles featuring the adult Yuki are gory affairs, with loud sound effects accenting every sword stroke. Huge spurts of blood follow the path of Yuki's blade and numerous limbs are hacked off. Yuki wears a white kimono that dramatically contrasts with the bright red blood that drenches her after battle. This is indicative of the failure to present Yuki as a human being. Clad in white and very pale, the character seems like a porcelain doll. The contrast between her white clothes and the bright red blood is visually striking and draws the eye to her in the frame, but the absence of any reaction from Yuki marks her as a fetish object. There is some potency on the image plane, but there is no emotional dimension to the figure, quite unlike Oichi from the 'Crimson Bat' series. In 'Lady Snowblood', the swordswoman is objectified, not personified.

In common with inhuman killers like Ogami Itto, Yuki does not feel pain. She doesn't cry out when injured and survives being shot and stabbed. The priest Dokai calls her a 'child of the Netherworlds', which echoes Ogami's claims to be standing 'at the crossroads to Hell'. The shift from stray dog to inhuman automaton in the *chambara* genre reflects a shift in Japanese cinema in the 1970s. These films are soulless and the lack of any attempt to criticise, never mind deconstruct, the *bushido* code speaks volumes of the success of the post-war Japanese education system in producing citizens unwilling or unable to question the status quo.

The Street Fighter (1974)

Directed by Ozawa Shigehiro and known in Japanese as *Gekitotsu! Satsujin ken*, which roughly translates to 'sudden attack: the killing fist', when released in the United States as *The Street Fighter*, this film had the dubious honour of being the first non-pornographic movie to earn an 'X' certificate. American distributors New Line Cinema, unhappy that the film could only be screened in 'adult' movie theatres, made whatever cuts the film board deemed necessary to lose the 'X' certificate. The result was a movie in which all the violence had been excised. Fights were over before they started. Opponents squared off, there would be an abrupt jump-cut and someone would be lying in a pool of blood. Twenty years later, American filmmaker Quentin Tarantino purchased the video release rights and the film was made available in its uncut version. Cut or uncut, it's a terrible movie, yet it has served to raise its star, Shinichi 'Sonny' Chiba, to the status of cult hero.

Muscle-for-hire Tsurugi Takuma, or Terry Surugi in the American-dubbed version, is hired to bust convicted killer Junjou out of jail. Terry springs Junjou and smuggles him to Okinawa, but when Terry meets Junjou's brother and sister to collect payment, they don't have the money. Terry is a stickler for fiscal responsibility, strong words are exchanged and Junjou's brother falls out of a window to his doom. Determined to try to make a buck out of a bad deal, Terry sells the sister into prostitution. The *yakuza* ask Terry to kidnap a wealthy heiress for them, but he hates the *yakuza*, refuses to work for them and beats several of them up for good measure. He offers his protection to the heiress, just to antagonise the gangsters, who kidnap her anyway. Terry rescues her, but not before being captured and losing his sidekick Ratnose, who dies trying to protect his boss. The *yakuza* hire Junjou, who happens to be a karate master, to fight Terry and they have a showdown. Terry wins. Hooray. The End.

What the above synopsis does not detail is the manner in which Terry dispatches his opponents. In the course of the film, he rips off a man's testicles, tears out an Adam's apple, crushes a skull and gouges out eyes. There are moments when the image switches to 'X-ray mode', so the audience can see the effect of Terry's blows on the internal structure of his opponents. The violence is never qualified or redressed by any moral dimension. Terry is not seeking enlightenment, he is not interested in protecting the weak and has no conscience, selling Junjou's sister into prostitution to make a dollar. Devoid of any wider context, the violence becomes gratuitous and exploitative. Whilst the character is muscle-for-hire, existing on the outskirts of society, it is difficult to equate him with the stray dog heroes of the *chambara* genre, like Sanjuro or Zatoichi. Sanjuro, despite his gruff exterior and poor manners, is a humanist. Zatoichi was forever rescuing orphans and the helpless, despite being a gambler and killer. Terry Surugi has none of these redeeming features. He cares for no one but himself and he takes on the *yakuza* not out of any sense of justice or moral righteousness, but because he hates them.

It is possible to view Terry's sociopathic behaviour as part of an attempt to cast Sonny Chiba in the mould of the hard-bitten Hollywood action stars of the 1970s – Clint Eastwood in *Dirty Harry*, or Steve McQueen. If so, it is badly misjudged, undermined by the character's complete amorality and the homoerotic nature of his relationship with sidekick Ratnose (Yamada Waichi). Terry expresses no interest in the women in the movie, while Ratnose, or Rakuda no Cho in the Japanese version, worships his boss. When Terry works out, the fawning Ratnose gazes at his boss's muscular, sweaty torso, and when Terry is captured, Ratnose gives information to the villains to save Terry from torture. He can't bear to see the big man suffer. Their relationship has sadomasochistic overtones as Terry constantly bullies, belittles and insults Ratnose, who dies trying to save his master's life. It is wildly camp and this further disqualifies the central character from the role of Hollywood-style tough guy.

The fight scenes reflect the influence of Hong Kong action movies, which by this time had surpassed their Japanese contemporaries. This was a strange reversal of fortunes; in the 1960s Hong Kong filmmakers had looked to Japan for technical expertise and stylistic sophistication. Four separate people are credited with contributions to the fight choreography, which still manages to be poorly executed. Terry must have studied at the same *dojo* as Tesshin from *Sanshiro Sugata, Part Two*, for he spends a lot of time grimacing and grunting. When he's not flexing himself, Terry is busy tearing off other people's body parts and breaking bones, but none of the fights are performed with great style or imagination. The climactic duel with Junjou (Ishibashi Masashi) uses slow motion to try to highlight the techniques, but neither performer is a particularly gifted screen-fighter and, despite the gore, they do not sell the punches convincingly.

The film was popular enough to spawn several sequels; *Return of the Street Fighter*, *Sister Street Fighter* and *The Street Fighter's Last Revenge*, all made in 1974, which gives some indication of the care with which they were produced. They are all as odious and relent-lessly gory as the original. Chiba continued to work regularly in Japan, appearing in countless martial arts and *yakuza* movies, such as *The Killing Machine* (1975), a rather lurid account of the life of Doshin Soh, founder of the *Shorinji kempo* style. He continues to work regularly in Hong Kong and Japan and appears in Quentin Tarantino's *Kill Bill – Volume One* (2003), a testament to his enduring status as a cult hero.

Pursuing the Youth Audience
– Japanese Cinema Post-Decline

The impact of television on domestic cinema was far more pro-nounced in Japan than elsewhere in the world; it saw the Japanese film industry lose the mass audience that it has subsequently never been able to reclaim. Popular series like the 'Zatoichi' films and 'Lone Wolf and Cub' made the transition from film to television. In *Dogs and Demons – The Fall of Modern Japan*, author Alex Kerr is full of condemnation for the current state of Japan's film industry:

> Once boasting masters such as Kurosawa Akira and Ozu Yasujiro, Japan has recently produced only a few films of moderate world suc-cess. The number of good films is so low that at the 1994 Kyoto International Film Festival the usual *Japan Film Today* program was replaced by a retrospective of older films – the most recent from 1964. (Kerr, 2001, p. 321)

Although the golden age of Japanese filmmaking is now half a century distant, there are still directors producing interesting works and attracting audiences in Japan and overseas. Itami Juzo made several excellent comedies before his untimely suicide in December 1997, including *Tampopo* (1985) and *Minbo – Or the Gentle Art of Japanese Extortion* (1992), which enjoyed successful art-house releases in the West. More recently, Japanese cinema has experienced international success in the horror genre, with movies like *Ring* (1998) and *Audition* (1999) becoming cult favourites.

Princess Blade (2001)

The *chambara* genre survived on television in Japan from the mid-1970s until the growing popularity of youth-oriented Hong Kong action films in Japan led to the genre being revisited in the cinema. *Princess Blade* was loosely inspired by the same *manga* by Kazuo Koike and Kazuo Kaminura that 'Lady Snowblood' was based upon and updates the stray dog protagonist.

Five hundred years in the future, in a country that has lapsed into isolationism and stagnation, reformers have taken to armed rebellion to try to force change, and the government has hired a clan of assassins, the house of Takemikazuchi, to suppress dissent. Princess Yuki (Shaku Yumiko) is heir to the clan, led by Byakurai. When Yuki learns that Byakurai murdered her mother, who wanted to disband the clan and live in peace, she is forced to flee. On the run, she meets Takeshi (Ito Hideaki), a bomb-maker for the rebels, led by Kidokoro. Takeshi and Yuki slowly form a bond and reassess their violent pasts. The Takemikazuchi clan catches up with Yuki and a battle begins while, back at his house, Kidokoro confronts Takeshi, who wants to quit the rebel cause, prompting Kidokoro to shoot him. Yuki defeats the Takemikazuchi clan and slays Byakurai, only to return and find Takeshi fatally wounded. He dies in her arms.

The setting, in a country that has adopted seclusion and stagnation, is a parallel with Tokugawa dynasty Japan. Further enforcing the film's genre credentials are the many sword fights. Despite being set in the future, the Takemikazuchi assassins use swords, not guns. As the six-shooter is the essential icon of the Western, so the sword is inseparable from the *chambara*. Like the other films adapted from the work of Kazuo Koike, including the 'Lone Wolf and Cub' and 'Lady Snowblood' series, *Princess Blade* is completely dour. Yuki never cracks a single joke. She is an isolated, dehumanised stray dog. Where this film differs from the previous works is that Yuki grows over the course of the narrative. In an early scene she kills Anka, a clan member attempting to defect, without the slightest trace of remorse, revealing no emotion at all. When injured, Yuki cauterises her wound with a hot knife, without flinching. 'Doesn't that hurt?' asks Takeshi. 'Yes, if you let it', she replies. She is much like Ogami Itto, a cold-blooded, stoical killer.

Yuki's emotional development is expressed visually; all the scenes with the Takemikazuchi clan are monochromatic, with washed-out colours reflecting the absence of warmth and compassion. The scenes with Takeshi are more colourful, employing a warmer palette, suggesting that it is Takeshi and his sister who bring emotion into Yuki's world. When Takeshi dies, Yuki experiences an epiphany and cries for the first time. The final shot is of Yuki standing by a lake holding her sword. This is a requirement of the *chambara* genre, which demands that its heroes end the film isolated in the frame, expressing the alienation wrought by their violent natures. Yet, unlike Ogami or Lady Snowblood, Yuki commences the story as an alienated protagonist, but finishes having rediscovered her lost humanity. This is a progression for the genre, and may be indicative of a decline in the cynicism of Japanese cinema.

The action sequences were choreographed by Donnie Yen, a performer trained in Hong Kong by Yuen Wo Ping. Yen's work in *Princess Blade* is impressive and contains the trademarks of his Hong Kong training. There are wire stunts, enabling the performers to execute aerial kicks in combination, and a large range of sword and unarmed techniques. The sword battles are filmed using a range of optical effects, including slow motion and altering the shutter angle of the camera to give the scenes a strobe-like quality. Shaku Yumiko performs much of her own action and the choreography possesses variety and energy.

The styling of the film is contemporary, rather than reflecting an attempt to anticipate future trends. Yuki and Takeshi's hairstyles and clothing are fashionable for the time when the movie was made. Whilst the film is set five centuries in the future, it offers a mixture of Japan's past and present, making allusions to the Tokugawa dynasty, and through its contemporary visual design, addressing itself directly at a modern, youthful audience.

Azumi (2003)

Azumi, directed by Kitamura Ryuhei and adapted from the *manga* by Yu Koyama, sees the *chambara* further tailored to appeal to a young audience. After the Battle of Sekigahara, a samurai called Gessai is charged with assembling and training a group of assassins to kill anyone who threatens to bring civil war back to Japan and unsettle the Tokugawa government. Gessai gathers ten young orphans and trains them in martial arts. Years later, the only girl in the group, Azumi, has emerged as the most capable fighter. Gessai takes the five students who survive the final stage of their training out of their mountain home to assassinate three warlords who plan to overthrow the shogun and replace him with Toyotomi Hideyori. Azumi slays the first warlord, but the second, Kiyomasa, proves more difficult when he sends assassins of his own to track down the group. At the conclusion Kiyomasa is slain, but only two of the assassins remain, Azumi and Nagara.

This is the *chambara* movie re-fashioned as a teen film. It is hard to imagine Kurosawa or Kobayashi making a samurai film with a teenage cast, but their films were intended for a mass audience composed largely of adults. With the loss of the mass cinema market in Japan and the ever-growing consumer power of the under-twenty-fives, it was perhaps inevitable that the *chambara* would be refashioned for the new, younger audience. Despite the youthfulness of the cast and the film's efforts to appeal to a young demographic, the movie supports a conservative ideology.

The film is quick to align itself emotionally with the young heroes against the adults. It is the grown-ups who cause all the suffering, from Gessai ordering the ten orphans to pair up and fight to the death to select the five best assassins, to the three *daimyo* plotting civil war. Azumi experiences the clash between *giri* and *ninjo*, and questions her mission when Gessai prevents the team from intervening when they witness a group of bandits slaughter a village of peasants. Gessai refuses to let the assassins reveal themselves, saying, 'Merely killing a hundred bandits will not change this nation'. Underlying this scene is the belief that the greater good outweighs the importance of the individual – the villagers die so the assassins can continue their mission to stop another civil war that would threaten all of Japan.

This idea is further developed when Amagi, one of the assassins, is poisoned and Azumi won't leave him, so he kills himself to ensure that she continues with their mission. Demonstrating the nihilism of *bushido*, Amagi puts the cause before his own life. At the end, after Gessai has been killed and Kiyomasa has been slain, Azumi chooses to hunt down the third and final *daimyo*, even though without Gessai she is now free to live her own life. She chooses duty before personal desire. This is the very conservative message underpinning the film; subservience to the needs of the group is paramount. The movie's support of the status quo is unquestioning: Azumi kills Kiyomasa because he threatens the shogunate. There is no real sense of youthful rebellion – the five orphans may be masterful fighters, and all their opponents in the film are adults, but the film's final message is one of obedience.

The movie makes extensive use of computer-generated effects, for rendering arrows in flight and for some of the backgrounds, showing that Japanese cinema is keeping pace with technological developments from the United States. The score is contemporary, rather than offering music of the early Tokugawa period. Much of the music is melodramatic, reflecting the desire to capture a young audience with broad emotional strokes that teenagers will find appealing. It is revealing that the film is yet another story adapted from a comic book. The generation of filmmakers coming to prominence since the 1960s has not used historical references per se, but has increasingly sought to emulate the tremendous popularity enjoyed by comic books. *Azumi* was a big hit and director Kitamura evidently succeeded in his efforts to attract the youth audience. A sequel, *Azumi 2 – Death or Love*, with Kaneko Shusuke replacing Kitamura as director, was released in 2005.

Red Shadow (2001)

Equally youthful in character was Nakano Hiroyuki's *Red Shadow*, a somewhat haphazard parody of ninja films. Predictably, the film is based on a *manga*, this time by Yokoyama Mitsuteru, which had already been adapted for television in the late 1960s. The movie concerns three ninja who are sent on various missions in the service of a local *daimyo*, Lord Togo. Like *Azumi* and *Princess Blade*, this is another movie tailored for the teenage viewer, with all three protagonists being young and attractive. The hero Akakage (Ando Masanobu) is handsome in the mode of clean-cut teen idol, whilst the female ninja Asuka (Aso Kumiko) wears a fishnet body stocking and leather mini-skirt. Hardly an authentic period costume, but intended to appeal to young male viewers.

Unlike *Princess Blade* most of *Red Shadow* is played for laughs. When the three ninja attempt to sneak into an enemy castle, they constantly bump their heads on the rafters and set off every booby trap in their path. The traps themselves are ridiculous and there is no sense of danger, only the spirit of nonsense, reinforced when they encounter a second group of ninja sneaking around, who proceed ineffectually to throw *shuriken* at the intruders.

The narrative touches upon the standard genre themes – the conflict between *giri* and *ninjo*, the notion of *shushigaku* – but these are incidental to the comedy. There is a brief moment of melodrama when Asuka is slain, but the silliness is swiftly resumed. The struggle to balance duty and desire is played out by Akakage and Aokage after Asuka's death when Aokage quits being a ninja, leaving Akakage to bear the burden of obedience to Lord Togo alone. Predeterminism is apparent in the unconsummated romance between Akakage and Lady Koto, the young, pretty *daimyo* whose life he saves. She knows she cannot marry a lowly ninja and he knows he has no claim to a high-class *daimyo*, revealing a conservative message about observing the status quo that underpins the story.

Like the music in *Azumi*, the score to *Red Shadow* is conspicuously contemporary, filled with electronic dance beats. Taken as a whole, the film makes no attempt to render an authentic vision of feudal Japan. The period setting is a pre-requisite of the story itself, concerning ninja and rival samurai factions, but is tangential to the style and mindset driving the movie. The film is only concerned with sat-isfying a modern, young Japanese audience and director Nakano maintains a tone of irreverence throughout, parodying the conven-tions of the cinematic ninja in a fashion similar to the approach of Jackie Chan and Yuen Wo Ping to the Hong Kong kung fu movie in the late 1970s. The lightness of mood is a much-needed break after so many grim *chambara* heroes stoically laying waste to entire armies. In the climax of *Red Shadow*, Lady Koto and Akakage capture the chamberlain, who wants to invade their neighbouring province, and Lady Koto argues vigorously against the destructiveness of war. There is no trace of the nihilism so widespread throughout Jap-anese cinema in the 1970s.

A Resurgence of Humanism

Roningai (1990)

Despite the over-abundance of exploitative and cynical *chambara* that dominated the 1970s, from the early 1990s there have been signs of a new wave of films to share the values of the humanist directors who led Japanese cinema after the Second World War. It is perhaps not surprising that many of these films have been the work of older directors, whose upbringing and education are likely to have been akin to those of Kobayashi, Kurosawa and Okamoto. These include Kuroki Kazuo and his remake of *Roningai*, or *Street of the Ronin*.

Kuroki was born in 1930 and his family moved to Manchuria in 1936, where he remained until returning to Japan for high school. Intending to become a minister, Kuroki entered the theology depart-ment of Doshisha University, but was so impressed by the films of Kurosawa Akira that he left college to pursue a movie career. Ini-tially working in documentaries, Kuroki moved to drama after the success of his acclaimed *Record of a Marathon Runner* (1964). *Roningai* was produced to mark the sixtieth anniversary of the death of Makino Shozo, the man regarded by many as the father of Japanese cinema. Makino Shozo was the first Japanese filmmaker to use a sce-nario (the silent-era version of a script), to pre-plan shots, and to make use of editing and camera movement to tell a story, where the earliest filmmakers had filmed static wide shots of stage actors performing theatrical scenes. His son, Makino Masahiro, filmed the first version of *Roningai* as a multi-part feature released in Japan in 1928 and 1929. There are no surviving prints of the original, but the scenario exists and was used as the starting point for Kuroki's film.

The movie concerns the inhabitants of a slum, particularly four destitute *ronin* and the prostitutes who congregate around an inn. A gang of shogunate samurai start murdering prostitutes at night and the local women appeal to the *ronin* for help, but they all have their peculiar excuses for not getting involved. It is only when Oshin, a prostitute with whom everyone is enamoured, is captured and condemned to death by the shogunate men that the *ronin* overcome their apathy and take up arms against their oppressors.

The cast is packed with *chambara* regulars, including Tanaka Kunie, from *Sword of the Beast*, *Sanjuro* and *Goyokin*; Katsu Shintaro from the 'Zatoichi' series; Harada Yoshio from *Hunter in the Dark*, and Ishibashi Renji who appeared in two of the 'Lone Wolf and Cub' movies. Kuroki uses this cast of established genre actors to play upon the conventions of the *chambara*, particularly with Katsu Shintaro, who portrays one of the *ronin*, named Bull. On first sight, Bull is another in Katsu's long line of tough guys, swaggering around, scowling belligerently. When challenged, Bull makes a great show of wetting the handle of his sword – a common habit among samurai to make their weapons easier to grip in battle. Kuroki plays on Katsu's screen persona by revealing that Bull is all talk and no action. In one early sequence Bull gets into a fight with Gennai (Harada Yoshio), another *ronin* down on his luck. They square off but neither is willing to draw their sword and risk real danger. Instead they kick and shove each other, before getting drunk together. When the shogunate samurai declare their intention to kill any prostitute seen out at night, Bull swaggers up to them, sprays water onto his sword handle, and tells the samurai to follow him outside. The audience expects a fight but instead the image cuts to Bull bowing on all fours to the head of the samurai, apologising for his rudeness and asking for a job, confounding the expectations that accompany Katsu whenever he appears on screen.

Kuroki displays the same interest in the downtrodden that was prevalent in Kurosawa's work, from the farmers in *Seven Samurai* to the characters of *The Lower Depths*. Here, the protagonists are the women forced to work as prostitutes to make a living and the *ronin* who scrape by any way they can. Magoza (Tanaka Kunie) breeds birds and his sister is a seamstress, while Horo (Ishibashi Renji) has to test swords on the bodies of the executed for wealthy samurai, a practice he finds repugnant. The wealthy and powerful are seen to exploit their positions, as the shogunate samurai bribe the local sheriff to turn a blind eye to their murderous activities. When the shogun's men capture Oshin they plan to kill her by tearing her apart between two bulls, revealing their callousness and cruelty.

Alienation was a defining feature of the 1970s *chambara* anti-hero, but in *Roningai* Kuroki condemns this trait. Gennai is apathetic and self-centred; Bull is desperate for self-advancement and joins the shogunate group, even though they are killing the women who are his friends. Magoza only thinks about getting back his old job at his former clan, while Horo is consumed by self-loathing. When Oshin is placed in mortal danger, Magoza's sister Obun (Sugita Kaoru) has to spur the men into action. The film affirms Kurosawa's belief in the inter-dependency of human beings. Alone, none of the characters can stop the shogunate men terrorising the locals, but together they triumph. In Kuroki's world, alienation is a negative quality that drains the vitality from life; *Roningai* marks a return to the values of the golden age of Japanese cinema and a rejection of the exploitation of the 1970s. Kuroki suggests that amongst poverty the beauty of the human spirit can survive, an idea he expresses by focusing the camera on the flowers that grow in the slum.

The story is set at the end of the Tokugawa dynasty and, in the scene where Bull meets a noodle seller, the script makes it clear that the age of the samurai is closing. The man tells Bull that he used to be a samurai, but became a noodle vendor because it was easier to make a living with noodles than a sword. Kuroki directs the final battle as the last hurrah of the samurai and offers the destitute *ronin* an opportunity for redemption before their class fades from existence.

The Twilight Samurai (2002)

Yamada Yoji, like Kuroki Kazuo, began his filmmaking career in 1961. Yamada was born in 1931 in Osaka and was responsible for the 'Tora-San' comedies, the longest running film series in the world. *The Twilight Samurai* was his seventy-seventh feature and enjoyed huge critical acclaim in Japan, where it swept the 2003 Japanese Academy Awards, winning twelve awards, including the one for Best Picture. It was released in the West to coincide with the Tom Cruise vehicle *The Last Samurai* and in any comparison the American movie fares poorly.

At the end of the Tokugawa dynasty a low-ranking samurai, Iguchi Seibei, struggles to support his two daughters and senile mother following the death of his wife. He devotes all his time to looking after his family, and his fellow samurai in the castle stores where he works call him 'Tasogare Seibei', meaning 'Twilight Seibei', because he is so dull. He accepts a challenge on behalf of his friend Iinuma Tomonojo from the violent ex-husband of Tomonojo's sister, Tomoe. Using a wooden sword against his opponent's real blade, Seibei wins the duel, which brings him to the attention of the clan warden when Yogo, the captain of the watch and a master swordsman, refuses to commit suicide following an internal rebellion. Seibei tries to turn down the clan's demand that he fight the renegade, but is threatened with expulsion if he refuses, forcing Seibei to confront Yogo in combat.

Sanada Hiroyuki plays Seibei and his excellent performance is remarkable in the light of his early career. He had started film work as a stunt man with Sonny Chiba and appeared in some terrible movies, including *Roaring Fire* (1982) and the entertaining, if nonsensical, Hong Kong production *Ninja in the Dragon's Den* (1982). Since then Sanada has matured into an accomplished actor and may be more familiar to Western viewers for his roles in the Japanese horror films *Ring* and *Ring 2* (1999).

Seibei is the antithesis of the *chambara* stray dog anti-hero. He is a quiet family man and epitomises the Japanese concept of *mono-no-aware* – the awareness of life's limitations, a sense of harmony with the world and an acceptance of change. The filmmaker whose works best exemplify this belief is Ozu, whose *Tokyo Story* is considered a distillation of the concept. When Tomonojo says 'The times are changing', Seibei replies, 'When they do, I'll give up samurai status and be a farmer. That's what I'm suited for.' This displays *mono-no-aware* and separates Seibei from the typical *chambara* protagonist. He is not consumed by ambition, like Gosha Hideo's characters, he is not an alienated killer like Ogami Itto, he is not even a hungry stray dog like Sanjuro. Seibei is a man who wants to live quietly in peace and raise his daughters. He is a reluctant warrior and thus a remarkable genre protagonist. His devotion to his daughters contradicts the advice of Yamamoto Tsunetomo in *Hagakure* – that samurai should only raise boys and not waste their time on girls – marking Seibei as an unconventional samurai.

When drawn into battle, Seibei continues to defy expectations. He duels Tomoe's ex-husband Toyotaro and subdues him with a wooden sword, leaving him bruised but alive; Seibei has no 'mania for death'. When forced to confront Yogo, Seibei finds he has much in common with the condemned samurai and admits that he would prefer to allow Yogo to flee rather than fight him. Contrast this with the character of Tatewaki in *Samurai Rebellion*, who cannot relinquish his sense of duty and allow his friend Isaburo to leave the clan's territory unchallenged. Seibei's compassion for Yogo's situation reveals a humanist element and director Yamada uses Yogo's situation to highlight the contradictions and cruelty of *bushido*. He has been ordered to commit suicide for having the misfortune to be subordinate to the leader of the internal rebellion and Yogo argues that he should not have to kill himself simply for having followed the orders of his superior, the duty of every samurai.

The scene is played out within Yogo's house, rendered as a netherworld, filled with shadows, suggesting that the samurai are trapped in the darkness of the feudal system. Seibei confesses that he sold his *katana* to pay for his wife's funeral and is only armed with a *kodachi*, a short sword. Seeing his chance and incensed that Seibei has the temerity to challenge him with a short sword, Yogo attacks. Seibei begs him to stop, but Yogo fights with the desperation of a man with nothing left to lose. The feudal system has taken his wife, his child and now his samurai status. Seibei has to kill Yogo, but after the battle he staggers home with no fanfare or sense of triumph. Yamada presents the duel not as a glorious victory, but as another source of suffering imposed on Seibei by his clan and by *bushido*. He is not an alienated anti-hero, remorselessly sending his enemies to hell; he is a petty samurai forced to fight by his clan. Yamada's con-demnation of *bushido* is much needed when so many Japanese films since the 1970s have been unable to critique the warrior code and its emphasis on the unquestioning subordination of the individual to authority. Yamada and Kuroki are both advanced in years and when these men retire, the vacuum left in their wake will be profound.

Aiki (2002)

Daisuke Tengan is the screen name of Imamura Daisuke, son of director Imamura Shohei. Daisuke's credits include the script for the horror film *Audition* (1999) and three screenplays for his father, *The Eel* (1996), *Dr. Akagi* (1997) and *Warm Water Under a Red Bridge* (2001). Prior to directing *Aiki*, Daisuke made the documentary *The Unbeatable Handicap*, about professional wrestling. In the press notes for *Aiki*, he recounts the origins of the movie:

> It was the summer of 1992, I'm sure. I was flicking through a comic book called 'Secret Traditional Martial Arts' which I had bought but never read, and I came across a strange article. It was about a Danish man who, completely paralysed from the chest down after a traffic accident, had learned a traditional Japanese martial art and earned a black belt in it – even though he was confined to a wheelchair. The article also included a photograph of him in a wheelchair. The man's name was Ole Kingston Jensen. He was unknown in Denmark. The style of martial arts was called Daitoryu Aiki Jujutsu.

Daisuke's screenplay is transposed from Denmark to Japan and his protagonist is Taichi (Haruhiko Kato), a young boxer. After his first professional fight, Taichi is hit by a car and left paralysed from the waist down. Unable to come to terms with life as a paraplegic, Taichi sinks into depression. When he tries to save a young woman from being raped by three thugs, he is beaten up and only saved by the intervention of a tough racketeer. Taichi and the racketeer become friends and Taichi starts looking for a way to defend himself in his wheelchair. After being rejected by several martial arts instructors, Taichi meets Hiraishi Masatsugu (Ishibashi Ryo), a master of *Aiki* jiu-jitsu, who is intrigued by the challenge of teaching someone in a wheelchair. As he learns *Aiki* jiu-jitsu, Taichi rediscovers his self-worth and begins a relationship with Samako (Tomosaka Rie), a temple girl with a gambling habit. At a martial arts demonstration, a *kempo* instructor confronts Hiraishi and declares *Aiki* jiu-jitsu to be a fraud. Hotheaded Taichi shoots his mouth off at the *kempo* master and a match is arranged between the two. After evading the *kempo* master's attacks by frantically wheeling away from him, Taichi throws him, winning the bout. Back in his *dojo*, Hiraishi is attacked by the vengeful *kempo* instructor and his students, but he subdues them all. The final shot is of Taichi training in his wheelchair on the path where he ran as a boxer.

This is an uplifting movie about the value of life and the importance of self-control. The title refers to *ki*, which means life energy, known as *chi* in Chinese. *Aiki* loosely translates as a state of harmony, when one's life energy is in perfect alignment. As a boxer, Taichi was full of aggression and when he turns this inward after his accident he starts to destroy himself, becoming isolated and drinking himself into oblivion. Taichi's journey is from spiritual darkness in the depths of depression, to enlightenment and he reaches this goal through martial arts. Hiraishi tells him that the secret to *Aiki* jiu-jitsu is 'By accepting your opponent, control your opponent'. Taichi's opponent isn't the *kempo* master or the thugs who beat him up. Taichi's opponent is himself; until he learns to accept who he has become, instead of being angry with himself for being paralysed, he will never develop. He is only able to make his Aiki jiu-jitsu work when he incorporates his wheelchair into the techniques, moving his wheelchair to gain the leverage to throw his opponent. The final shot of him in the wheelchair on the running path demonstrates his acceptance of himself and his spiritual release.

Daisuke uses the character of the *kempo* instructor to elaborate on the theme of the futility of uncontrolled aggression. The *kempo* master is a bully who beats up his students to feel like a big shot. By contrast Hiraishi, the *Aiki* jiu-jitsu *sensei*, is a quietly spoken, unassuming man who arrives at the *dojo* carrying his briefcase from the office. The showdown between the *kempo* school and the *Aiki* master is outstanding. When the *kempo* students attack, Hiraishi moves forwards, accepting their attacks and throws them all into a heap. The *kempo* master is horrified, but attacks anyway, only to join the pile of bodies. The sole witness to the fight is a cleaning lady, who breaks into spontaneous applause. The conflict between rival martial arts

schools is so common in martial arts films that it has become stereotypical and Daisuke has fun with the convention. When the *Aiki*
master defeats the entire *kempo* class, without seriously harming any
of them, it is difficult not to share the cleaning lady's admiration for
the skill with which both performers and director execute the
sequence.

Aiki is in the same vein as *Sanshiro Sugata* and reflects a humanistic outlook similar to that of Kurosawa. Taichi's friends include the
gambling Samako, the racketeer (who is essentially a *yakuza* by
another name) and the *Aiki* instructor who is a salaryman. The
diversity of the characters is typical of the broad range of society that
Kurosawa brought to the screen. It is a sharp contrast to the nihilism
of the *chambara* films of the 1970s and makes a welcome addition to
the genre.

Closing the Circle

Fourteen years after Katsu Shintaro's last outing as the blind
swordsman and six years after Katsu's death, Kitano Takeshi
brought the character back to life. Kitano's film, simply titled *Zatoichi* (2003), is not a remake of any of the earlier movies, but presents
a distinctly postmodern approach to *chambara* cinema.

The story contains the requisite elements that defined the original
series. Ichi, played by Kitano, wanders into a remote village where
the ruthless Ginzo gang are squeezing protection money from the
local farmers and eliminating their rivals. Ichi befriends a gambler,
Shinkichi, and his aunt Oume, before encountering two orphans,
Osei and Okinu, searching for the bandits that murdered their family. When Ichi stirs up trouble against the Ginzo, the gang hire a
ronin, Hattori (Asano Tadanobu) to duel him. After slaying the
yakuza and Hattori, Ichi exposes the leader of the bandits and blinds
him, leaving him to spend the rest of his life as an outcast.

On the surface, the plot follows the expected format, but Kitano
deconstructs the standard generic elements. In his production notes
he comments on his approach to the title character, 'Zatocihi is practically invincible. He can take anybody on. The question is how? ...

I finally decided the secret to Zatoichi's strength is "This is a film!"' Throughout the movie, Kitano asserts his awareness of the directorial power he wields as filmmaker in a world of his own devising. A pertinent example is the interaction of incidental music with the performers on screen. On three occasions the sounds of peasants working becomes the rhythm of the score. In the first instance, a group of farmers are seen digging a field, the sound of their tools hitting the soil keeps time with the music. This is repeated when the same group stamp out a beat in the mud, keeping time with the score, and for a third time as they rebuild Aunt Oume's house, knocking out the rhythm with their hammers. The interplay between incidental music and motivated sounds produced within the film's world makes the audience aware of Kitano's manipulation of both levels, breaking the illusion of naturalism.

Kitano pushes this idea further at the conclusion. In his production notes, he comments, 'I used to make fun of Japanese period dramas, which all had identical endings. For example, when the hero leaves town and walks on a road along a rice field, the farmers ploughing the fields suddenly started singing and dancing while they worked.' Kitano deconstructs this motif by abandoning the period *mise-en-scène* and staging a tap dance routine on a stage, with the principal cast (excluding Zatoichi) and the members of the Japanese tap dance troupe, the Stripes, performing a contemporary routine backed by modern music. The generic form of the peasants dancing remains, but the staging is so overtly self-aware that the motif becomes deconstructed. The traditional sequence survives only as a postmodern nod to the expectations of the genre.

A vital difference between this film and the original series lies in the nature of Zatoichi himself. Aside from the obvious physical differences – Kitano's Ichi has blond hair and a red cane sword, where Katsu's Ichi had black hair and a wooden cane sword – Kitano's Ichi is not the emotional centre of the story where Katsu's Ichi drove his movies, narratively and emotionally. Kitano's performance as Ichi is reserved and distant, a typical performance from him, who is understated (or wooden, as his critics have it) in all his films. Where the original Ichi was boisterous, prone to falling in love and possessing a ribald sense of humour, Kitano's character is detached. Most of the screen time and character development are given to the orphans

Osei and Okinu and the bulk of the humour is provided by Shink-ichi. Ichi is present only in physical terms and this sense of detachment – of Kitano being present in the film plane but always looking at the film world from the outside – is most perfectly enunciated in Ichi's duel with Hattori, the *ronin*. When they face off Kitano allows the audience inside Hattori's mind as he imagines the technique he will use to counter Ichi's reverse-grip *iaido* attack. Hattori and the audience see him block Ichi's stroke and slay him, then the image returns to the two men standing opposite one another. Ichi changes from a reverse grip to a conventional one and kills Hattori. It appears that Kitano/Ichi is watching the film, just as the audience does, allowing him to see what Hattori has planned. This refers back to Kitano's comment on the secret behind Ichi's invincibility in the production notes, 'This is a film!' a fact of which Kitano as director and performer is constantly aware.

The film is not entirely satisfying; Kitano's refusal to involve Ichi emotionally is frustrating and there is a sense that Ichi is fighting to fulfil the demands of the genre, but the film is nevertheless an interesting addition to the Zatoichi canon. The movie enjoyed a successful release in the West, winning the Silver Lion Special Director's Award and the Leone Del Pubblico Audience Award at the 2003 Venice Film Festival. The movie offers a postmodern approach to Zatoichi in particular and *chambara* in general, indicating that a contemporary audience may be unwilling to accept a straightforward *chambara* film on its own terms. The genre has become too familiar and can only be sustained by a radical approach like Kitano's.

Japanese cinema is enjoying a new surge of international interest and critical acclaim for the first time since the heyday of Kurosawa and Kobayashi in the 1960s. It remains to be seen if the humanism that defined that era will survive the passing of the last of the directors from that time or if the new filmmakers, like Kitamura Ryuhei, will follow the exploitation path of the 1970s.

Hong Kong

A Note About Names

The official language of China is Mandarin and since July 1997 this has been the official language of Hong Kong. However, the main language spoken in Hong Kong is Cantonese. There is no official system for transliterating Cantonese into English, so differing spellings of Cantonese names are common. To make matters worse, many Hong Kong stars have English names too. Sometimes these are of their choosing. On other occasions the names are invented by distributors to make their films more appealing to Western audiences. Lau Gar Fei is sometimes written as Lau Kar Fei, or Liu Chia Hui when using the pinyin system. Some film distributor in the 1970s decided to call him Gordon Liu, although Gordon Lau has also been used. Sometimes the Anglicised name is used with the Chinese name, for example Andy Lau Tak Wah, but this is akin to writing James Brown James. So, for the purposes of this book, I will use the Anglicised name where that is the one most readers will be familiar with, in such cases as Bruce Lee and Jackie Chan. Otherwise, I will use the Cantonese approximation whenever possible, as that is how the individual would identify themselves.

Key Terms

Kung fu loosely means 'hard work' in Cantonese, but is commonly used to refer to Chinese martial arts. There are countless different forms of kung fu and the Glossary describes the styles frequently seen in the movies. The title used for a kung fu master is *sifu*, denoting considerable respect.

The triads are the Chinese organised crime groups, comparable to the mafia and the Japanese *yakuza*. Their influence in Chinese communities is profound and their involvement in the entertainment industry omnipresent. During the boom in the Hong Kong film industry of the early 1980s, many stars were forced to act in movies produced by triad bosses who really did make offers that could not be refused. The triads' infiltration of the Royal Hong Kong Police was so successful that in 1974 the British government set up the Independent Commission Against Corruption (ICAC). At the time of the ICAC's inception it was estimated that thirty-five per cent of Chinese police officers in Hong Kong were either triad members or affiliates. There is a Chinese proverb that translates as 'the officials draw their power from the law; the people from the secret societies'. The triads have become a popular subject for contemporary Hong Kong action films.

Confucianism is a major element in Chinese culture and is present in many kung fu movies. It is based upon ancestor worship and the adherence to a set of classic texts that Confucius believed contained the guidance for human beings to live in harmony. Four central concepts provide the foundation of Confucianism: '... the Way (*dao*), ritual/propriety (*li*), humaneness *(ren)* and virtue (*de*) ... Devoting himself whole-heartedly to solving human problems, Confucius propagated the value of education, virtue and self-cultivation' (Yao, 2000, p. 26). Of greatest relevance to the martial arts genre is virtue, in particular the concept of martial virtue, as it relates to the self-cultivation of a moral and upstanding character through the discipline of martial arts training.

China and the Monks of Shaolin

China's recorded history goes back to 2500 BC, so what follows is a selective account, focusing on the periods relevant to the martial arts genre.

In AD 1250 the Mongols invaded China, where they held power until they were repelled by the Ming dynasty. The first Ming emperor was a Buddhist monk called Chu Yuan Chang, but upon his ascension to the throne in 1368 he assumed the name Hung Wu. The Ming dynasty lasted until 1644 when the Manchus invaded China and established the Ch'ing dynasty. The conquering Manchus met with resistance from organisations determined to restore the Ming to power, including the monks from Shaolin Temple (Siu Lam in Cantonese, but Shaolin is commonly used in the West).

The first Shaolin Temple was built during the T'ang dynasty (AD 618–907) in Songshan in Hunan province. The founding and eventual destruction of the temple are surrounded by legend, but the temple was probably destroyed during the reign of the Ch'ing emperor Kang Hsi. A renegade monk, Ma Yee Fuk, collaborated with imperial troops and showed them the secret passageways to the temple. When the building was set alight, the fleeing monks found their exits blocked by flames and the imperial soldiers. Only five monks escaped and they established a second temple in Fukien province. Their adopted creed became 'Overthrow the Ch'ing – Restore the Ming – Act according to the Will of Heaven'.

It is the students and monks from the second temple, in Fukien, that are the subject for many kung fu movies. The head abbot was Chi Shan, who established the Lohan Hall, through which students had to pass before graduation. In one outlandish form or another, numerous films detail the perils of the Lohan Hall. The most famous martial artists from the Fukien Temple were the monk San Te and fighters including Hung Hey Kwun, Hu Hui Chen, Fong Sai Yuk and two of his brothers, Fong Hau Yuk and Fong Mei Yuk. In 1768 the emperor sent his troops to attack the second temple for harbouring and training anti-Ch'ing revolutionaries and it was burnt to the ground. For a second time, the imperial troops were aided by a renegade monk, Bak Mei, who had left Shaolin to join the rival Wu Tang group. The surviving Shaolin fighters dispersed throughout southern China, spreading Shaolin martial arts. Canton became a centre for the descendants of the Shaolin rebels and it was there that Wong Kai Ying and his son Wong Fey Hung rose to fame.

In 1840 the Opium War broke out between China and Great Britain, as the Chinese authorities tried to stop the British selling opium in exchange for tea. The war ended in 1842 with the British triumphant and they acquired the island of Hong Kong. Matters further deteriorated for the Chinese when they were defeated by the Japanese in 1894, leading to the Treaty of Shimonoseki, in which China renounced all claim to the Korean peninsula. The European powers joined in the scramble for Chinese territories and Britain secured a ninety-nine-year lease on a section of the mainland, known as the New Territories.

In 1900 the growing resentment of foreign influence in China, in the wake of increasing foreign land claims and religious missions, led to the Boxer Rebellion, or Taiping Rebellion. The rebels were members of the I Ho Chuan Society, who believed that their combination of kung fu and magic would make them invulnerable to gunfire. They found support in the empress dowager, who issued edicts in their favour. After besieging the foreign compound in Beijing, the Boxers were defeated by a coalition of non-Chinese troops and driven out of the city before the rebellion collapsed.

In 1911 a revolt in Canton spread throughout southern China. On 1 January 1912 the Republic of China was founded by Sun Yat Sen, but Sun's Nationalist Party was unable to secure control, faced with the growing threat of the Chinese Communist Party and the invading Japanese. Sun died in 1925 and was replaced by Chiang Kai Shek, but he too was unable to unite and pacify China. In 1949 the Communists, led by Mao Tse Tung, drove Chiang's supporters out of the mainland to Taiwan. Many Chinese from Canton and southeast China fled the mainland and settled in Hong Kong under British rule.

Hong Kong remained under Britain's authority until July 1997, when it was returned to the Chinese. In the intervening century, the island and its people had developed a distinctive character. Hong Kong became a thriving international financial centre and whilst the official language was English, most of the Chinese population spoke Cantonese. The islanders developed their own unique culture, an esoteric blend of Chinese, British and American influences. The local pop music, Cantopop, is a huge industry where the biggest stars sell millions of albums throughout Asia and to Chinese ex-patriot communities throughout the world.

It is worth bearing in mind the distinction between Hong Kong and China. The movies to be discussed here are Hong Kong productions, for whilst they may be shot on location throughout Southeast Asia, they are the product of the Hong Kong film industry.

The Process of Genre

Film theorist Christian Metz proposed that a genre passes through four stages in its cinematic life cycle – experimental, classic, parody and deconstruction. The experimental stage comprises the first films to utilise the key elements that come to be regarded as defining the genre: iconography, narrative structure, *mise-en-scène*. The classic period includes the films that best exemplify the genre, where the key elements are fully integrated. This is followed by parody, which uses the genre expectations for humour, before deconstruction, where the essential elements are taken apart and re-assembled in an unfamiliar manner that retains the stylistic prerequisites for the genre but renders them meaningless by their removal from their accepted context.

The martial arts films of Hong Kong provide an ideal model for the application of Metz's theory and Hong Kong cinema has performed this cycle twice. The first cycle began in the 1940s, when Cantonese-language films first featured martial arts displays, and concluded around 1982. The second cycle, beginning in 1982, has only recently come full circle.

Kwan Tak Hing and Wong Fey Hung

Chinese folk hero Wong Fey Hung was born in Canton in 1847, the son of Wong Kar Ying, a famous martial artist who was a member of the Ten Tigers of Canton, a group of the top kung fu men in the region. Father and son were versed in *Hung Kuen*, the style spread by the anti-Ch'ing fighter Hung Hey Kwun, so there was a direct connection between Shaolin Temple and Wong Fey Hung.

When Fey Hung reached adulthood he took over his father's medicine clinic, Po Chi Lam, and started teaching martial arts. His senior student, Lam Sai Wing, opened a branch of Po Chi Lam in Hong Kong and was important in spreading *Hung Kuen*, writing the first books on the system. Fey Hung taught martial arts to the 5th Regiment of the Canton army and the civilian militia, which was responsible for guarding the local Chinese from the expanding foreign population. Aside from that, very little is known about the activities of the real Wong Fey Hung, who died in 1924. Like Robin Hood, most of what is currently accepted about him is at best a mixture of folklore and history. His adventures were first brought to public attention in a series of stories in Hong Kong newspapers. One of these, in the *Kung Shueng Daily News*, caught the eye of director Hu Peng, who made the first film about the legendary hero in 1949, *The True Story of Wong Fey Hung*. Actor and martial artist Kwan Tak Hing played Wong Fey Hung and the film was a hit. Kwan Tak Hing went on to play the same character over eighty times throughout the 1950s and 1960s. Two other directors, Wang Feng and Luo Chi, contributed to the series, which finished in 1970 with *Wong Fey Hung – Bravely Crushing the Fire Formation*.

Kwan Tak Hing continued to play the character on television and reprised the role in *The Skyhawk* (1972), *The Magnificent Butcher* (1979) and *Dreadnought* (1981). Kwan Tak Hing effectively became Wong Fey Hung, his screen persona filling the cultural and historical void left by the absence of verifiable information about the hero. The two names, Kwan Tak Hing and Wong Fey Hung, became inseparable, until Kwan Tak Hing the man had become Wong Fey Hung the myth. Kwan's portrayal of Fey Hung became the standard against which all subsequent interpretations were measured, including the parody by Jackie Chan and Yuen Wo Ping in *Drunken Master* (1978), and Tsui Hark's revival of the character in the 1990s.

The original series had a regular cast that included Lau Chan, a kung fu master trained by Lam Sai Wing, Wong Fey Hung's senior student. Lau Chan played his *sifu* on screen, forming a link between the films and the real Wong Fey Hung. Lau Chan was the father of Lau Gar Leung, Lau Gar Wing and the adopted parent of Lau Gar Fei, all of whom were major players in the Hong Kong film industry in the 1970s. Another supporting player whose career carried over into the 1970s was Yuen Siu Tien, the father of Yuen Wo Ping, who played the title character in *Drunken Master*. Shih Kien, who played Mr Han in *Enter the Dragon* (1973), was a regular actor in the series, always playing villains.

The films in the original series set the path for the kung fu movies that followed. Earlier Chinese films, such as *Burning of the Red Lotus Monastery* (1928) used special effects for their action scenes, with the performers demonstrating superpowers, shooting bolts of energy from their hands and flying through the air. There was no attempt to demonstrate authentic Chinese martial arts. Some films borrowed theatrical staging from the Peking Opera tradition, which meant that fights looked more like dancing than combat, with graceful movements and no sense of impact or realism. The 'Wong Fey Hung' series was the first to employ authentic martial artists and to include demonstrations of Chinese kung fu as a recurring element. A typical example is *How Wong Fey Hung Pitted a Lion Against the Dragon* from 1956, directed by Hu Peng. There are fights featuring a range of empty-handed techniques and fights performed with the broadsword, spear, pole and butterfly knives. The sequences are performed with speed and agility, although there are no sound effects to enhance the action. The choreography has the actors continuously interact with the environment, which, combined with the speed of the performances, creates the illusion that the fights are out of control, a quality essential to an exciting action sequence. There is a battle in a teahouse with Wong Fey Hung and his students against the villains led by Chin Chi Lok (Shih Kien, the perennial bad guy). Teahouses became extremely popular locations for fight scenes, since they provide numerous props with which to interact (seen more recently in *Crouching Tiger, Hidden Dragon* (2000)). Jackie Chan and Sammo Hung would become masters of staging fights with a huge range of props and the genesis of this style of screenfighting is found in *How Wong Fey Hung Pitted a Lion Against the Dragon*. When the fight breaks out, tables are overturned, benches smashed and the teahouse is practically levelled. Lam Sai Wing (Lau Chan) punches through a table and then smashes it over someone's head. When the villainous Chin pulls out two daggers, Wong Fey Hung picks up a cooking pot and fights with that. This spirit of improvisation, using whatever is to hand whether or not it's a traditional martial arts weapon, would be expanded by Chan and Hung in the 1980s.

The portrayal of women in the series set the stage for the female action stars that became commonplace in Hong Kong cinema. In this film, Fey Hung and his gang meet Lo Ming and her father, two out-of-towners who help them against the bad guys. Lo Ming is as competent as any of the men and holds her own in a sword duel against Chin Chi Lok. She is entirely more dynamic and self-reliant than any of her contemporaries in Japanese cinema. Where Otsu and Akemi trail after Miyamoto Musashi, frequently swooning at the drama of it all, Lo Ming dispatches Chin Chi Lok with a throwing dart. It is impossible to imagine Otsu appearing at the end of *Duel at Ganryu Island* and taking care of Kojiro. The strong portrayal of women may be because of the input of Mo Giu Lan, the last wife of the late Wong Fey Hung. Mo Giu Lan was only a teenager when she married the elderly Fey Hung, but she became an accomplished martial artist and performed several Lion Dances in the series.

How Wong Fey Hung Pitted a Lion Against the Dragon is shot on soundstages, not on location, a technique that would be very popular at Shaw Brothers Studios later on. This gives many of the scenes a somewhat artificial appearance, lacking the clutter and depth of perspective that lends naturalism to location shooting. Unlike the kung fu productions of the 1970s, the film is shot with synchronous sound, rather than having dialogue and sound effects dubbed in later. The script is underdeveloped, a major criticism levelled at kung fu cinema in general, but the narrative is not the principal point of interest. It was the demonstrations of Chinese martial arts that attracted audiences. Whilst the plots are often weak and un-dramatic, they contain a strong moral core. Fey Hung defeats the villains because he is the superior person, not just in kung fu, but in terms of his moral character. Fey Hung is the embodiment of Confucian philosophy; a patriarch who is admired and adored by the locals and he epitomises the concept of *wu de*, or martial virtue. This is similar in some respects to Sanshiro Sugata or Miyamoto Musashi in Japanese cinema, whose victories in combat are inseparable from their growth as human beings.

The use of film language in *How Wong Fey Hung Pitted a Lion Against the Dragon* is unsophisticated. The staging is distinctly theatrical with the camera covering dialogue in flat wide shots. Scenes with numerous actors conversing are composed with the characters lined up, facing the camera as if performing on stage and playing to the audience. The editing is simplistic; there is no use of montage, and very little camera movement. In terms of technical accomplishments, it is a far cry from the films coming out of Japan at this time. The technical virtuosity of Kurosawa's *Seven Samurai*, made in 1954, was beyond the reach of Hong Kong filmmakers of the same period. They worked with basic equipment and low budgets, hence the use of soundstages that appeared again and again throughout the 'Wong Fey Hung' series, ensuring the maximum return on the initial investment in set construction.

Another aspect of the series that became forever linked with the conceptualisation of Wong Fey Hung was the theme music. 'Under the General's Orders' is a Cantonese melody that has become Wong Fey Hung's personal score. When Tsui Hark revived the character in his 1991 film, *Wong Fey Hung*, he employed 'Under the General's Orders' for the opening and closing credit sequences. The theme has since been used in all the sequels and spin-offs that followed Hark's movie. In his article on the original series, Yo Mo Wan noted the importance of the theme's Cantonese origin:

> Quite apart from their subject matter, this strong regional flavour, including of course the lively and vivid Cantonese dialect, clearly distinguishes these films from productions from mainland China or Taiwan. Few Hong Kong productions have succeeded in embodying or reflecting this regional sensibility to the degree accomplished in the Wong Fey Hung series. (Chan, Ng and Sek, 1980, p. 81)

In addition to the theme, *How Wong Fey Hung Pitted a Lion Against the Dragon* features a song performed by two characters at a party. It is a set piece, unrelated to the narrative flow and staged in a most theatrical manner. Songs have continued to play a prominent role in Hong Kong cinema ever since and their presence is not limited to any one genre. With the 'Wong Fey Hung' series they were part of a deliberate attempt to record and pass on Cantonese culture, providing a connection between the displaced Cantonese citizens of Hong Kong with their native artistic heritage. The series is set in Canton but was produced on soundstages in Hong Kong. There are no Westerners in the films, despite Hong Kong being under British rule at the time they were made. For the generation of filmgoers who made the series successful, China, and in particular Canton, was their first point of reference when defining their identity. This is a vital point, for it established that Hong Kong cinema concerned itself with Chinese history, rather than with contemporary Hong Kong. Virtually all of the major recurring heroes in Hong Kong cinema were from Canton, including Wong Fey Hung, the Ten Tigers, and the Shaolin fighter Fong Sai Yuk. The character of Fong Sai Yuk featured in a series that rivalled the popularity of the Wong Fey Hung movies, with the earliest production dating from 1928 and the silent film *Fong Sai Yuk's Battle in the Boxing Ring*.

Certain fictional characters were introduced to the 'Wong Fey Hung' stories by Hu Peng's films that became permanent fixtures in the mythology that surrounds the figure. Buck-toothed Soh, one of Fey Hung's followers studying medicine at Po Chi Lam, has become part of the canon of characters linked with the legend. Soh was included in Tsui Hark's 1991 film, played by Cheung Hok Yau, and by Chan Kwok Pong in *Once Upon a Time in China and America* (1997) directed by Sammo Hung. Hu Peng's contribution to Hong Kong cinema proved to be tremendously significant. Much of what followed in the kung fu genre built on his foundation. The decision to showcase authentic Chinese martial arts marks this body of work as the experimental stage of Christian Metz's model of the process of genre. Many of the key ingredients of the kung fu film can be found here – the displays and demonstrations of kung fu forms, the use of props, the conflict between rival masters and the importance of martial virtue.

The Classic Kung Fu Movie

Run Run Shaw was born in 1918 in Ninbo, Shanghai, the third of seven children. His eldest brother, Runme Shaw, set up a silent film company in Singapore, followed by the Unique Film Company in Shanghai in 1924. By 1939 the Shaws operated 139 cinemas across Singapore, Malaysia, Thailand, Indonesia and Indo-China. After the Second World War, Shaw Brothers became the principal distributor for Hollywood films in Southeast Asia.

In 1957, the company moved its headquarters to Hong Kong, where it was so successful that within ten years Shaw Brothers had a virtual stranglehold over Hong Kong cinema. Its films began to out-gross the American imports at the box office. The studio had a roster of in-house writers, directors and stars, all of whom were kept very busy. Movies spent approximately forty days in production and actors were often required to make several films simultaneously. It was a boom period for Hong Kong cinema, with large audiences eager for local product. By the end of the 1960s, the studio had twelve soundstages, all in continual use. In 1966, Shaw Brothers produced more than forty feature films. Unlike the films in the 'Wong Fey Hung' series, they were shot without synchronous sound and were dubbed during post-production. This allowed each film to be dubbed into several languages to ensure it reached the widest possible audience throughout the region. The biggest hits were romances and musicals, including *The Kingdom and the Beauty* (1958), *Yang Kwei Fei* (1961) and *Madam White Snake* (1962).

The studio made several co-productions with companies outside Hong Kong, notably co-producing Ridley Scott's *Blade Runner* (1982) with Ladd Productions. In 1973 Run Run launched the television station TVB and in the 1983 the studio ceased film production to concentrate on television. Sir Run Run Shaw (he was knighted in 1976) died in Hong Kong in 1991. In 1995 Shaw Brothers resumed filmmaking, it remains the major distributor for American films in Singapore and has a wide range of business interests throughout Southeast Asia, including real estate and cinema ownership.

At Shaw Brothers, two divergent streams of martial arts films developed. The first group of movies, exemplified by the films of King Hu, combined displays of martial arts techniques with the fantasy elements and special effects of the earliest Chinese films. The stories were adapted from novels about the adventures of mythical swordsmen, yet these were soon overtaken in popularity by the more naturalistic style of kung fu cinema begat by director Chang Cheh. These films picked up from the 'Wong Fey Hung' series in their lengthy and elaborate detailing of Chinese martial arts techniques.

King Hu

Born in Beijing in 1931, King Hu left China in the wake of the Communist Revolution and joined Shaw Brothers Studios, starting as an actor and scriptwriter. King's work is important for several reasons – his influence on subsequent Hong Kong martial arts films, particularly the swordplay genre, is considerable. Secondly, King gave strong roles to women, a pattern established by the 'Wong Fey Hung' series and expanded upon by King Hu, although Chang Cheh's movies effectively put an end to that trend at Shaw Brothers.

Come Drink With Me (1965)

Hu's first feature as director was *Sons of the Good Earth*, a period drama, but it was *Come Drink With Me* that became a landmark in Hong Kong cinema. It offered a dynamic and fresh approach to the presentation of martial arts, combining the fantasy elements of the earlier Mandarin language films with the martial arts that were essential to the popularity of the 'Wong Fey Hung' series. King Hu's style heavily influenced Tsui Hark, who drew upon his work as the inspiration for the 'New Wave' of Hong Kong cinema in the 1990s. In 1992 Tsui Hark, Ching Siu Tung and Raymond Lee remade King's film *Dragon Gate Inn* (1966).

   Come Drink With Me drew upon Japanese *chambara* films and earlier Chinese movies to create a new style that was referential whilst possessing its own unique character. The story's heroine is Golden Swallow (Cheng Pei Pei), who is sent to rescue the local governor's son from a group of bandits that are holding him hostage. She encounters a beggar, Drunken Cat (Yueh Hua), who comes to her aid. The bandits' leader, Liao Kung, is from the same martial arts school as Drunken Cat and they have a long-standing feud. After several violent clashes, Golden Swallow rescues the governor's son and Drunken Cat slays Liao Kung. The plot is secondary to the action set pieces. The martial arts choreography was the work of Han Ying Chieh, who appears as one of the bandits. Han was a graduate of the Fulian-Cheng Peking Opera School and started working as a stuntman in 1946. He appeared in the 'Wong Fey Hung' series, usually in non-speaking roles since his native tongue was Mandarin, not Cantonese. He is probably best known in the West for playing the main villain in *The Big Boss*, but he was a respected figure in Hong Kong cinema prior to working with Bruce Lee. Han's background in Peking Opera was well suited to King Hu's filmmaking style. King described his approach to the staging of martial arts:

> I've always taken the action part of my films as dancing rather than fighting. Because I'm very interested in the Peking Opera, and particularly its movement and action effects, although I think it's difficult to express them adequately on stage, where the physical limitations are too great. A lot of people in Hong Kong have misunderstood me, and have remarked that my action scenes are sometimes 'authentic' and sometimes not. In point of fact, they're always keyed to the notion of dance. (Chan, Ng and Sek, 1980, p. 103)

The influence of Peking Opera permeates the fight scenes, both in the music and the choreography. The action is highly rhythmic, obviously choreographed, as opposed to being an attempt to look like a real fight. Performers spin, come together like dancing partners, exchange techniques, and then separate again. It is very elegant, although extremely bloody. The huge spurts of blood are stylistic devices taken from Japanese films such as *The Sword of Doom* or Uchida's 'Miyamoto Musashi' series. By the end of the final confrontation between Drunken Cat and Liao Kung, the victorious Cat is drenched in blood.

Trampolines are used extensively in the action scenes to allow high flips and somersaults. These are visually appealing and further confirm that King is more concerned with style and rhythm than naturalism. Several tricks are used to enhance the fights, including slowing down the camera during filming, which speeds up the scenes when they are projected. Several sequences use reverse motion to allow the performers to demonstrate superhuman dexterity, for example when Golden Swallow catches coins with a pair of chopsticks. The characters possess a range of superpowers. Drunken Cat and Liao Kung can snap swords and pierce rock with their bare hands. This is a far cry from the down-to-earth presentation of martial arts in the 'Wong Fey Hung' series, which showcased authentic Chinese techniques. King Hu is not interested in using *Come Drink With Me* to record Cantonese culture. The presentation of martial artists as beings with superhuman abilities is an element borrowed from the novels upon which his films are based and is one of the defining characteristics of this style of martial arts films; this is an obvious difference between King's approach and that of Chang Cheh or Bruce Lee.

There are other major differences between this film and the 'Wong Fey Hung' movies. *Come Drink With Me* has no connection with the Canton region, but references an idea of China as its setting. It is post-dubbed, not shot with synchronous sound and makes effective use of sound design to enhance the action scenes with loud sword strokes. It has a considerably higher budget than any of Kwan Tak Hing's outings, with location shooting and meticulously detailed sets and costumes. The cinematography is outstanding and King's command of film language is far in advance of anything in the earlier films. The direction of the performers, the use of camera movement, the shot composition and lighting marked a new peak for a Hong Kong martial arts production.

Following the release of *Come Drink With Me*, which was a huge hit for Shaw Brothers, King left the studio to make films independently. *Dragon Gate Inn* and *A Touch of Zen* (1969) were in the same vein as *Come Drink With Me*, and saw King Hu continue his collaboration with Han Ying Chieh. 1972's *The Fate of Lee Khan* saw the pair adapt their style in the wake of Bruce Lee's enormous impact on the martial arts genre. Whilst the film still employed trampolines for displays of acrobatics, the action choreography was more naturalistic, with an emphasis on fighting techniques rather than on superpowers. The film features a whole cast of strong female figures, including Mao Ying, who later appeared as Bruce Lee's sister in *Enter the Dragon* (1973).

The Valiant Ones (1975) was based upon an historical incident concerning a group of Chinese martial artists trying to eradicate a gang of bandits during the Ming dynasty. It is the least sophisticated of King Hu's films, with a straightforward narrative and simplistically defined heroes and villains. The choreography by Han Ying Chieh and Sammo Hung does not feature the fantastic elements of *Come Drink With Me* or *A Touch of Zen*, reflecting the changing climes in kung fu cinema with Chang Cheh's Shaolin films dominating the box office. The final duel between Xu Lian (Han Ying Chieh) and Yu Dayou (Roy Chiao) relies upon frantic editing for pacing rather than showcasing the choreography. The film is nihilistic in the same manner as Chang Cheh's films, because the heroes sacrifice themselves to kill the bandits, much like the Shaolin heroes dying in battle with the Manchus, but it seems derivative and formulaic when compared to *Come Drink With Me*, or *The Fate of Lee Khan*. King Hu eventually returned to the martial arts genre with 1990's *Swordsman*, the film that helped launch the New Wave of period films in Hong Kong, but Hu left the production during shooting due to poor health and Tsui Hark and Ching Siu Tung finished the project. King Hu died in 1997, having left his mark on Hong Kong cinema. He enjoyed critical success in the West, with *A Touch of Zen* winning the Grand Technical Prize at the 1969 Cannes Film Festival, although he never achieved the mass popularity attained by Bruce Lee or the Shaolin films of Shaw Brothers during the kung fu boom of the 1970s.

Chang Cheh and the Shaolin Heroes

Chang Cheh was born in China in 1923 and before the Communists came to power he worked in theatre, staging Peking Opera productions. He wrote his first screenplay in 1947 for the Shanghai Cathay Film Production Company and, following the Communist Revolution, moved to Taiwan where he continued writing and began his directing career with *Storm Cloud Over Alishan* (1949). Chang's films were unusual for Taiwanese productions because they were completely focused on men, where the main output of Taiwan's film industry was romantic melodramas starring and aimed at women. In 1956 Chang moved to Hong Kong and continued writing, his output including screenplays, newspaper film reviews and novels. In 1962 he joined Shaw Brothers, where his career took off after teaming up with actor Wang Yu. They made a series of martial arts films together, beginning in 1963 with *Tiger Boy* and concluding in 1969 with *The Return of the One-Armed Swordsman*. Their most significant contribution to developing the genre was *The One-Armed Swordsman* (1967). Unlike the 'Wong Fey Hung' series, still going strong at the time, *The One-Armed Swordsman* is not concerned with martial virtue, Confucianism or functioning as a substitute for authentic

Chinese history. It is a bloody tale of revenge, influenced by the Japanese *chambara* genre, about a swordsman (Wang Yu) who loses his right arm in battle. He survives, learns to fight with his left arm and exacts his vengeance. The narrative is hardly complicated, with good and evil clearly delineated, and the nihilistic nature of the central character owing much to the anti-heroes of Japanese cinema. Unlike the virtuous Wong Fey Hung, the protagonist here, called Kong, is as violent as his enemies. In the climactic duel he slaughters them all, with blood and limbs flying everywhere, in an attempt to emulate the gory swordfights of the later *chambara* films. The choreography of the sword battles, by Lau Gar Leung and Tang Chia, is not as sophisticated as that of their Japanese counterparts like Kuze Ryu. The special effects are not terribly convincing, the bright red blood looks artificial and the camerawork and editing are not as polished as contemporary Japanese productions or King Hu's work. There is none of the attention to detail in the costumes or music found in the movies of King Hu, but it succeeds on its own terms as a straightforward action film.

When Wang Yu struck out on his own in 1970, directing and starring in *The Chinese Boxer*, Chang turned his attention to the heroes of Shaolin Temple. *Heroes Two* (1973), *Men from the Monastery* (1974), *Shaolin Martial Arts* (1974), *Five Shaolin Masters* (1974), *Disciples of Shaolin* (1975) and *Shaolin Temple* (1976) all dealt with different parts of Shaolin history. Chang's films all stick closely to the accepted history of the temple and the films attempt to recreate Chinese history on the screen, albeit without the aesthetic flair of King Hu. Chang's films are literal presentations, extremely male-centred, with women on the periphery, and he presents the Shaolin heroes as noble patriots and martyrs. *Heroes Two* details the creation of the Tiger-Crane form of *Hung Kuen* kung fu, featuring two of the most prominent Shaolin heroes, Hung Hey Kwun and Fong Sai Yuk combining their martial arts to kill the villainous Manchurian Che Kang, a master of the Tibetan White Eyebrow kung fu style. Hung is a master of Tiger Fist, Fong is versed in Crane Fist, but individually they are no match for Che Kang. It is only when they combine their styles and attack in unison that they are able to kill him. The choreography was by Lau Gar Leung and Tang Chia. Leung, the eldest son of Lau Chan from the 'Wong Fey Hung' series, was himself an expert in *Hung Kuen*

4. Hung Hey Kwun (Chen Kuan Tai) sends another Manchu reeling in Chang Cheh's *Heroes Two*.

kung fu, so the recreations of the Tiger-Crane form in the film are rooted in authentic martial arts, albeit adapted for screenfighting. Chen Kuan Tai, a martial arts champion off-screen, winner of the 1969 light-heavyweight championship at the Southeast Asian Chinese Martial Arts Tournament, played Hung, and the nineteen-year-old Fu Sheng played the youthful Fong. The film was a hit and led to the more ambitious *Men from the Monastery*.

Men from the Monastery (1974)

Men from the Monastery covers much of the same period as *Heroes Two* and reunited Chen Kuan Tai and Fu Sheng in their roles from the earlier film. The story is drawn from the Ch'ing dynasty novel *Evergreen*, which details several key events from Shaolin's history. The film introduces each major Shaolin hero in his own sequence, beginning with Fong Sai Yuk taking on the Wu Tang affiliate Lei Lao Hu. The second section introduces Hu Hui Chen, who goes to Shaolin to learn kung fu so that he can avenge the death of his father at the hands of the men from the Jinlung Tang textile factory. Finally, Hung Hey Kwun brings all the Shaolin patriots together after the temple is burnt by the imperial troops. A showdown between the Shaolin men and their Wu Tang rivals sees both sides wiped out, with Hung Hey Kwun the only survivor. Titles over the final shot tell the viewer that Hung went on to spread Shaolin martial arts throughout the region and that his *Hung Kuen* style is practised to this day.

There are a lot of fight scenes in the film and the story is simplistic. The Shaolin heroes are noble, good and true, the Wu Tang and Manchu villains are evil, cruel and treacherous. There is no attempt to critique the violence of the Shaolin fighters, as the bad guys always strike first, thereby placing the blame for the ensuing bloodshed on their shoulders. Chang takes the same unquestioning approach to his subject that Japanese filmmaker Inagaki Hiroshi took to Miyamoto Musashi. His heroes are pure and devoted to their cause, unconcerned with material matters. There is the same ambivalent attitude to women; when Fong Sai Yuk saves a girl from a gang, she is brimming with gratitude. He pats her on the head and walks off with his arm around his kung fu buddy. The implied homosexual nature of their relationship is never confirmed, but Fong obviously isn't interested in girls. The life of the real Fong Sai Yuk had elements in common with that of Miyamoto Musashi. Fong was capable of extraordinary violence – when he was just fourteen years old he killed Lei Lao Hu. In Chang's account, Lei Lao Hu is set up as a villain whose henchmen murder one of Fong's friends. This serves to qualify and condone Fong's subsequent violence, whereas historically Fong killed Lei in a duel, angry that Lei had been boasting about his *Wu Tang* style martial arts. Chang is not willing to address the more unsavoury aspects of the story, preferring to keep his heroes noble and his villains despicable.

The fighting sequences are more naturalistic than those in *The One-Armed Swordsman* or King Hu's work. There are no superhuman leaps or fantastical skills. Instead there are countless displays of authentic Chinese martial arts, more in keeping with the 'Wong Fey Hung' series, in that the film acts as a catalogue of *Hung Kuen* techniques. The choreography was again the work of Tang Chia and Lau Gar Leung, reflecting their attention to form and accuracy.

In the climactic battle between the Shaolin men and their antagonists, Chang used monochromatic filters, a technique he had started to experiment with during *Heroes Two*. *Men from the Monastery* is a colour film, but the screen goes completely red for a moment when one of the Shaolin men is killed, and then the image returns in black and white. Hu Hui Chen is stabbed in the stomach and mortally wounded; the film stays in black and white as Lee Choi Ping binds up Hu's stomach and he fights on. Hu kills all his Manchu opponents, before collapsing against a post, which is where he dies, still on his feet. The image returns to colour as the scene shifts to Fong Sai Yuk and Hung Hey Kwun, who are still locked in combat with the villains. The decision to use black and white seems somewhat random, but it is possible to consider this scene as an attempt by Chang to reinforce the notion that the film is not merely a recreation of a scene from Chinese history, but that the audience is viewing history directly. Black-and-white film suggests old newsreel or documentary footage and thus Chang asserts the verisimilitude of his staging of Hu's death. Furthermore, the 'Wong Fey Hung' series was shot in black and white and that came to be viewed as the definitive account of the legendary hero, replacing the lost history. In

Chang's film, it is not an entirely successful technique, as this is the only occasion in the movie in which it is employed, so it seems inconsistent with the overall naturalistic, unobtrusive direction.

It is even more difficult to explain the manipulation of the visual plane in *Heroes Two*, where a red filter is used. There is no connotation for the use of red to invoke historical authenticity. Cinematographer Arthur Wong commented in an interview, 'If there is a lot of blood in that scene, to prevent the audience seeing too much blood he would use the colour red for the whole scene'. This is difficult to balance with the torrents of blood found in many of Chang's films from the same period, such as the blood-soaked climactic battle in *The Boxer from Shantung* (1972).

The visual device of the hero stabbed in the gut who binds up his wound to fight on recurs throughout Chang's work. All of Chang's heroes possess a tolerance for pain and injury that is superhuman, but unlike Ogami Itto in the 'Lone Wolf and Cub' series, Chang's heroes always die. In *Men from the Monastery*, this reflects the accepted account of Hu Hui Chen's life, for he is generally considered to have died in battle. However, the prevalence of such scenes in Chang's films suggests a nihilistic philosophy at work. It is present in *The Boxer from Shantung*, *Man of Iron* (1972), *Disciples of Shaolin* and *The Chinatown Kid* (1977). In all these films, the hero is stabbed in the stomach during the climactic battle, but binds up his mid-section and fights on, only succumbing to his wounds once the villains all lie dead. It is possible to conceive of this device as part of the martial arts tenet that defeating others means defeating oneself. The hero only triumphs in combat because he overcomes his own suffering, but it is more convincing to argue that these scenes reflect an inherent nihilistic masochism. All the heroes choose to die; they never walk away from conflict, no matter how serious their injuries. They choose to stay and fight, becoming active participants in their own destruction. There is an undeniable vanity in these films, a sense of gloriousness in the deaths of the heroes that may spring from the fact that the Shaolin rebels never succeeded in driving out the Ch'ing dynasty and restoring the Ming. Of all the Shaolin heroes to emerge from the Fukien Temple, only Hung Hey Kwun lived past his thirties. The others all died in battle, pursuing a goal that was never within reach.

The Chinatown Kid (1977)

This sense of hopelessness, of pursuing an impossible end at any cost, permeates Chang's work, not just the films about Shaolin Temple. *The Chinatown Kid* is a contemporary story, rather unusual for a Shaw Brothers martial arts film. It is noteworthy for both its contemporary setting and for its style and subject matter. The protagonist of the film is Tan Tung (Fu Sheng), an illegal immigrant in Hong Kong. He runs foul of a local triad boss, and when he is arrested carrying drugs planted on him by the triads, he flees to the United States. In San Francisco's Chinatown, Tung meets Yang Ching Wen, a Taiwanese student and together they convince a Chinese restaurant owner, Mr Chan, to hire them illegally. The triads in San Francisco are having a turf war and Tung joins the White Dragon Triads, who are impressed by his fighting skills. As Tung rises in the gang, Wen turns to heroin to cope with the stress of working and studying. Tung finds out about Wen's drug problem and orders the White Dragons to stop dealing drugs. They try to have Tung arrested, but he eludes the police and storms into the triad headquarters, intent on destroying the gang single-handedly. He kills the local boss, but is stabbed in the gut. Wen arrives and the pair takes out the whole gang in a violent battle. Tung succumbs to his stomach wound and dies.

The production values of *The Chinatown Kid* are typical of a Shaw Brothers production of the time. Some of the exterior scenes are shot on location in Hong Kong, but all the scenes set in San Francisco are shot on Hong Kong soundstages. Certain elements in *The Chinatown Kid* are familiar motifs from Chang's Shaolin films with Tung's stomach wound being the most obvious. The film differs from Chang's earlier works in the character of his heroes: Tung and Wen are both flawed, a contrast to the noble men of Shaolin. At the start, Tung is a naive young man from the mainland, who wants nothing more than to be able to afford a digital watch. He has an inner morality, demonstrated when he rescues and saves from a life of prostitution a girl kidnapped by the triads. When Tung joins the White Dragons in San Francisco, he is a successful gangster for a short time until his conscience interferes. When he runs into Wen, who is still working at the restaurant, Tung expects his old friend to be pleased by his newfound wealth. Instead, Wen is disgusted because Tung has become a gangster, telling him 'You've got every-thing, all right. Except honour.' If the Shaolin heroes had anything, it was honour; they were righteous patriots. It is apparent that Chang Cheh does not hold the triads in the same high regard as the Shaolin heroes.

Wen, like Tung, is a flawed hero. When Tung confronts the Ching Wo Triad members who are pressuring Wen and Mr Chan for pro-tection money, Wen wants to help Tung fight the gangsters. Mr Chan threatens to fire him if he gets involved and Wen backs down, leaving Tung to fight alone. This is morally more sophisticated than any of Chang's period films, where good and evil were perfectly delineated. Here, the morality of his protagonists is ambiguous and imperfect. Wen has to choose between his job and his friend, and he chooses his job. There is none of the idealism of the films about Shao-lin. Wen becomes a heroin-user to cope with his stressful lifestyle, reflecting a contemporary and cynical outlook. The screenplay, which Chang co-wrote with I Kuang, offers Wen a chance to redeem himself in the finale, when he fights side by side with Tung against the White Dragons, but Tung dies in the battle and Wen flees the scene to avoid arrest. *The Chinatown Kid* is a dark film, where the tri-ads are all treacherous, the cops are bullies and the poor are victims. Tung's mantra is 'When you are poor, you must struggle', and all the poor characters in the film – Tung's grandfather, the girl kid-napped into prostitution – find that life is harsh and unforgiving.

The fight choreography is a significant shift away from traditional Chinese martial arts. The 1986 English-dubbed Warner Home Video release of the film lists Liu Chia-Ting and Tai Chi-Hsien as fight cho-reographers. It is likely that Liu Chia-Ting is Lau Gar Wing, who worked with Chang Cheh on *The Boxer from Shantung* and whose brother Lau Gar Leung was a regular collaborator with Chang until he began his own directing career in 1976. The fight scenes in *The Chinatown Kid* contain elements from traditional kung fu, but they are mixed in with a rough, street-fighting approach. There are throws, joint-locks, Thai boxing knee strikes, head butts, and kicking techniques from *Tae Kwon Do*, performed by a host of talented screenfighters, including Sun Chien as Wen, and Philip Kwok and Lo Meng as the rival gang leaders. To some extent the combination of styles is Bruce Lee's legacy, since Lee was the first kung fu star to mix techniques freely from different systems. In addition, the choreography is intended to convey a sense of realism, to look like a real fight, rather than offering a catalogue of Chinese martial arts techniques. It would be anachronistic and stylistically inaccurate for the Shaolin heroes to employ such a wide range of fighting styles, but the contemporary context of *The Chinatown Kid* demands a shift in the choreography. It is not as extreme as what was to follow in the 1980s, but this film is certainly a significant work in moving the Hong Kong martial arts film forwards. The action scenes also use guns and knives, a precursor to the gangster films of John Woo.

The vital difference between *The Chinatown Kid* and the gangster films of the 1980s is that Chang's film does not address the question of identity that is central to the later works. All the characters in *The Chinatown Kid*, whether they are from the mainland like Tung, from Taiwan like Wen, or living in the United States like Mr Chan, are identified as being Chinese, linked by a common cultural heritage. There is none of the uncertainty about identity, or the search for self-realisation that are essential traits in Hong Kong cinema after 1981. Chang's heroes, whether they are the patriots of Shaolin, or innocents abroad like Tan Tung, are all 'Chinese'.

Chang's films are secular, unconcerned with the spiritual and the lyrical. There are no musical set pieces, no songs to lift the spirits of his violent heroes. He is interested in nihilism and the strength of will to follow a path to its bitter end. This was a trait shared by the films of Wang Yu after he parted from Chang Cheh and produced his own movies. *The Chinese Boxer* (1970), written and directed by Wang Yu, is an interesting example of the kung fu movie immediately prior to the rise of Bruce Lee. The story is either a rip-off of, or riposte to, Kurosawa's 'Sanshiro Sugata' films. Wang Yu stars as Lei Ming, a young kung fu student whose master is killed by a trio of villainous Japanese *karateka*. Lei Ming trains in the Iron Palm technique to toughen his hands and develops his agility (apparently by performing the high jump), before taking on the karate masters in the inevitable showdown. The plot is hopelessly formulaic and villains and heroes are drawn without depth or complexity. Chinese actors play all the Japanese characters, including the lead villain Kitashima, portrayed by Lo Lieh in a ridiculous wig that references the character Tesshin in *Sanshiro Sugata, Part Two*. The martial arts choreography, by Tang Chia, looks very weak compared with what Bruce Lee would accomplish in the next two years. Wang Yu is not a very talented screenfighter and the choreography makes excessive use of hidden trampolines and some clumsy wirework to allow the performers to leap through the air.

Wang's later works are slightly better, even though they too rely upon ideas borrowed from Japanese *chambara* and Chang Cheh. *Blood of the Dragon* (1978) has all the essential qualities of one of Chang's stories – a violent, flawed hero called Lung Tai (Wang Yu), who is battling the Mongols. He is injured before the final battle, but chooses to stay and fight to the death, claiming, 'I would rather die on my feet than live the life of a Mongol whore!' He kills all his enemies and stands on a battlefield littered with bodies, before slowly falling to the ground, dead. It's a warrior's death, full of vanity and pride, dying unconquered and unbowed. The film was written and directed by Lao Pao Shu, but its debt to Chang Cheh is enormous. Wang Yu was never really able to establish an independent screen identity after his collaborations with Chang and his popularity waned with the passing of the traditional kung fu movie in the 1980s.

Lau Gar Leung

Three of the most prominent martial arts filmmakers to emerge in the wake of Chang Cheh's success were the sons of Lau Chan, the actor who played Lam Sai Wing in the 'Wong Fey Hung' series. The eldest, Lau Gar Leung, was born in Canton in 1934, his younger brother Lau Gar Wing was born in 1944 and adopted brother Lau Gar Fei joined the family as an infant. All three were versed in the *Hung Kuen* style of kung fu, which their father had studied under Lam Sai Wing, and the two older brothers appeared in the 'Wong Fey Hung' series.

Lau Gar Leung's first job as martial arts choreographer was on *South Dragon, North Phoenix* (1963), where he shared the credit with Tang Chia. In 1966 Leung and Tang Chia began their lengthy collaboration with director Chang Cheh on *The Magnificent Trio*. When Chang turned his attention to the Shaolin heroes, beginning with *Heroes Two* in 1974, Leung and Tang were in their element, for the Shaolin films offered ideal vehicles for the performance of the *Hung Kuen* style that was Leung's family tradition. A trademark of the films on which Leung worked, either as choreographer or director, was an opening title sequence demonstrating different forms of Chinese martial arts. These sequences featured the actors in full period outfits performing kung fu routines in bare studio settings. The contrast between the costumed performers and the empty soundstages focuses the viewers' attention on the performer as martial artist, stating Leung's intention to mark the authenticity of the kung fu content of these films.

Leung was the first Hong Kong choreographer to become a director in his own right with *The Spiritual Boxer* (1976). The overriding theme of Leung's work is the importance of family and the concept of kung fu as part of a family's heritage. *Executioners from Shaolin* (1977) concerns the creation of the Tiger-Crane form, the subject of Chang Cheh's *Heroes Two* three years earlier. Where Chang's film is straightforward and follows the accepted account of the lives of Hung Hey Kwun and Fong Sai Yuk, Leung's doesn't show an immutable and fixed history. Rather, history becomes the source material for the filmmaker to adapt, twist and reshape. Leung's account shifts from Chang's male-centric story about Hey Kwun and Fong Sai Yuk to focus on the relationship between Hey Kwun and his wife, Fong Wing Chun. Factual information about Fong Wing Chun is scant, but she was born in Canton and was Fong Sai Yuk's niece. Since Sai Yuk's brothers were much older than him, Wing Chun was approximately the same age as her uncle.

Executioners from Shaolin (1977)

In *Executioners from Shaolin*, Leung opens with a fight in a studio, again showcasing the martial arts. He breaks with his established practice by using this opening sequence to set up the narrative, for the combatants are Chi Shan, the abbot of Shaolin Temple, and Bak Mei, the traitor, played by Lo Lieh. Chi Shan kicks Bak Mei in the groin, but the blow has no effect and Bak Mei traps Chi Shan's foot, breaking his leg before killing him. This is a startling opening to the film, with the limbo of the studio setting and Bak Mei's violent triumph. It sets into motion the quest for vengeance that drives the story. On the run from the destruction of Shaolin Temple, Hung Hey Kwun (Chen Kuan Tai) and Fong Wing Chun (Lily Li) marry. On their wedding night, Wing Chun refuses to consummate the marriage unless Hung can prise her legs open. Unfortunately for him she's a master of the Crane style, which uses a stance with the knees locked together, and Hey Kwun struggles to force her to open her legs using his Tiger style. Leung never shows how Hey Kwun succeeds in sleeping with his wife, but they have a son, Hung Wen Ting (Wong Yu – not to be confused with Wang Yu, the one-armed swordsman). Hey Kwun is obsessed with killing Bak Mei and neglects his son, who is raised by his mother. Wen Ting learns his mother's feminine Crane style kung fu and his appearance is a bizarre mixture between male and female, with his hair in pigtails and wearing girls' clothes. When Hey Kwun is killed fighting Bak Mei the duty of vengeance falls upon Wen Ting. He knows his Crane style is insufficient to defeat Bak Mei, so he studies Tiger style from a battered kung fu manual that belonged to his father. Parts of the manual are missing, so Wen Ting fills in the gaps using Crane style, creating the Tiger-Crane form of *Hung Kuen*. Wen Ting confronts Bak Mei and kills him using the new style.

The most obvious connection between this and the Shaolin films by Chang Cheh is the presence of Chen Kuan Tai as Hung Hey Kwun. He was closely linked with the character, playing him in *Heroes Two* and *Men from the Monastery*. There was not the same level of identification of Chen as Hung as there was of Kwan Tak Hing as Wong Fey Hung, simply because the number of films in the 'Wong Fey Hung' series far exceeded Chen's appearances as Hung. The strong portrayal of Fong Wing Chun and the sexual nature of her relationship with Hey Kwun were elements peculiar to Leung. In his film there are no normal patterns of sexuality; Hey Kwun finds himself forced to exchange martial arts techniques with his wife on their wedding night, Bak Mei is a eunuch, and Wen Ting is a boy who looks like a girl. It is possible to suggest that Wen Ting is able to defeat the asexual Bak Mei because he is his opposite – where Bak Mei is sexless, Wen Ting is both male and female and thus able to negate/kill Bak Mei. Gender and sexuality, like history, are flexible in Lau Gar Leung's hands, not linear and rigid; this is a significant progression.

Shaolin Mantis (1978)

Despite the title, *Shaolin Mantis*, sometimes known as *The Deadly Mantis*, has nothing to do with the Shaolin Temple. It concerns Wei Fung (David Chiang), a scholar and martial artist, who is ordered by the Ch'ing emperor to infiltrate the Ming-supporting Tien clan and steal a list of rebels. Wei tries to refuse but the emperor warns him that if he doesn't succeed within twelve months, his entire family will be executed. Wei enters the Tien household as tutor to the strong-willed young woman Chi-Chi. The head of the clan, Tien (Lau Gar Wing) learns that Wei is working for the Ch'ing and plans to kill him. Chi-Chi pleads for Wei's life and Tien spares him on condition that they marry and Wei never leaves the house. After the wedding, Wei finds the list of rebels and Chi-Chi and her mother help Wei fight his way out of the mansion, until they face Tien. Chi-Chi is killed but Wei escapes and hides in a wood. Here he is fascinated by a praying mantis and develops Mantis style kung fu. He returns to face Tien and slays him. Wei presents the list to the emperor, but his father is so ashamed that he poisons himself and Wei, damning him as a traitor to the Ming cause. Wei battles the imperial guards as the poison takes effect and the image freezes on Wei in a Mantis pose.

This is an even darker film than *Executioners from Shaolin*. The central theme is the importance of the family and familial loyalties create all the conflict. Wei chooses to save his father and sacrifice the Ming rebels; Chi-Chi chooses her husband over her blood relatives; Chi-Chi's mother turns against her own husband, Tien; and Wei's father poisons his son. Like *Executioners from Shaolin*, the film distorts normal patterns of the family, which for Leung is another subject, like history, that he can manipulate within his film world. This is a morally complicated film that does not offer a simple solution to Wei's dilemma when he is forced to choose between family and country. Chi-Chi's decision to help her husband against her family is understandable in light of the Chinese custom of the bride joining the groom's family after marriage. For Wei, death is the only release from the burden of guilt that his situation has placed on him. This is comparable to Japanese films exploring the conflict between *giri* and *ninjo* and the film shares the darkness and despair common to *Harakiri* and *Samurai Rebellion*.

The action sequences in *Shaolin Mantis* are outstanding, with choreography by Lau Gar Leung and Tang Wei Cheng. Aside from the displays of Mantis style, there are numerous weapons forms, including the halberd, double sword forms, spear and trident. There is a title sequence with David Chiang using a Mantis form, typical of Lau Gar Leung.

Shaolin Challenges Ninja (1978)

The director's next film to address family conflict was a comedy, *Shaolin Challenges Ninja*, starring his adopted brother Lau Gar Fei. The story is set in pre-Communist China and concerns Tung (Lau Gar Fei), a young Chinese man whose father has arranged his marriage to a Japanese girl, Kuda (Yuka Mizuno). When he discovers that she is a martial artist, they argue over whose techniques are superior – the Chinese or the Japanese. Kuda returns to Japan, where she encounters Sanzo, her *sensei* (Kurata Yasuaki), who has designs on her. Tung, desperate to bring Kuda home but not wanting to lose face, sends her a challenge, hoping she'll return if she feels Japan's honour is at stake. Sanzo reads the challenge and sets off for China with six other Japanese fighters to defend their country's honour. Tung has to face seven duels, each with a master of a different style or weapon. Kuda supports her husband and returns to the family. Tung triumphs and he and the Japanese fighters learn a new respect for each other.

Unlike the tragic *Shaolin Mantis*, this film is primarily comedic, particularly in the first half, where Lau has fun with the culture clash between husband and wife. At the wedding the Chinese guests are horrified when Kuda wears a white dress, worn for funerals in China, instead of the red dress traditionally worn by Chinese brides. At dinner, Kuda kneels on the floor, while Tung sits on a chair. Ultimately Kuda chooses her husband over her country; when the Japanese fighters challenge Tung, she returns to China and thereafter dresses in Chinese clothes.

It is significant that Lau maintains a light tone once the fighting has begun. Unlike many Hong Kong films of the 1970s, such as *When TaeKwonDo Strikes* (1973) or *The Valiant Ones*, that cast the Japanese as monstrous villains, Lau humanises the Japanese characters. Kuda is beautiful and charming, and Sanzo is motivated every bit as much by jealousy as by nationalistic fervour. The Japanese characters in Hong Kong films of the 1970s were usually played by Chinese actors, but Lau fills his cast with Japanese performers. Xenophobic hatred is absent, although in keeping with the traditions of the genre, the hometown hero, Tung, wins all his battles. Lau is not about to alienate his audience by having the Chinese hero lose. However, no one dies, the duels are fought as an exchange of techniques, to test whose fighting styles are superior, but they end without bloodshed. Perhaps Lau wanted to make a more upbeat film after the darkness of *Shaolin Mantis*, and *Shaolin Challenges Ninja* is uplifting and highly entertaining.

The fight choreography is some of Lau's finest. The cast are all superb screenfighters, including Yuko Mizuno as Kuda, who performs her fight scenes with skill and verve. The range of techniques is huge, as Tung takes on a Japanese *kendo* master, a *karateka*, a *budoka* who uses a *nunchaku* and a *tonfa*, a spear master, a *sai* master, a gigantic *judoka* and finally Sanzo, a master of *ninjutsu*. In the first duel Tung defeats the Japanese swordsman, who offers his weapon to Tung as a sign of respect. Unable to understand Japanese and not comprehending the gesture, Tung doesn't take the sword, insulting the Japanese and widening the gulf between the two sides. In the climax, when Tung has outsmarted Sanzo, the swordsman offers his blade to Tung a second time. Tung bows and accepts the sword, closing the film with an affirmation of the importance of respect and understanding. Unlike earlier kung fu films, in which nationalistic zeal was sufficient cause to fight to the death, Lau rejects pride. It is pride that creates the friction between Kuda and Tung, and pride that prevents Tung from going to Japan to ask her to come home. Pride has become a folly, not something worth dying for, a major shift for the genre.

My Young Auntie (1980)

My Young Auntie was another comedy that saw Lau turn the traditional Confucian notion of respect for one's elders on its head. Jing
Dai Nan (Hui Ying Hung) is the youthful widow of Yu Yan Sang,
charged with ensuring that her late husband's considerable estate
passes to his virtuous brother Yu Jing Chuen (Lau Gar Leung) and
not to the villainous Yu Wing Sang (Wang Lung Wei). Despite being
a young woman, Dai Nan's marriage to the elderly Yu Yan Sang
means, under Confucian custom, that she is considered to be
Chuen's aunt, although he is much older than her. This is typical of
Leung, turning familial relationships on their heads and he further
explores this inversion of roles when the young Dai Nan trains
Chuen and his three brothers, all of whom are old men, to prepare
them to take on Yu Wing Sang. The classic master–pupil relationship in the kung fu genre is of the old, wise *sifu* training the young
protégé, not the other way around.

The film displays a modern sensibility and addresses the clash
between Chinese and Western values. Dai Nan is old-fashioned and
full of respect for Confucian thought, while Chuen's son, Charlie
(Hsiao Hou), has adopted Western clothes and an English name
after studying in Hong Kong. Charlie's speech is a mixture of Cantonese and English and the middle of the movie is devoted to
exploring the disparity between Dai Nan and Charlie, who are polar
opposites, despite being contemporaries. The film is set in Republican China, not Hong Kong, but it touches on the issue of identity as
it addresses the cultural gap between Charlie and Dai Nan. Further,
it freely mixes comedy, martial arts and music, a precursor to the
comedy/action films of the 1980s.

Legendary Weapons of Kung Fu (1982)

Legendary Weapons of Kung Fu, also known as *Eighteen Legendary
Weapons of China*, is set during the Boxer Rebellion and concerns the
I Ho Chuan Society, whose leaders are trying to combine kung fu
with Taoist magic to make their followers immune to gunfire. One
of their senior members, Lei Kung (Lau Gar Leung), has disbanded
his branch of the society and gone into hiding, adopting the identity
of Yu, a woodcutter. The vengeful I Ho Chuan leader dispatches

three assassins after Lei Kung, and a fourth member Fong (Hui Ying Hung) sets out to help him. The assassins are Ti Hao (Hsiao Hou), Ti Tan (Lau Gar Fei) and Lei Yung (Lau Gar Wing). After winning over Ti Hao and defeating Ti Tan, Lei Kung faces off against his brother Lei Yung in a ritualistic duel. Kung wins, but tells his brother to return to the I Ho Chuan and tell them he has slain Lei Kung, leaving him to live in peace.

This is Leung's most ambitious film and the first kung fu movie to rely on intertextuality to create meaning on the visual plane. The film is about the limits of kung fu, both as a martial art and as a genre. On the first level, Lei Kung leaves the I Ho Chuan because he knows that kung fu and magic will never be able to withstand gunfire. Martial skill has been outstripped by technology. On the second level, Lau Gar Leung as director exposes and deconstructs many of the key elements of the traditional kung fu movie, dismantling the work of his predecessors King Hu and Chang Cheh. Lau Gar Leung refuses to admit the possibility of magic in his film world. In King Hu's work, the martial artists shoot energy bolts, fly and break steel weapons with their bare hands. In Lau Gar Leung's movie, the characters carry pyrotechnical devices that they use to create explosions and bursts of smoke. Lau shows these devices, instead of hiding them, drawing attention to their artificiality. His characters use ropes to climb, instead of flying, affirming that they are human beings, not superheroes. The most telling sequence is the one in which the con artist Wu and his cronies perform their staged battle to convince the locals that Wu is Lei Kung. They use phoney weapons that are either too blunt to hurt Wu or that are designed to break when he bends them, creating the illusion that he has fantastic strength. The climax of the battle sees Wu stabbed in the stomach, in a manner that is unmistakably a comic reference to Chang Cheh. Wu's palpably fake intestines spill out of his robe, along with a great deal of brightly coloured blood, but he summons up all his strength, wraps them up, tucks them back in, and fights on. The fact that the character of Wu is played by Fu Sheng, who performed a disembowelment sequence for Chang Cheh in *The Chinatown Kid*, intensifies the parody to the point of deconstruction. The disembowelment makes no sense if the viewer is not familiar with Chang's movies, relying upon the relationship between Chang's work and that of Leung to create meaning. In this one sequence Leung reveals all the conventions and limitations of the traditional kung fu film and laughs at them. It is akin to a magician showing exactly what he has up his sleeves; Lau leaves nothing to the imagination. He shares the fakery with the audience, demanding that they lose their suspension of disbelief and forcing them to reassess the accepted conventions of the kung fu 'fight'.

With this film, Leung touches upon a theme central to Hong Kong cinema after 1981 – identity. Where in *Executioners from Shaolin*, history had become mutable in Leung's hands, in *Legendary Weapons of Kung Fu*, identity becomes flexible. All the central characters, Lei Kung, Ti Hao and Fong Shao Ching, have identities that change as the story progresses. Lei Kung, the retired kung fu master, has become Yu the woodcutter and has abandoned martial arts. There is no conventional master–pupil relationship; instead Lei Kung is both master and student. He has to re-learn his martial arts, using his past experience as a guide, and reverse the transformation from woodcutter to fighter. Ti Hao's transformation is from unquestioning killer to free thinking human being. As a member of the I Ho Chuan, he is expected to follow orders without hesitation and kill himself upon demand. Lau Gar Leung is not prepared to endorse this mindless self-destruction, just as his onscreen counterpart Lei Kung rejects the nihilism of the I Ho Chuan. Fong's identity shift is cosmetic and is the one manner in which Leung respects the conventions of the Hong Kong martial arts film. In her search for Lei Kung, Fong disguises herself as a man, and in the tradition of Hong Kong movies, her disguise fools everyone, even though it's painfully apparent to the audience that Fong is a woman. This convention can be traced back to *Come Drink With Me*, and it reflects a Peking Opera sensibility, wherein men played female roles and the audience was expected to accept their impersonation without question.

Leung's work after *Legendary Weapons of Kung Fu* included two more films starring Lau Gar Fei: *Eight Diagram Pole Fighter* (1983), and the third entry in his films about the monk San Te, *Disciples of the Thirty-Sixth Chamber* (1985). He made one final period film with *Shaolin Temple Part Three*, starring Jet Li, in 1986, before switching to the more popular contemporary action film with *Tiger on the Beat*

(1988). He continued to make contemporary films until 1994, when he was hired to direct Jackie Chan in *Drunken Master Part Two*. It was not a successful collaboration and Leung left during production, leaving Chan to finish the movie. Leung made his own *Drunken Master Part Three*, but that was well below his usual standards and failed at the box office.

Drunken Monkey (2003)

In 2003 Shaw Brothers and Lau Gar Leung reunited to produce the studio's first kung fu movie in two decades. *Drunken Monkey* is a mixed affair, offering some excellent martial arts displays, but suffering from a weak middle section and a poor script. The story concerns the Chun-Yuen Delivery Service, run by Man Bill (Lau Gar Leung), who is betrayed and left for dead by his greedy assistant Man Pao and partner-in-crime, the opium smuggler Master Yu. Bill is found and nursed back to health by Siu Man (Shannon Yao) and lives quietly in seclusion. A year later, two students, Ka-Yip and Tak seek out Man Bill to help Ka-Yip finish his manual of Monkey kung fu. Man Bill is drawn back into conflict with Man Pao and Yu, leading to a final battle between the two sides.

The film opens with a classic Lau Gar Leung title sequence, featuring the principal cast performing kung fu in a studio, immediately declaring the kung fu lineage of both the director and the film itself. Lau then cuts to the Chun-Yuen Delivery Service in action. He mixes genre iconographies, in this case the kung fu genre and the American Western, by dressing the Chun-Yuen men as cowboys, with Western-style hats, long coats, riding horses. Being a kung fu film, they have Chinese swords instead of rifles on their saddles, displaying Lau's proclivity for playing with the boundaries of the form. The first twenty minutes are action-packed and reference Chang Cheh when Man Bill is stabbed in the gut but fights on despite the injury. The studio title sequence, the kung fu techniques and the stomach wound all suggest Leung is trying to create a traditional kung fu film, until the movie makes a sudden shift in tone with the introduction of Ka-Yip and Tak, slowing down with a series of ill-conceived comedy sequences.

The mid-section, centred on the high jinks of the pair, reflects a more modern style of cinema and undercuts the traditional kung fu narrative flow that Leung developed in the preceeding twenty minutes. The comedy is poorly realised and does not match up to Leung's earlier works, relying upon a lot of mugging from the cast, and there is none of the social satire of *Shaolin Challenges Ninja* or the parody of *Legendary Weapons of Kung Fu*. There is a sense that the comedy sequences in *Drunken Monkey* are a tired tip of the hat to the demands of the audience.

The role of the family and the master–pupil relationship are both present in *Drunken Monkey*. Their interconnection is revealed in the paternal relationship between Bill and Siu Man, whom he effectively adopts as his daughter after she finds him in the aftermath of his fight against Man Pao and Yu. Bill repays her kindness by training her in martial arts. When Ka-Yip and Tak convince Bill to become their *sifu* he adopts a similar role in their lives and the final sequence sees the four Monkey kung fu fighters, Bill, Siu Man, Ka-Yip and Tak, re-founding the Chun-Yuen Delivery Service. Their familial relationship has been nurtured through their common martial arts heritage and has been forged by combat. In this movie, the role of *sifu* has become explicitly paternal, an idea Leung explored in the earlier *Challenge of the Masters*.

The direction of the fight sequences is excellent, combining the handheld camerawork, wirework and fast-paced editing of modern action cinema with Leung's traditionally rooted choreography. There is a good deal of common ground between the techniques of *Drunken Monkey* and Lau's earlier *Mad Monkey Kung Fu*, perhaps reflecting a decision by Leung to bring his career full circle. The presence of Lau Gar Fei as Hung Yat Fu, a detective investigating opium smuggling, further enforces the movie's claim to invoke the legacy of the traditional kung fu film. There is a terrific sequence in which Hung Yat Fu and Man Bill are forced to fight, leading to an exchange of techniques from *Hung Kuen* kung fu and Monkey style that is one of the highlights of the movie and shows that, despite their advancing years, Lau Gar Leung and Lau Gar Fei are still the masters of their craft. It is to be hoped that *Drunken Monkey* will not be the last entry in Leung's remarkable career and he is so highly regarded in the Hong Kong film industry that everyone addresses him as *sifu*, a mark of the utmost respect.

Bruce Lee and Golden Harvest

Raymond Chow was born in Hong Kong in 1929 and his impact upon Hong Kong cinema rivals that of Sir Run Run Shaw. Chow left Hong Kong to attend university in the United Kingdom, but returned home after graduation to work as a journalist. In 1959 he switched careers and joined Shaw Brothers. He became head of production, second in command to Run Run Shaw, but where Chow was keen to develop into the international market, Shaw wanted to move in to television and concentrate on Southeast Asia. In 1970 Chow left Shaw Brothers and founded his own production company, Golden Harvest. This was a bold move, since at the time Shaw Brothers dominated both the production and distribution of films in Hong Kong. Luck was on Chow's side when he signed the actor best known in Hong Kong for his role as Kato in the American TV series *The Green Hornet* – Bruce Lee.

Lee Jun Fan was born in San Francisco on 27 November 1940, to Lee Hoi Chuen and Grace Lee. Lee Hoi Chuen was a Cantonese Opera performer on tour in the United States. The following year the family returned to Hong Kong, where Lee Jun Fan, who had been given the name Bruce for his birth certificate by a nurse in San Francisco, spent his childhood. He followed in his father's thespian footsteps, working as a child actor in Hong Kong movies, starting with *The Beginning of a Boy* when he was six. His last role prior to his departure for the United States was in *The Orphan* (1958), playing a juvenile delinquent.

As a youth Bruce studied *Wing Chun* kung fu with master Yip Man, although he had enough energy left to get himself expelled from La Salle College. At his next school, St Francis Xavier, Bruce was part of a confrontation between students from the *Wing Chun* style and their rivals from a *Choy Li Fut* kung fu school. Bruce beat one of the *Choy Li Fut* students very severely and his parents decided it was time for him to leave Hong Kong. In 1959, aged eighteen, Bruce boarded a ship for San Francisco.

On arrival in the United States, Bruce worked at a restaurant until he enrolled in the University of Washington in Seattle, where he met his future wife, Linda. In Seattle, Bruce opened his first *kwoon* (martial arts school), teaching a system he called *Jun Fan* kung fu, a variation of *Wing Chun*. In 1964, he married Linda, despite the objections of her family, who didn't want a Chinese son-in-law, and opened his second kung fu school in Oakland, California. In 1966, they moved to Los Angeles, where Bruce gave private lessons to actors including James Coburn and Steve McQueen for $250 an hour. By this time Bruce's approach to martial arts had changed sufficiently for him to coin a new name for his method. *Jeet Kune Do* means 'The Way of the Intercepting Fist' and was intended to reflect Bruce's flexible approach to martial arts. Lee thought the classical, traditional forms were too rigid and intransigent and was keen to point out that *Jeet Kune Do* was a philosophy, not a style; he felt that the ultimate goal of any martial artist was self-expression, not mindless adherence to the unchanging forms of the past.

In 1966, Bruce landed the part of Kato in the television series *The Green Hornet*, starring Van Williams. Although Lee played the sidekick, his martial arts performances were the highlights of the series. When the show was cancelled Lee began developing other projects, including what would become the *Kung Fu* television series. Lee had hoped to play the lead role, which was given to David Carradine, who is neither Chinese nor a martial artist. Apparently the producers felt that Bruce was too Asian to be accepted by the American public. The second project was a screenplay entitled *The Silent Flute* (1978), developed by Lee with his friend and student Stirling Silliphant. The project never came to fruition during Lee's lifetime, although an altered version was filmed after Lee's death, again with David Carradine. Silliphant did a great deal to promote his *sifu*; for the film *A Walk in the Spring Rain* (1970), Silliphant wrote in a fight scene that Lee choreographed. Then for *Marlowe*, starring James Garner, Silliphant created the character of Winslow Wong for Lee and the scene in which Wong trashes Marlowe's office is the most exciting sequence in the movie. Thereafter, Lee appeared in several episodes of the television series *Longstreet*, playing himself, to all intents and purposes, as the martial arts instructor to the detective played by James Franciscus. Stirling Silliphant wrote the scripts and again he found opportunities to showcase Lee's talents. The opening episode was even called 'The Way of the Intercepting Fist'.

Still, Lee was trapped in supporting roles, as villains or sidekicks, and he felt dissatisfied, not to mention financially insecure. On a visit to Hong Kong in 1970, Lee was surprised to discover that he was famous in his homeland. His role as Kato in *The Green Hornet* had been hugely popular in Hong Kong and Lee made several appearances on Hong Kong television, giving interviews and demonstrating his martial arts. Run Run Shaw made Lee an offer to sign with Shaw Brothers, for US$2,000 per film, with a contract that would make Lee part of the Shaw Brothers in-house roster. Instead, Lee accepted the offer of US$7,500 per film for two films from Raymond Chow, who had just set up Golden Harvest studios. Linda Lee writes in her biography of Bruce:

> And so on a hot and humid day in July, Bruce found himself in the little village of Pak Chong north of Bangkok. It was here that he met Raymond Chow for the first time. The two men shook hands and afterwards were able to laugh at Bruce's first words. With sublime assurance and the utmost confidence, he declared, 'You just wait, I'm going to be the biggest Chinese star in the world.' (Linda Lee, 1993, pp. 100–1)

The Big Boss (1971)

The first project for Chow and Lee was very low budget, even by the Hong Kong standards of the time. The decision to shoot *The Big Boss* in Thailand was financial, to keep production costs low. Given Lee's experience in the United States, the working conditions must have seemed Neolithic. He wrote to Linda during the shooting: 'The film I'm doing is quite amateur-like. A new director has replaced the uncertain old one; this new director is another so-so one with an almost unbearable air of superiority' (Linda Lee, 1993, p. 103).

The new director was Lo Wei, who replaced Wu Chia Hsiang. Lo started directing in 1957 with *River of Romance* and joined Shaw Brothers in 1965. There he made his first martial arts movie, *Dragon Swamp* (1968), but he would have been long-since forgotten had it not been for his involvement with Bruce Lee. Lo Wei was, to be blunt, a hack. The films he made without Bruce Lee are formulaic, with sloppy direction and lacklustre action scenes, including several movies starring the young Jackie Chan, all of which failed at the box office.

The story for *The Big Boss*, or *Fist of Fury*, as it was wrongly labelled in the United States, details the misfortunes of a group of

Chinese workers in Thailand, among them, fresh from home, is Cheng Chao An (Bruce Lee). They work in an ice factory that is a front for heroin smuggling. Anyone who discovers the heroin operation is murdered and the Chinese workers are dropping like flies. Cheng, who has promised his mother that he'll keep his nose clean, tries to avoid trouble, but when a riot occurs at the factory instigated by the unhappy Chinese demanding to know the whereabouts of their missing countrymen, Cheng explodes into action and flattens the Thai thugs. The manager of the factory tries to silence Cheng by promoting him to foreman. The factory owner's son kidnaps Chow Mei (Maria Yi) – one of the group of Chinese immigrants that Cheng lives with – for his lascivious father, murdering all of Cheng's relatives in the process. Cheng sets out to avenge them, killing the villain's henchmen before squaring off with the big boss himself. Cheng slays the gangster, consumed with such fury that he pummels his opponent's corpse even after he is dead. As the closing credits roll the Thai police arrive to arrest Cheng.

The plot is underdeveloped but there were a handful of aspects that helped separate *The Big Boss* from the movies produced at Shaw Brothers. The most important was Bruce's martial arts techniques, but the film was also considerably racier than anything made by Chang Cheh or King Hu. In one sequence, the factory manager takes Cheng out for dinner to distract him from the matter of the missing workers. Cheng gets drunk and ends up bedding a prostitute. Aside from the clear implication that Cheng has lost his virginity, unthinkable for any of Chang Cheh's repressed heroes, the prostitute is seen topless. This may have been Lo Wei hoping to guarantee a decent box office by adding some gratuitous nudity, but it could equally have reflected Lee's Western sensibilities and his understanding that sex appeal and potency were vital elements in the screen personas of American movie stars.

The action director on *The Big Boss* was Han Ying Chieh, King Hu's regular collaborator. Lee was used to handling his own fight scenes and cannot have taken kindly to Han Ying Chieh's traditionally rooted choreography. There is a marked difference between Han's direction of the fight scenes without Lee's character and those in which Lee participates. Han plays the main villain, the big boss of the title, and in his fight sequences he makes frequent use of off-screen trampolines to perform high leaps and flips. These acrobatics were anathema to Lee, who wanted his fight scenes to reflect his personal approach to martial arts, which was geared towards maximum efficiency and effectiveness. Lee knew how to adapt his style for the screen, for he understood the importance of selling a punch, but a major part of what made the film remarkable was Lee's fighting style. Where all his contemporaries in Hong Kong cinema were limited to Chinese martial arts, Lee drew upon a myriad of systems from all over the world. In particular he was a devastating kicker, a skill developed from studying French *savate* and Thai boxing. At Shaw Brothers the in-house style was *Hung Kuen* kung fu, which made scant use of kicks; Lee's fast, aggressive brand of screenfighting was like nothing the audience had seen before. The film's tremendous success is inexplicable without Lee's appeal. The plot is weak at best – no matter how many workers vanish, no one ever goes to the police – and the direction is without flair. Nevertheless, upon release *The Big Boss* broke box office records:

> Within three weeks, the take at the box office was ahead of the previous record-breaker, *The Sound of Music*, which had grossed $2.3 million in Hong Kong in less than nine weeks. In fact, *Boss* took in over $3.5 million in Hong Kong alone within 19 days … (Linda Lee, 1993, pp. 107 and 112)

Fist of Fury (1972)

After *The Big Boss*, Lee returned to the United States to film three more episodes of *Longstreet*, before starting work in Hong Kong on his second film for Raymond Chow, *Fist of Fury*. In the United States the shipping labels for Lee's first two Golden Harvest films were mixed up, so *Fist of Fury* became *The Chinese Connection*, which was supposed to be the American title for *The Big Boss*.

The story for the film was loosely inspired by the life of Fok Yuen Gap, a kung fu master who lived in Shanghai in the early twentieth century during the city's occupation by the British and Japanese. Fok founded the Ching Wu kung fu school and was famous for winning challenge matches against rival masters, including a Russian wrestler. The movie opens with Fok's funeral and the return home of his most gifted student, Chen (played by Lee) who is devastated by his teacher's sudden death. Suspicions of foul play are heightened when a group of Japanese martial artists show up carrying a plaque reading 'The Sick Man of Asia' that they present to the Ching Wu School. None of the Chinese are prepared to start trouble with the Japanese who control the city – no one apart from Chen, of course. He goes to the Japanese *dojo* and beats the hell out of every-one there, literally forcing the Japanese to eat their words when he stuffs the paper from the plaque down their throats. Back at the Ching Wu School, Chen discovers that the cook is a Japanese agent who poisoned Fok, and he kills him. While Chen is away from Ching Wu, the Japanese attack the school and demand that Chen is handed over. He returns to the Japanese *dojo* and kills everyone who crosses his path, including a Russian karate champion and Suzuki, the school's senior instructor. When the Japanese militia arrive, Chen charges into a hail of gunfire rather than face arrest. The image freezes on Chen leaping into the air as he hurls himself at the Japanese.

Fist of Fury enjoyed a bigger budget than its predecessor and was shot on studio sets in Hong Kong, sparing Lee the discomfort of the Thai countryside. Lo Wei stayed on as director and Han Ying Chieh received the martial arts choreography credit, but it is clear that Lee was asserting his own ideas even more than he had on *The Big Boss*. Relations between Lee and Lo Wei were severely strained during production. Jackie Chan worked as a stuntman on the film during the early days of his career and in his autobiography remembers Lo Wei:

> ... Lo was a hard-core gambler who favored horse racing; while scenes were being shot, he'd turn on the radio to listen to the post-to-post coverage from the Happy Valley Racetrack, utterly unconcerned about the action going on around him ... It was clear that Bruce had nothing but contempt for the man who called himself 'the Dragon's mentor' ...
>
> ... Lo Wei might have been the director of the movie, but Bruce Lee was in charge, and everyone on the set knew it. (Chan and Yang, 1999, pp. 168 and 169)

The difference between the action scenes without Lee and those in which he participates are even more marked than in *The Big Boss*. The sequence in which the Japanese fighters attack the Ching Wu School sees the Chinese performers using traditional kung fu tech-niques that bear no resemblance to Lee's screenfighting style.

5. The dramatic freeze frame that closes *Fist of Fury*, as the defiant Chen (Bruce Lee) chooses death rather than surrender.

Furthermore, the film introduced the weapon that Lee single-handedly popularised in the martial arts genre, the *nunchaku*. The irony is that while the story casts Chen as the *Chinese* hero who triumphs over foreigners with his *Chinese* kung fu, many of Lee's techniques were skills from non-Chinese systems.

The narrative is simplistic and purely driven by revenge, but the story was crafted to appeal to Chinese audiences on the most base, jingoistic level. The Japanese are all despicable villains, from the vain, strutting interpreter to the bullies at the *dojo*. The Chinese antipathy towards the Japanese can be traced back to the Sino-Japanese War, the Japanese occupation of Shanghai that followed, the invasion of Hong Kong during the Second World War and the subsequent human rights abuses. Whilst it relies upon stereotypes and lacks depth, *Fist of Fury* satisfies the Chinese desire for retribution. In one memorable sequence, Chen smashes a sign outside the Bund in Shanghai that reads 'No Dogs or Chinese' and lays out several taunting Japanese. The film plays to the vanity of its intended audience with great effect and was an even bigger box-office success than *The Big Boss*, taking over HK$3.5 million in two weeks.

Way of the Dragon (1972)

Having fulfilled his contract with Raymond Chow, Lee set up his own production company, Concord, to gain full creative control over his next project. It was co-produced by Concord and Golden Harvest, for while relations with Lo Wei had deteriorated beyond repair, Lee was still close to Raymond Chow. For *Way of the Dragon*, Lee assumed the duties of writer, director and star, playing Tan Lung, a country boy from the New Territories, Hong Kong, sent to Rome by his uncle to help out Chen Ching Wa (Nora Miao), whose Chinese restaurant is in trouble. The plot is still rather half-baked, with Ching Wa's restaurant under threat by a group of Italian mobsters who, for whatever reason, feel that they've just *got* to have that restaurant. They won't take no for an answer and have been frightening off customers, inspiring the waiters to learn karate to try to drive them away but they're no match for the thugs until Lung arrives. He thrashes all the gangsters, until the villains decide to hire three foreign *karateka*. They trick Lung and four of the other Chinese into an ambush. Lung defeats the first two fighters, then heads into the Colosseum for the climactic duel against Colt (Chuck Norris), the toughest of the three. While Lung is fighting, it is revealed that Ching Wa's uncle has been working with the gangsters and he stabs two of the waiters, Tony and Jimmy. After a lengthy battle in the Colosseum, Lung defeats Colt and is forced to kill him when the American refuses to surrender. Lung heads back to his friends, only to find them dead. The head gangster arrives in time to shoot the treacherous uncle, before the police show up. The final sequence sees Lung bidding farewell to Ching Wa and Ah Goon – one of the waiters, the comic relief – before he returns to Hong Kong.

Once again, the film is unsatisfying in terms of narrative structure and plot development. The first half is comic in tone, playing on Tan Lung's country-boy naivety as he struggles to deal with the foreign customs of the Italians. He can't read the menu at a restaurant and ends up ordering six bowls of soup. He doesn't know how to use an indoor toilet and gets picked up by a prostitute after Ching Wa tells him to be friendlier to the locals. The comic scenes are largely successful and Lee was certainly a better director than Lo Wei in handling dialogue. Where the film is exceptionally good is in the action scenes, choreographed by Lee, with an assistant martial arts instructor credit to his friend Unicorn Chan, who played Jimmy, one of the waiters. Lee showcases an even greater range of techniques than he displayed in *Fist of Fury*, although again there is the dichotomy between the intense Chinese jingoism of the screenplay and Lee's use of non-Chinese martial arts. In the story, the waiters all practise Japanese karate prior to Tan Lung's arrival and they are no match for the European thugs. Tan Lung teaches them 'Chinese boxing' and the waiters finally get the best of the foreigners. Yet, the 'Chinese boxing' is the screen version of Lee's *Jeet Kune Do* philosophy and it is a hybrid form. Lee performs techniques from French *savate*, Chinese *Wing Chun* kung fu, Thai boxing, Western boxing and uses the Okinawan *nunchaku*.

The three *karateka* are played by Whang Ing Sik from Korea and two Americans, Robert Wall and Chuck Norris. Lee's fights with the three of them are splendid and the duel with Norris sees Lee display his martial arts philosophy concerning adaptability and not relying upon set forms. At the start of their battle Tan Lung fights in a stiff, rigid manner and the heavier, stronger Colt overpowers him, drawing first blood. Tan Lung revises his strategy and the viewer is able to watch Tan Lung's martial arts evolve on screen. He abandons his traditional style and starts to bounce on his toes, light and loose. When Colt attacks, still using a rigid, hard karate style, Tan Lung easily evades and parries Colt's techniques. Tan Lung has become adaptable, by abandoning the limitations of traditional martial arts. When Tan Lung starts to break Colt down, he employs an enormous variety of techniques. He ties up Colt's arms using *Wing Chun*, batters his legs using *savate* kicks, then knocks Colt down by switching to high kicks. When he starts losing, Colt attempts to adapt his style, but instead of finding his own method he tries to copy Tan Lung's footwork. For Lee, this is imitation, not development, and it does not save Colt from a further beating. After breaking Colt's arm and leg, Tan Lung wants to stop fighting. Demonstrating an economy of direction, Lee handles the exchange between the two fighters without dialogue. Their eyes meet and Tan Lung shakes his head, telling Colt he does not wish to continue. Colt smiles, shouts his battle cry and lunges at Tan Lung, who catches Colt in a guillotine choke and kills him. Lee does not play this scene with any sense of glory or victory. Tan Lung is saddened at Colt's decision to choose death, not life, and covers his body with the *karateka*'s jacket in an act of respect. The music reinforces Tan Lung's sadness, for while Lee was willing to play on the nationalistic sensibilities of his audience, he was not prepared to trivialise the loss of life. This was unusual for a Hong Kong production in 1972, and stands in sharp contrast to many other films of the period, in which non-Chinese are all villains only deserving of a bloody demise. It is probable that the ideological shift in *Way of the Dragon* reflects Lee's sensibilities, since he had control over both script and direction for the first time. Whilst *Way of the Dragon* has plenty of faults – not least the decision to have the uncle turn traitor, which seems unnecessary – it is the most cohesive of Lee's films. He had not intended for the film to be distributed beyond the Asian markets, which explains the script's pandering to the nationalism of the Chinese audience, but its popularity throughout the world speaks to the brilliance of the action sequences and Lee's tremendous onscreen magnetism. The movie was a huge success, taking more than HK$5 million in Hong Kong alone.

6. Colt (Chuck Norris) and Tan Lung (Bruce Lee) in their classic duel from *Way of the Dragon*.

By the close of 1972 Bruce Lee was a superstar throughout Southeast Asia and in Hong Kong he could not go out in public without being mobbed. He had Robert Baker as his bodyguard, but was still under a great deal of pressure. He started work on a project entitled *The Game of Death* and commenced shooting some of the action scenes. The story involved a trio of martial artists fighting their way up a pagoda, on each floor encountering a martial artist who had to be defeated before they could continue. Each martial artist would have a particular style, until the trio reached the final level where the fighter would be like Lee himself, a martial artist with no fixed style, without limitations.

Enter the Dragon (1973)

Filming on *The Game of Death* was interrupted when American producer Fred Weintraub contacted Lee about the possibility of making a martial arts film for an American audience. A co-production deal was worked out, bringing Lee's company Concord together with the American producers Warner Brothers and Sequoia Productions. Warner Brothers were unwilling to let Lee direct, so an American, Robert Clouse, was brought in. The screenplay by Robert Allin was originally titled 'Blood and Steel', then renamed 'Han's Island'. It was only as a result of Lee's tenacity that Warner Brothers decided to use the name Lee himself coined for the project, *Enter the Dragon*.

The story borrows from Ian Fleming's James Bond adventure *Dr No* and concerns a Chinese martial artist, Bruce Lee, who is recruited by the British government to infiltrate a tournament held on the island of the reclusive Mr Han (Shih Kien), who is suspected of running all kinds of nastiness from his lair. Lee heads to the island, along with two Americans, Roper (John Saxon) and Williams (Jim Kelly). At the tournament, Lee kills Han's bodyguard Oharra (Bob Wall), who was responsible for the death of Lee's sister. Han kills Williams, before trying to recruit Roper to run their heroin operation in America. Lee is trapped when he runs amok in the island's underground drugs facility and he teams up with Roper to take on Han's army of goons. In the finale, Lee squares off with Han in a hall of mirrors and kills Han by kicking him onto a spear.

The script and direction are dreadful, full of the worst American clichés and misconceptions concerning the Far East. The story sees Lee acting as an agent of the British government, disenfranchising him of the role as a *Chinese* hero that he had established in his first three kung fu films. The revenge plot concerning Lee and Oharra is unconnected to the rest of the narrative and exists only to justify Lee's violent retribution against Oharra in their duel. The art direction is perhaps the worst element, particularly the colour coding of the karate *dogi*. Aside from the incongruity of Chinese martial artists wearing Japanese uniforms, Robert Clouse had a brainstorm concerning the colour of the outfits:

> To get more colour into the fight scenes and separate our principal characters from the stuntmen and extras who wore traditional white gis, I suggested yellow gis. My rationale was it was Han's tournament on his island and he could require any form of dress he wished. Everyone accepted that but Bruce. He refused to get into a yellow gi. (Clouse, 1987, p. 126)

Lee had good reason not to wear one of the canary-coloured karate suits. They looked ridiculous. Thirty years after the film was made, they still look ridiculous. Traditional *dogi* come in two colours – white or black – and they are Japanese uniforms. This one element perfectly demonstrates the complete ignorance of Chinese culture at work in the minds of the Americans on the project. Lee refused to wear a yellow *dogi* because he knew his fellow Chinese would laugh at him. Clouse even had the performers who were meant to be Han's security guards wear *beige* karate *dogi*.

Clouse did no better in his direction of the fight scenes. Mercifully, Lee was given free rein to choreograph the film and there are several scenes where the martial arts direction is excellent. Yet Clouse failed to understand the most basic rule in the filming of fight sequences – if you shoot a fight in a medium shot or medium close-up, then the audience can't see the movements of the performers. In many sequences Clouse opted to shoot Lee in a medium close-up, negating the impact of the fight choreography by keeping many of Lee's actions effectively off-screen. When the film works it is because of Lee's presence. His animal magnetism and explosive choreography are the only interesting ingredients in the movie. The film was Lee's least successful release in Hong Kong, where the Chinese didn't take kindly to the mangling of their culture.

On 10 May 1973, during the process of dubbing the dialogue for *Enter the Dragon* at Golden Harvest Studios, Lee collapsed and suffered violent convulsions. He was rushed to hospital, where he was diagnosed with a swelling of the brain. Lee was given the drug Manitol and he regained consciousness. On 20 July Lee was at the flat of Hong Kong actress Betty Ting-pei, where he complained of a headache. She gave him a painkiller and Lee laid down to rest. He never woke up and was pronounced dead at Queen Elizabeth Hospital. Lee was buried in Seattle at Lake View Cemetery before *Enter the Dragon* had even been released. It was a sudden and unexpected end for the first worldwide martial arts star. His impact on Hong Kong cinema was without equal. He secured the financial success of Golden Harvest, which became the largest film production company in Hong Kong when Shaw Brothers switched to television. He revolutionised the martial arts world, on and off screen, with his ideas about adaptability and his willingness to combine different styles. He broke open the world market for martial arts films, creating the kung fu craze of the 1970s and paving the way for the Western distribution of Hong Kong movies. Lee himself became a film icon and his work is still referenced today.

The Game of Death (1978)

The footage for Lee's unfinished film sat idle until Raymond Chow decided that the project might still be a money-spinner. Chow teamed up with Robert Clouse, who wrote a new screenplay that incorporated some, but by no means all, of Lee's footage. Clouse's story bore no resemblance to Lee's concept and his finished film is even worse than *Enter the Dragon*. The plot concerns Billy Lo, a kung fu movie star who has been targeted by gangsters who want him to make films for them. Billy fakes his own death and takes the bad guys apart. It's dreadful and the attempts to make it appear that Lee himself is in the film are risible. Footage from Lee's three Hong Kong productions are periodically used for close-ups, but this means that his haircut changes from shot to shot. The scene in which a photo of Lee's face is glued on to a mirror to obscure the identity of the body double is like a bad joke.

The action scenes are competently handled by Sammo Hung, who played Lee's opponent in the opening of *Enter the Dragon*, and so had first-hand experience of the late martial artist's fighting style. Several performers substituted for Lee, including Kim Tai Chong and Yuen Biao, all of them forced to hide their faces from the camera, either by keeping their heads down or by sporting a variety of disguises, from large dark sunglasses to motorcycle helmets. They all perform a reasonable imitation of Bruce Lee's screenfighting style, but it is never more than imitation.

The supporting cast are awful, particularly Gig Young, who sounds drunk in all his scenes. The whole production does not possess the slightest respect for the man whose work is being so thoroughly degraded. Mercifully, almost thirty years after Lee's death, the original footage for *The Game of Death* was dug out of the vaults at Golden Harvest and edited according to Lee's script notes. The resulting forty minutes offer a glimpse of what Lee hoped to accomplish with the project, which sees him expand upon his philosophy of *Jeet Kune Do*. The trio of martial artists fighting their way up the pagoda are Lee, James Tien and Chieh Yuan. Their opponents are played by Dan Inosanto, who portrays a master of *kempo*, Fillipino *escrima* and the *nunchaku*; Han Jae Ji, who uses the Korean art of *hapkido*, and Lee's student Kareem Abdul-Jabbar. Kareem was a professional basketball player and he towered above the rest of the cast.

Lee elaborates on his ideas about martial arts through several devices. Firstly, his character wears a black and yellow tracksuit, rather than a martial arts uniform, showing that Lee was not limited by any single style. In the duel with Inosanto, Lee employs a flexible bamboo rod against Inosanto's rigid *escrima* sticks. He defeats the *hapkido* master by adapting to his style when the *hapkido* fighter becomes stuck in a set pattern of attack. Finally, he takes on the massive Kareem Abdul-Jabbar, who does not wear a martial arts uniform for he too has a style of 'no style'. Lee defeats the giant when he realises his opponent is sensitive to sunlight, so he punches holes in the rice-paper windows, letting the light in and blinding Kareem. It is a shame that Lee did not live to finish *The Game of Death* or to see the huge success his work went on to enjoy in the United States. Lee dreamt of becoming an international film star and it is a bitter irony that he was only able to do so posthumously.

The Kung Fu Comedy and Jackie Chan

Returning for a moment to Christian Metz's theory regarding the process of genre, his third stage, after experimental and traditional, is parody. It is time to introduce two figures whose careers had a major impact on the martial arts film, Yuen Wo Ping and Jackie Chan.

Yuen Wo Ping is the son of Yuen Siu Tien, a regular from the 'Wong Fey Hung' series. Wo Ping was born in 1945 and was one of five brothers, all of whom learnt martial arts from their father. Wo Ping's first work in the film industry involved playing small roles in the 'Wong Fey Hung' films and a very youthful Wo Ping can be spotted in Wang Yu's *The Chinese Boxer*, where his character is killed by one of the Japanese *karateka*. The assistant director on *The Chinese Boxer* was Ng See Yuen, who left Shaw Brothers in 1971 to become an independent producer. Ng's inaugural production, *Mad Killer*, gave Yuen Wo Ping his first job as martial arts choreographer. The pair worked together on *The Bloody Fists* (1972), before Wo Ping returned to Shaw Brothers. Ng established the Seasonal Film Corporation in 1975 and produced the immensely popular *The Secret Rivals* (1976). In 1978, Ng borrowed the services of a young actor called Jackie Chan, who was signed to Lo Wei's company, to appear in Yuen Wo Ping's directorial debut, *Snake in the Eagle's Shadow* (1978). Kung fu movies were never the same again.

Jackie Chan was born in Hong Kong in 1954 and was a graduate of Yu Jim Yuen's Peking Opera School. He started his film career in *Big and Little Wong Tin-Bar* (1963) at the age of eight. After leaving Master Yu's school, Chan worked as a stuntman and bit player in martial arts films under the name Chan Yuen Long, following the tradition of students adopting part of their master's name as their own. In 1976 he joined Lo Wei's company and began using the name Jackie Chan as Lo attempted to groom him for stardom. The films produced by Lo with Chan were poorly directed, hopelessly formulaic efforts, including one of many attempts to cash in on Bruce Lee's legacy, *The New Fist of Fury* (1976). The subsequent films made by Lo Wei's company, *Shaolin Wooden Men*, *To Kill With Intrigue*, *Snake and Crane Arts of Shaolin*, *Spiritual Kung Fu*, *Half a Loaf of Kung Fu* and *The Magnificent Bodyguards* singularly failed to make Chan into a star. As a result, Lo was only too happy to let Ng See Yuen borrow Chan for *Snake in the Eagle's Shadow.*

Snake in the Eagle's Shadow (1978)

The film has a standard, generic plot about a young orphan, Chen Fu (Jackie Chan), who lives at the Hung-Tai kung fu school where he is the class punching bag. A group of Eagle Claw fighters come to town, hunting and killing their rivals from the Snake Fist style, one of which is an old beggar Pai Cheng Cheh (Yuen Siu Tien). Pai befriends the hapless Chen Fu and teaches him Snake Fist. After Chen Fu has used his new skills to defend the Hung-Tai School, Pai and Chen face off with the Eagle Claw killers, led by Sheng Kuan (Hwang Jang Lee). Chen combines the Snake Fist techniques with a style of his own invention based on the movements of a cat and kills Sheng Kuan.

The story has all the essential ingredients of a traditional kung fu film, the master–pupil relationship, the extended training sequences, and a showdown in which the techniques are tested in mortal combat. The opening title sequence shows Chan playing Snake Fist forms against a red studio background, an unmistakable reference to the Shaolin films of Lau Gar Leung and Chang Cheh. However, the tone of the movie is markedly different from the Shaw Brothers films. The key component of the kung fu comedy is the de-mythologising and diminishing of the kung fu hero. The historical heroes, Hung Hey Kwun and Fong Sai Yuk, are tragic heroes, their stories frequently ending in death. They approach their fates with a grim determination; Hu Hui Chen's death scene in *Men from the Monastery* is a perfect example. By contrast, Chen Fu is a bumbling oaf, stumbling his way through life, but somehow managing to stay alive and come out on top.

Yuen Wo Ping mocks several concepts key to the traditional kung fu film, including notions of loyalty and martial virtue. A recurring joke is the speed with which the fickle students switch between the Hung-Tai and Hing-Wei schools as the fortunes of each establishment rise and fall, ridiculing the notion of being devoted to one's martial arts school and *sifu*. Martial virtue is decidedly lacking in the kung fu instructors, who only care about looking tough in front of

7. Beggar Pai (Yuen Siu Tien) tormenting his pupil Chen Fu (Jackie Chan) during a training sequence from *Snake in the Eagle's Shadow*.

their students. Master Lee is a bully and when Master Lung is asked to perform a demonstration of brick breaking, he hurts himself so badly that when he has to shake hands afterwards he screams in pain, parodying the Iron Palm technique from *The Chinese Boxer*.

The choreography in *Snake in the Eagle's Shadow* plays with the traditional forms, but is still grounded in Chinese martial arts. Hwang Jang Lee is a Korean *Tae Kwon Do* adept, but he uses Eagle Claw hand techniques in addition to his tremendous kicking skills. Chen Fu's style, his amalgamation of Snake Fist and Cat's Claw, is pure invention, but retains elements of the authentic Snake Fist style. The action scenes are enhanced by Chan's considerable acrobatic talents but the film is still a kung fu movie, a pedigree asserted in the title sequence.

Drunken Master (1978)

Snake in the Eagle's Shadow was a huge hit and director and star capitalised on its success with the follow-up, *Drunken Master*. Where *Snake in the Eagle's Shadow* parodied the traditional kung fu film, the target of the humour in *Drunken Master* is the most revered of all Hong Kong cinematic icons – Wong Fey Hung. Chan plays the young Fey Hung as a boisterous troublemaker, more interested in chasing girls than studying martial arts. In desperation his father Wong Kai Ying sends Fey Hung to study with Sam Si (Yuen Siu Tien), the drunkard of the title. Fey Hung tries to escape Sam Si's clutches, only to fail time and again, and struggles to endure the old man's tortuous training methods. The zenith of Sam Si's drunken style is the 'Eight Drunken Gods' form, of which Fey Hung only learns the first seven movements, turning his nose up at the last form, the feminine 'Fairy Ho' style. When the assassin Thunderfoot (Hwang Jang Lee) shows up to kill Wong Kai Ying, Fey Hung comes to his father's rescue and has to invent his own version of 'Fairy Ho' to defeat the villain.

The film's approach to the character of Wong Fey Hung is positively iconoclastic. Where Kwan Tak Hing was proud, severe and majestic, Chan's portrayal is that of a blundering rascal who tries to take the easy option every time. He cheats when forced to practise horse-stance training, the very foundation of the *Hung Kuen* system of which Wong Fey Hung was a master. When he has learnt drunken boxing he finds that the more he drinks, the better he fights, a perversion of the Confucian concept of self-cultivation. Chan's performance of his own 'Fairy Ho' style is hilarious and grotesque, as he minces around in a terrible parody of femininity. Staggering about, intoxicated, he batters his opponent using a range of bizarre techniques with names like 'Old Lady Sits on the Toilet'. It is an outstanding display of Chan's athleticism and very funny. This manner of behaviour would have been unthinkable for Kwan Tak Hing as

8. The young Wong Fey Hung (Jackie Chan) struggles to hold his Horse Stance while being plagued by one of his kung fu teachers (Dean Shek) in Yuen Wo Ping's *Drunken Master*.

9. Wong Fey Hung (Jackie Chan) tests his Drunken Fist kung fu against the King of Sticks in one of the many imaginatively choreographed sequences from *Drunken Master*.

Wong Fey Hung, the very model of Confucian temperance. In *Drunken Master* the hero triumphs not through martial virtue, but by getting drunk and pretending to be an intoxicated woman. Whilst the film is still amusing without understanding the dismantling of the Wong Fey Hung mythos (the English language version of the film refers to the lead character as Freddie Wong), the humour is greatly enhanced by an intertextual appreciation of the relationship between Chan's portrayal of Wong Fey Hung and the legacy established by Kwan Tak Hing.

The film has a period setting, but there are signs of Hong Kong cinema's impending shift to a contemporary paradigm. Whilst the set design and costumes approximate the film's nineteenth-century period, Chan sports an anachronistic 1970s hairstyle. This reflects the film's self-conscious youthfulness, a sense of irreverence that exists both in Chan and in the Hong Kong audience. The character is not intended to act as a conduit between the viewer and Canton's distant history; rather he is the spirit of contemporary Hong Kong transposed into a period *mise-en-scène*. Numerous films copied this model, including *The Magnificent Butcher* (1979) and *Knockabout* (1979), all reflecting the growing self-awareness of the citizens of Hong Kong that their identity was no longer strictly 'Chinese'. It is worth noting that *Drunken Master* is still firmly rooted in Cantonese culture. The early action scenes see Chan use techniques from *Hung Kuen* kung fu, even if they are deliberately distorted. A later sequence sees Fey Hung and Sam Si perform a poem, 'About to Drink Wine', the presence of which provides a further link to the original 'Wong Fey Hung' series. The casting of Yuen Siu Tien, a regular from that series, further reinforces the referential nature of Wo Ping's work.

The Young Master (1980)

Drunken Master was even more successful than *Snake in the Eagle's Shadow*, allowing Chan to assume the director's mantle for his next starring vehicle, *The Fearless Hyena* (1979). Chan was still under contract to Lo Wei, so the film was produced for Lo's company, not without friction between producer and star. A split was inevitable and Chan signed with Golden Harvest, giving him creative control over *The Young Master*. The film is a broad comedy, full of slapstick and much mugging from the cast. Whilst there are plenty of martial arts techniques on display, the film is different from the projects Chan made with Yuen Wo Ping on several counts. There is no central master–student relationship and no development of new kung fu techniques. Where *Drunken Master* hinges on the interplay between Sam Si and Fey Hung, and on the importance of Fey Hung learning Sam Si's Drunken Fist style, the central character of *The Young Master* does not grow as either a martial artist or human being in the course of the story. Chan plays Dragon, an orphan who lives at a kung fu school with his friend Tiger (Wei Pei). The film begins with a Lion Dance contest, but immediately reveals the absence of martial virtue when Tiger, the senior Lion Dancer from Dragon's school, accepts a bribe to lead their opponents' team. Tiger needs the money to keep seeing the prostitute with whom he is smitten. When his *sifu* finds out, Tiger is expelled from the school and joins a gang of criminals, led by Kam (Whang Ing Sik). Dragon is sent to bring him home, leading to a series of misadventures when the local police mistake Dragon for Tiger. Dragon succeeds in securing Tiger's pardon by promising Sang Kung, the local official, to bring Kam into custody, setting up the climactic duel between Dragon and Kam.

The film contains many conflicting elements, indicative of a free-form approach to history and iconography. Chan continues to sport a modern hairstyle and the soundtrack is filled with contemporary Hong Kong pop songs, rather than traditional Cantonese music. When Dragon uses a long skirt to fight two villains, he acts like a matador and the soundtrack switches to a piece copying Spanish flamenco styles. This is wildly inappropriate for the film's Republican China setting, but it highlights Chan's light-hearted approach and the changing identity of a youthful audience with a fading connection to Canton. He's more interested in film as entertainment than film as history.

The final duel is well staged and Whang Ing Sik is an excellent screenfighter, yet unlike the climactic battles in *Snake in the Eagle's Shadow* and *Drunken Master*, here Chan's character triumphs not through the mastery of a new fighting style, but through sheer bloody-mindedness. Kam is clearly a better martial artist than Dragon and hammers him mercilessly. Dragon refuses to stay down and throws himself at Kam with abandon, limbs flailing, all kung fu technique forgotten in his desperation. When he subdues Kam it is not through any application of martial arts skill, but by pure ferocity. Kung fu skill and martial virtue have fallen by the wayside. The final fight is about the irrepressibility of the young, not the cultivation of the self.

Following *The Young Master*, Chan travelled to Hollywood, where he unsuccessfully attempted to break into the American mainstream. For *The Big Brawl* (1980) he had the misfortune to be paired with Robert Clouse, director of *Enter the Dragon*. Chan describes working with Clouse in his autobiography:

> ... Clouse, had scripted and storyboarded every scene in advance, deciding exactly where the cameras would be placed and how the action would move ... We ran through one scene in which I was supposed to move from a car to the door of my father's restaurant, which was being held up by mobsters. As I walked around the set, I saw in my mind how the scene could go. Through broken English and physical demonstrations, I showed Clouse my idea: I'd leap forward out of the car, roll into a somersault to stay beneath the line of sight, and then backflip to a position near the door. 'No, Jackie,' he said. 'Just get out of the car and *walk*.' (Chan and Yang, 1999, p. 258)

Despite having a bigger budget than Chan's Hong Kong movies, the American film has little to recommend it. Chan's acrobatics are marvellous, but the script is weak, Clouse's direction is poor and Chan's opponents are all lumbering brutes, too slow and clumsy to provide him with a suitable match. Shortly afterwards Chan appeared in *The Cannonball Run* (1981), an American comedy about a car race with a large cast of Hollywood players, including Burt Reynolds, Sammy Davis Jr. and Farah Fawcett. Chan and fellow Hong Kong star Michael Hui were cast as two Japanese entrants, offering a perfect example of the producer's ignorance of the outside world. The pair even converse in Cantonese, not Japanese, but this was of no consequence to director Hal Needham. Chan has one fight scene to show off his considerable athletic prowess, but it is all too brief. A disillusioned Chan returned to Hong Kong and Golden Harvest, for whom he made *Dragon Lord* (1982).

The film is a kung fu comedy in a similar fashion to *The Young Master*, but it has very little martial arts action. Rather, it offers a collection of comedy set pieces, involving Dragon (Chan) and his pal Cowboy (played by Chan's long-time stuntman, Mars) getting into trouble. They play tricks on each other and compete for the attention of a girl called Alice (Sidney Yim). Supposedly set in an unspecified period of Republican China, perhaps after the imperialists but before the Communists, the anachronistic elements are even more pronounced than in the ealier film, including two action set pieces modelled on present-day sports. The first sees four teams competing to catch a bun, which plays like an acrobatic version of American football. The second is a shuttlecock game modelled on soccer that even includes cheerleaders in traditional Chinese dresses.

Concepts of martial virtue and self-improvement are notable by their absence; Dragon is a lazy, mischievous boy who only practises kung fu when his father is watching. Chan brought back Whang Ing Sik to play the main villain and the choreography of their duel sees Chan move even further away from traditional Chinese martial arts than he had in *The Young Master*. Whang still makes an impressive villain as he employs his *Tae Kwon Do* skills, knocking Chan head over heels, and once more Chan simply hurls himself at his opponent, fists whirling. The wild, out-of-control nature of the scene is a stark contrast to the rhythmic and formal choreography of the Shaw Brothers Shaolin films. The climactic battle is not a rite of passage that marks the transition from youth to adulthood for, after winning, Dragon remains an undisciplined, wayward boy. He has learnt nothing nor experienced any kind of enlightenment. The ostensible reason for Dragon fighting Whang's character is to stop Whang from selling Chinese cultural treasures to foreigners, yet the final scene sees Dragon and Cowboy blowing up the very same antiques using firecrackers, oblivious to their value. They start and finish the narrative as kids constantly getting into trouble. There is no *sifu* figure, no development as human beings, and the romantic subplot between Dragon and Alice is never resolved, for to do so would be to force Dragon to grow up and face the responsibilities that accompany maturity.

Unfortunately for Chan, *Dragon Lord* failed at the Hong Kong box office and it is not his best work, lacking focus and any cohesive plot. It was his last kung fu film for over a decade. Whilst all these kung fu comedies – those of Yuen Wo Ping and Jackie Chan – contained stylistic elements that betrayed the influence of contemporary Hong Kong, they had nevertheless chosen pre-Communist China as their setting and subject. It was time for Hong Kong cinema to stop merely hinting at the modern character of the city and its people, and to address them directly.

The Shift to a Contemporary Cinema

The traditional kung fu film was going strong at the end of the 1970s, with Shaw Brothers, Golden Harvest and the independent producers all contributing to the genre but, by the mid-1980s, the genre was virtually dead, replaced by films that were aggressively contemporary, even when dealing with period stories. For the generation of filmmakers who created and developed the traditional kung fu film, the first point of reference had always been China, and more specifically Canton, the birthplace of virtually every important filmmaker in the traditional genre, with the exception of Bruce Lee. The directors were part of a generation of refugees and immigrants who left Canton in the wake of the Communist Revolution and settled in Hong Kong. It is important to note that none of the films of Lau Gar Leung, Chang Cheh or their contemporaries dealt with the reality of China under Communism. Period films were set either during the Ch'ing dynasty or in early Republican (and pre-Communist) China, like *The Boxer from Shantung* or *Fist of Fury*. The uncertainty of their situation in Hong Kong, faced with a return to Chinese control in 1997, was not something filmmakers in the 1970s were ready to address. Communist China did not exist on their screens.

A sea change occurred in the 1980s when Hong Kong's filmmakers began to address the central concern of the Hong Kong Chinese population – what does it mean to be a citizen of Hong Kong? This apparently sudden awakening of the public's consciousness can be traced to several sources. The growing prosperity of Hong Kong in the 1970s meant that more people were joining Hong Kong's growing middle class and found they had to devote less energy to keeping food on the table. Their increased financial security allowed socio-political awareness to take hold. More crucially, in 1981, the

Conservative government in London passed a law concerning the rights of all Hong Kong citizens who held British passports. Chris Patten, the last British governor of Hong Kong, wrote in his book *East and West* about the shift in the public's awareness following this decision:

> Their sense of Britishness was choked off by the British government's decision in 1981 ... to redefine the rights that possession of a Hong Kong British passport imparted ... Hong Kongers were left with a second-class document that only allowed them access to British consular protection and easier travel across international frontiers ... it gave the distinct impression that Britain cared less about its colonial subjects than they deserved ... If the average Hong Kong citizen thought of himself as a Hong Kong Britisher, this was despite the efforts of British politicians to prove him wrong. (Patten, 1998, p. 28)

The changes in the law meant that holding a British Hong Kong passport no longer allowed the holder to relocate to the United Kingdom. In 1982, Margaret Thatcher's Conservative government began negotiations with China on the transition of Hong Kong to Chinese rule. The uncomfortable question of Hong Kong's future was abruptly brought into sharp focus. Whilst it was clear that the politicians in London did not consider the citizens of Hong Kong to be their fellows, it was equally clear that the people of Hong Kong did not consider themselves to be part of Communist China. Hong Kong was perhaps the perfect model of the capitalist free market. There was no welfare state, never mind any equivalent to the totalitarianism found on the mainland. In the years following the Second World War, Hong Kong had grown in a direction that stood in sharp contrast to developments in China. The city was a financial centre, home to multinational banks, investment firms and a volatile stock exchange. It may not have been democratic, but it enjoyed freedoms unthinkable under the Chinese Communist Party. So, if the people of Hong Kong weren't British and they weren't Chinese, what were they? This became the central question of Hong Kong cinema in the 1980s and it was ever present in the minds of the people of the city. Chris Patten remembers the intensity aroused by this issue:

> Wherever I went as 'mayor' for five years, I was pursued by the same questions. Visit a school or hospital, talk of disability or training, what really mattered to the media was always the same. I would stand outside some welfare centre that I had opened talking about the needs of

the elderly and observe the pens of the attending press corps still poised unmoving in their hands; nor was there any sign of interest from the TV film crews. Then the first questions, and we were off and running – running always over the same ground: democracy, freedom, China. A one-issue media would daily drag the 'mayor' back to the main problem of his governorship and would then accuse him of never talking about anything else. (Patten, 1998, p. 53)

Compounding the shift in the self-perception of the residents of Hong Kong was the work of the new generation of filmmakers. The directors who came to the fore in the late 1970s and early 1980s had been raised in Hong Kong, not China. Their first point of reference was no longer an idealised vision of pre-Communist China, but the city of Hong Kong itself. As a result, when they made films set on the mainland, instead of addressing China and the past, they invariably found themselves talking about Hong Kong and the present. The first films to consciously address themselves to an idea of Hong Kong were comedies, notably the films of the Hui Brothers, Ricky, Michael and Sam. They created the enormously popular 'Mr Boo' series, full of parodies of other films and making great use of the Cantonese language's capacity for wordplay. Their most significant film in terms of its thematic impact on the film industry was *Security Unlimited* from 1981. The film is a pure comedy, not a kung fu comedy, but its importance in the wider arena of Hong Kong film makes it worthy of mention. The principal story is about a trio of security guards trying to track down a gang of crooks, yet there is a subplot in which they encounter a group of illegal immigrants from the mainland. For the first time in Hong Kong cinema, there was a clear distinction between people from Hong Kong and people from Communist China. The growing political self-awareness of the island finally found expression on screen. *Security Unlimited* was a massive hit and it was the starting point for a major shift in Cantonese language film.

Whilst Hong Kong filmmakers were still unwilling to address Communist China directly, they engaged with the uncertainties of Hong Kong's future by exploring the concept of identity – what does it mean to be a citizen of Hong Kong, when the city itself is neither purely Chinese nor British?

Project A (1983)

If there is one film that can be considered the first contemporary Hong Kong martial arts film, then it is *Project A*. The movie was directed by Jackie Chan, although it has been reported that when the production ran over budget and behind schedule, Golden Harvest appointed Sammo Hung as uncredited co-director to bring the project back under control. The story is set in 1903 and concerns the Royal Hong Kong Coast Guard's attempt to deal with pirates in the South China Sea. Chan plays Ma Lung, a member of the coast guard, who teams up with Tsu (Yuen Biao), a captain in the Hong Kong Police, and Fei (Sammo Hung), a black-market dealer. The three hatch a plot to rescue a group of British gentry kidnapped by the pirate Sanpao (Dick Wei), and succeed in destroying the pirates' lair and disposing of Sanpao.

The film is significant in theme and in the action choreography. On the first point, the script clearly distinguishes between the British authorities and the Hong Kong Chinese who work for them. The incompetence and untrustworthy nature of the British colonel who runs the coast guard and police is contrasted with the resourceful spirit of the Hong Kong Chinese. Sanpao kidnaps the British admiral before he even reaches Hong Kong, indicating that the British can't look after themselves, never mind their citizens in the colony. When the British colonel plans to pay Sanpao's ransom to secure the release of the hostages, Ma scolds him, 'The ransom money was given by the public to fight pirates. You can't abuse their trust. It's dishonest! You stand for law and order, yet you offer the pirates' accomplice a knighthood! Does the Queen pay you for that?' Clearly, the British are incapable of safeguarding the colony and it falls to the Hong Kong Chinese to sort out the mess created by their colonial governors.

The action choreography in *Project A* was a radical departure from everything that had come before in Hong Kong cinema. There is no trace left of traditional Chinese martial arts as Hung and Chan created a new form of screenfighting that was a true hybrid. The best illustration from *Project A* is the fight between the members of the coast guard and the police. The sequence is not set in a teahouse, but in a saloon; it is a cross between a kung fu fight and a barroom brawl. The influence of the American Western is apparent, as bodies fly over the bar, bottles, chairs and tables are smashed and fists fly. The performers really sell the blows, swinging wild punches that betray the influence of John Wayne's screenfighting style. The nihilistic, masochistic heroes of Chang Cheh and Wang Yu are nowhere to be found. When Ma and Tsu break chairs over each other, they hide their pain until out of sight, then writhe in agony. The sequence is acrobatic in the extreme, a trait in which it surpasses anything attempted in an American Western, and its freewheeling energy was unlike anything staged before in a Hong Kong action film.

A later sequence in which Ma is pursued through the back alleys of Hong Kong on a bicycle sees Chan drawing inspiration from Hollywood's silent era, particularly Buster Keaton. The climax of the chase is a spectacular stunt in which Ma falls from a clock tower that references the Harold Lloyd film *Safety Last!* (1923). Chan performed the stunt himself and shows it twice in the film and once more in the closing credits. Chan's willingness to perform such dangerous stunts is an essential quality in his appeal. It is particularly significant in *Project A* that the sequence references work beyond the scope of the kung fu genre. It is difficult to ascribe the title 'kung fu film' to *Project A* because it refuses to be bound by the expectations that accompany the genre. There is no *sifu* figure, no training regimes, no development of martial arts techniques and no displays of authentic Chinese martial arts. The fight sequences are explosive and completely freeform. In the final battle where Ma, Tsu and Fei take on Sanpao, the fighters punch and kick, but without attention to traditional kung fu forms. Chan has compared his style to jazz, declaring the traditional kung fu forms to be classical music. It is an accurate analogy.

Project A was a smash hit in Hong Kong and it heralded the demise of the traditional kung fu genre. Yuen Wo Ping's *Drunken Tai Chi* (1984) was passed over by audiences, who had lost their appetite for displays of Chinese martial arts. Chan and Hung's new screenfighting style, their hybrid of kung fu, kickboxing and acrobatics, was the new vogue. With the passing of Chinese martial arts from the screen, so the Shaolin heroes disappeared. The film brought with it a sense of modernity, as it addressed the relationship between the citizens of Hong Kong and their British governors. Communist China was notable only by its absence.

10. A defining moment in Hong Kong cinema: the barroom brawl from *Project A*. Kung fu is nowhere in sight.

A Modern Action Cinema

Hung and Chan followed *Project A* with the action comedy *Wheels on Meals*, directed by Hung. It reunited them with Yuen Biao in a story set in modern-day Spain in which the three come to the rescue of an heiress. Like the 'Lucky Stars' films, the movie is a collection of comedy and action set pieces that builds to a spectacular final battle. Hung brought in two Americans, Keith Vitali and Benny Urquidez, to play the hired muscle that take on Chan and Biao in the finale. The duel between Chan and Urquidez is frequently cited as the best fight scene Chan has ever performed. Urquidez was a champion kick-boxer and his battle with Chan is an outstanding example of the new Hong Kong style of screenfighting. Where the traditional kung fu films frequently established their martial credentials right from the first frame, featuring displays of kung fu forms during the opening titles, Hung begins *Wheels on Meals* with the two characters Thomas (Chan) and David (Yuen Biao) performing their morning exercises. The scene makes it clear that the parameters have shifted. The work-out begins with Biao striking a *Wing Chun* wooden dummy, a traditional piece of equipment for Chinese martial arts. Chan then squares off in front of the dummy, hits it once, shrugs and walks away, leaving kung fu behind. The pair performs a sequence of exercises culminating in a display of kickboxing. It's completely contemporary and a declaration that the film has broken with the traditions of the past.

Wheels on Meals established the pattern for many subsequent films by Chan and Hung. Plot and narrative are secondary concerns, given less importance than the staging of action and comedy routines. In the book *Hong Kong Babylon*, Chan described his approach to planning a film:

> When the audience see my movie, they are more interested in action than story, so a lot of time, my story very simple. First thing, how many fight scene? Of course, there is a big fight scene at the end, a middle one, a light fight scene, a little big scene – maybe five fighting in the whole movie. Then I plan it ... Then, how many comedy [scenes] I put inside? OK. Then we start the story. (Dannen and Long, 1997, p. 60)

The films that succeeded *Wheels on Meals* all kept to this pattern, action – comedy – action – comedy – repeat. The script is never the primary text and if the films are approached on a narrative level, they are unsatisfying. The stories are weak with a lack of attention to plot and character development. The actors rely on pre-existing screen personae for the audience to identify with them. Chan is the nice guy caught up in a bad situation, triumphing through will-power and determination. Hung is the bumbling oaf, happy-go-lucky but deadly when roused. The appeal of the films and the reason for their enormous popularity throughout Asia is the remarkable execution of the action scenes. The final fight scenes in *Police Story* (1985), *My Lucky Stars* (1985), *Heart of the Dragon* (1987) and *Dragons Forever* (1988) have few equals in any other nation's cinema. This can be attributed to the unique background of the filmmakers, who came out of the Peking Opera School system. In addition to Chan and Hung, this includes Yuen Biao, Yuen Wah and Corey Yuen. Their training in acrobatics, martial arts and gymnastics left them perfectly equipped for their roles as action choreographers and performers. They worked their way up the system from stuntmen to directors. Chan's classmates were the last group of students to attend a traditional Opera training school and there will never be another generation of filmmakers quite like them.

For a time in the late 1980s Chan concentrated on making fewer films with more ambitious scope. The results were mixed. *Mr. Canton and Lady Rose* (1989), based upon Frank Capra's *Lady for a Day* (1933) and *Pocketful of Miracles* (1961), is one of Chan's personal favourites and contains his most accomplished direction to date. However, it had a huge budget by Hong Kong standards, spent nine months in production (a very long time for a Hong Kong movie), and whilst it performed well at the box office, its high cost meant that it wasn't very profitable for Golden Harvest. Chan spent even more money on *Armour of God II: Operation Condor* (1991), which certainly wasn't used for script development. The comedy–action formula is very much in evidence and the film was a creative step backwards after *Mr. Canton and Lady Rose*.

Chan's subsequent output, with the exceptions of *Police Story III – Supercop* (1992), *Crime Story* (1993) and *Drunken Master II* (1994), is all highly formulaic, created as entertainment with an eye on the box office. *Rumble in the Bronx* (1996), *Mr. Nice Guy* (1997), *Who Am I?* (1998), and *Gorgeous* (1999) all feature good action sequences, but rely upon Chan's personal charm to carry the scenes when he isn't fighting. *Crime Story*, directed by Kirk Wong, was a rare foray into the police thriller genre for Chan, who is excellent in a dark and serious movie about corruption.

Police Story III – Supercop paired Chan with Hong Kong's most famous female action star, Michelle Yeoh. Directed by Stanley Tong, it features jaw-dropping stuntwork, including Yeoh jumping a motorbike onto a moving train and Chan dangling from a ladder attached to a helicopter high above Kuala Lumpur. Yeoh's character is a police officer from Communist China who teams up with Chan's Hong Kong cop. In the intense anxiety prevalent in Hong Kong in the run up to the handover in 1997, Chan and director Tong seemed to want to set people's minds at rest. Yeoh's character is smart, resourceful and attractive. She's no cold-blooded tool of the Communist state. Chan makes a joke at the end of the film after the pair have recovered the villains' stolen money – when discussing whose government the money should be given to, Chan says that it doesn't matter, 1997 is just around the corner. The movie offers no criticism of the Chinese Communist Party and aside from that one gag, makes no other references to Hong Kong's return to Chinese control. Yet it seemed to suggest that Chan himself, publicly at least, was not nervous about 1997.

Drunken Master II (1994) was a belated sequel to Yuen Wo Ping's *Drunken Master* from 1978. Lau Gar Leung was the director when the film started shooting, but Chan had taken full control by the time the project wrapped. The film was made during Hong Kong's New Wave in the early 1990s, when period stories came back into fashion, but like all the other movies made at the time, it is resolutely contemporary. *Drunken Master II* is a true kung fu film, Chan's only return to the genre after 1982. It features displays of traditional Chinese martial arts, particularly the *Choy Li Fut* and *Hung Kuen* systems. The final duel in which Wong Fey Hung (Chan) battles his off-screen bodyguard Ken Lo, does not see Fey Hung developing or improving his Drunken Fist style, but is more akin to *The Young Master* or *Dragon Lord*, in that Chan's character triumphs through determination and tenacity. The film was a big hit, but since then Chan's Hong Kong films have all had modern settings. When the American distributor New Line Cinema began to dub Chan's films into English and release them in the United States, they picked up *Rumble in the Bronx* (1996), *Mr. Nice Guy* (1997) and *Jackie Chan's First Strike* (1996), but did not release *Drunken Master II* in the West, despite the high regard in which the movie is held by Chan's fans. Their explanation was that the film was too Chinese in character for Western audiences. It's their loss, as *Drunken Master II* is a highlight from the latter part of Chan's career.

In addition to the evolution in screenfighting, the modern-day films swapped classical Cantonese music for Cantopop. Music and song maintain a strong presence, but they no longer offer a link to pre-Communist Cantonese culture. Jackie Chan, like many Hong Kong actors, has a successful singing career and he performs several title songs himself, including the theme for *Police Story*. As the 1980s progressed, more and more Hong Kong pop stars developed film careers, including Leslie Cheung, Cheung Hok Yau (Jackie Cheung), Andy Lau (Lau Tak Wah) and Anita Mui. The film stars who followed Chan, Hung and their contemporaries were more often than not singers first. As such, they were well suited to the entertainment industry, but could not match the remarkable physical talents of the Peking Opera School graduates.

Yuen Wo Ping made a late shift to contemporary action movies after the box-office failure of *Drunken Tai Chi*. His modern-day films all employed the hybrid screenfighting style, melding elements at random. In *Tiger Cage II* (1990) Wo Ping stages a duel between two martial artists armed with Japanese swords. The incongruity of a sword duel in Hong Kong in 1990 is not addressed. The fight itself is of primary importance, not narrative cohesion. All of Wo Ping's contemporary films feature action scenes performed with flair and imagination, even as they suffer from repetitive plots about cops fighting corruption. When the New Wave ushered in a return to period films, Wo Ping was back in his element and enjoyed considerable success with *Wing Chun* (1994) and *Iron Monkey* (1993) to name but two.

Sammo Hung

Hung Kam Bo, better known by his nickname Sammo, was born in Hong Kong in 1950. He attended the Peking Opera School run by Master Yu Jim Yuen, with Jackie Chan, Yuen Biao and Corey Yuen. School is perhaps not quite the correct word. Master Yu's regime was brutal and unforgiving. Mistakes or misdemeanours were punished by beatings and the boys endured conditions that would see their master imprisoned for child abuse if practised today. Information about life at the school can be found in Jackie Chan's autobiography, or in Alex Law's excellent film *Painted Faces* (1988), in which Hung plays his old master.

Hung started film work at the age of eleven in *Education of Love* (1961). After leaving Master Yu's school, Hung became a stuntman, a role for which the harsh training had left him well prepared – he was a talented acrobat and martial artist with a high tolerance for pain and injury. In 1970, Hung joined the fledgling Golden Harvest as martial arts instructor on Huang Feng's *The Fast Sword*. Thereafter, he worked constantly as a choreographer, frequently appearing in the films as a villain. He was the regular martial arts instructor on the films of Huang Feng, including *Hap-Ki-Do* (1972), *When Tae-KwonDo Strikes* (1973), *The Tournament* (1974) and *The Himalayan* (1976). The films have standard genre stories, but are interesting for showcasing non-Chinese martial arts.

In 1977 Hung graduated from choreographer to director with *The Iron-Fisted Monk*, written by Hung and his mentor Huang Feng. The movie follows the format of the Shaolin films made at Shaw Brothers and has elements in common with *Men from the Monastery* (1974). The story is set during the Ch'ing dynasty and concerns Husker (played by Hung), a miller who goes to Shaolin Temple to learn kung fu after his uncle is murdered by a group of Manchu bullies. Husker returns to his hometown, where he meets Tak, the monk who sent him to Shaolin, and Leung, who works at the local dye factory. When the Manchus attack the dye factory and kill all the workers, Husker and Tak retaliate by storming into the villains' lair and tearing them apart.

The plot is formulaic with the Manchus being relentlessly evil, leading up to the intended catharsis as Husker and Tak deliver a violent retribution. What separates the film from Chang Cheh's work or that of Lau Gar Leung, are the relationships between the major characters and the nature of the violence. Firstly, unlike Chang Cheh's noble Shaolin heroes, Hung's characters are cynical and self-centred. Husker constantly tries to get one over his instructor at the temple and plays tricks on the monks. He trains in martial arts motivated by a desire for revenge and self-preservation, not self-cultivation. He hates the Manchus because they have wronged him – it's personal, not patriotic. Hung's films are lacking in the idealism of the Shaw Brothers Shaolin movies and they are far more profane. Sex and violence against women are prevalent in *The Iron-Fisted Monk*. There are two intensely unpleasant rape scenes, a considerable amount of female nudity and a scene in which a customer at a brothel tries to convince a prostitute to perform oral sex. Such scenes would have been unthinkable for Chang Cheh or King Hu, whilst Lau Gar Leung addressed sexuality indirectly. Where Shaw Brothers films were prudish, Golden Harvest's output was more

11. The climactic moment of revenge in Sammo Hung's directorial debut *The Iron-Fisted Monk*.

exploitative, going back to *The Big Boss*. Furthermore, the most frequent criticism of Hung has been the high level of violence against women in his films; the rape scenes in *The Iron-Fisted Monk* support this assertion.

What makes the film work is the quality of the fight sequences, which see Hung using traditional Chinese martial arts, particularly the *Hung Kuen* style. There are demonstrations of Crane, Mantis, Snake and Tiger techniques, all performed with tremendous speed and excellent timing. This is very much a traditional kung fu movie, as were the rest of Hung's works prior to 1982. *Warriors Two* (1978) was the first of a pair of films about the *Wing Chun* kung fu style, along with *Prodigal Son* (1981). *Warriors Two* saw Hung begin to develop his own style, in particular his talent for balancing the comic and the tragic, a hallmark of his work. *Prodigal Son* is a marvellous film, with brilliant fight sequences performed by Yuen Biao, Lam Ching Ying and Frankie Chan. The movie remains a highlight of both Hung's career and the traditional kung fu film.

In terms of the process of genre, Hong Kong cinema began its second cycle in the early 1980s, as filmmakers started to contemporise their movies. Hung and Jackie Chan were vital to this process. Hung's 1983 comedy, *Winners and Sinners* – also called *Five Lucky Stars* – was a vehicle for a group of Hong Kong comedians modelled on the films of the Hui brothers. Whilst most of the screen time is devoted to the comic antics of the Lucky Stars, there were several action set pieces performed by Hung and Chan, which saw them injecting their martial arts skills into a contemporary *mise-en-scène*. The film spawned several sequels, *Twinkle, Twinkle Lucky Stars* and *My Lucky Stars* in 1985, both directed by Hung, and *Lucky Stars Go Places* (1986), produced by Hung and directed by Eric Tsang. The action set pieces do not gel smoothly with the comedy and in *My Lucky Stars* Chan's character disappears after the opening fight and only returns for the action-packed final showdown. Between the two the audience is 'treated' to a collection of comedy routines from the Lucky Stars. It would not be correct to describe these films as kung fu comedies, for they are not concerned with the de-mythologising of the kung fu hero and do not feature traditional Chinese martial arts. Rather, they move freely between slapstick, farce and martial arts action that showcases the new, hybrid style of screenfighting created in *Project A*.

Prior to the switch to a contemporary cinema, Hung had begun to expand the boundaries of the kung fu film. Like Lau Gar Leung, Hung tested the flexibility of the form by combining the martial arts film with other genres. He began with *Encounters of the Spooky Kind* (1980), blending horror and kung fu. The opening title sequence establishes Hung's intention to break new ground, as he does not begin with a display of martial arts forms. He starts with a disturbing scene in which two ghosts attack the protagonist Cheung (played by Hung), tearing and biting at him. It turns out to be a nightmare, but the horror of this initial scene sets the tone for the rest of the tale. Cheung's wife is having an affair with his boss, Master Tam, and when Cheung almost catches them together, Tam decides to have Cheung killed. To make it look like an accident, he hires Chin Hoi, an evil wizard, to dispose of Cheung, who is saved by the intervention of Tsui (Chung Fat), a good wizard. The story builds to a duel between the wizards, with Cheung and Tam caught up in their spell casting. Tsui kills Chin Hoi, but is mortally wounded, while Cheung kills Master Tam. Cheung's wife appears and pretends to be pleased to see her husband. He beats her and the image freezes on Cheung hurling his wife through the air.

The film was tremendously influential and was much imitated. The iconography that Hung used for the Taoist magic rituals and his presentation of Chinese vampires became the standard that all filmmakers subsequently copied. The hopping vampires originated in the myths of Ming dynasty China and Hung brought them to the screen with invention and wit, making them funny and frightening. The film makes extensive use of special effects and wirework to enhance the action, techniques that are now commonplace. In the climactic duel, Tsui and Chin Hoi summon Taoist deities to possess Cheung, Tam and Chin Hoi's assistant, to help them fight. The scene is the perfect synthesis of kung fu and magic and reveals Hung's skill at blending genres. Hung's company Bo Ho Films produced *Mr. Vampire* (1985), which used the same techniques for the vampires and led to numerous sequels.

Eastern Condors (1986)

Hung continued melding genres and in 1986 made one of his darkest works, *Eastern Condors*, combining the martial arts movie with a war film. In 1976 a group of Chinese illegal immigrants, having been arrested in the United States, are offered US residency in return for taking part in a secret raid to destroy an American arms cache in Vietnam. Codenamed the Eastern Condors, they parachute into Vietnam moments before their leader learns that the mission has been aborted. He parachutes with his team anyway and they join up with three female Cambodian guerrillas and set off in pursuit of the arms silo. The Condors find themselves tailed by the Vietcong and their numbers dwindle as they fight through the jungle. The Vietcong catch up with the Condors at the weapons cache, leading to the final battle. The silo is destroyed, but only three of the team survive and they are left waiting for the American helicopter that they hope will retrieve them.

Hung brought together an extraordinary cast, including Yuen Wo Ping, Corey Yuen, Lam Ching Ying (from *Mr. Vampire*), Yuen Biao, Yuen Wah, Dick Wei (Sanpao in *Project A*), Kurata Yasuaki (from *Shaolin Challenges Ninja*), Hsiao Hou (from *Legendary Weapons of Kung Fu*), and kickboxer Billy Chow. The pace is relentless as Hung moves from battle to battle, scarcely pausing for breath. There are references to American war films, notably Sam Peckinpah's *Cross of Iron* (1977), both in the bloodiness of the action scenes and the use of Peckinpah's technique of freezing the image while the sound continues. Both films are bleak and violent, with a sense of despair about the nature of humanity. The most disturbing sequence in *Eastern Condors* sees two Vietcong children using prisoners for a game of Russian roulette, which references Michael Cimino's *The Deer Hunter* (1978).

The film is decisively modern and deals with the issue of identity so widespread in Hong Kong cinema during the 1980s. Many of the characters are not who they appear to be and loyalties shift at a moment's notice. A telling example occurs when one of the Condors captures a young boy during a battle. He releases the child, who turns and stabs him. His mistake was to confuse youthfulness for innocence, demonstrating that nothing is what it seems.

Yeung Lung (Haing S. Ngor) pretends to be insane, until he exposes the traitor amongst the group. When the team reach the arms silo, the leader of the Cambodians turns against the Condors, determined to keep the weapons for her cause rather than let them be destroyed. She shoots the leader of the Condors to stop him setting his explosives, a sudden change in her allegiance. This sense of uncertainty about roles and identities is so omnipresent in Hong Kong cinema of the time that it is possible to argue that it is the externalisation of the citizens' anxiety about their ill-defined place in the world.

After the last battle, the three survivors sit waiting for the US army to retrieve them, unaware that their mission was cancelled. The movie closes with a sense of futility and a pervasive distrust of those in authority. This can readily be construed as a criticism of all governments that neglect those they govern, applicable to both China's authoritarianism and Great Britain's decision to abandon the people of Hong Kong. There is a version of *Eastern Condors* released in the West that features a helicopter superimposed over the final shot, an attempt to temper the film's dark cynicism.

Pedicab Driver (1989)

Hung's last piece of genre experimentation was *Pedicab Driver* (1989), blending the martial arts film with a romantic melodrama. The central story concerns a young pedicab driver whom everyone calls Malted Candy (Mok Sui Chung), who falls in love with Hsiao-Tsui (Fennie Yuen), unaware that she is working as a prostitute to clear her family's debts. With the aid of his friends Tung (played by Hung), Rice Pudding (Mang Hoi) and Shan Cha Cake (Lowell Lo), the lovers are married. Their happiness is short-lived when the vengeful triad boss who owned Hsiao-Tsui, Master Five (John Shum) sends his men to kill the couple on their wedding night. Arriving too late to save their friends, Tung and Rice Pudding storm Master Five's house and exact their bloody retribution.

The bulk of the narrative deals with the romances between Malted Candy and Hsiao-Tsui, and Tung and his sweetheart Ping (Nina Li). Against this backdrop, Hung deconstructs the work of one of Hong Kong's most important kung fu filmmakers – Lau Gar

Leung. In a memorable sequence Tung and Ping crash into a gambling house when fleeing from Master Five and his thugs. Ping drops her money and when Tung tries to pick it up from the piles of cash on the floor, he is forced to confront the master of the house, played by Lau Gar Leung. The two men fight for Ping's money and Hung gives Lau Gar Leung the same treatment that Leung gave to Chang Cheh in *Legendary Weapons of Kung Fu*. The fight begins with Hung and Leung exchanging flurries of strikes and kicks in the modern, hybrid screenfighting style. As the two square off for the second time, Leung drops in to a *Hung Kuen* stance. Cantonese music fills the soundtrack as Leung adopts a series of classic kung fu poses, asserting his martial arts pedigree. In response, Hung performs a grotesque parody of Monkey style, screeching and contorting his face, an unmistakable reference to Leung's film *Mad Monkey Kung Fu*. When Hung finishes his monkey imitation, Leung looks mortified, stepping outside the narrative, for he knows when he's being belittled as a filmmaker. Hung launches back in to the fray, continuing to employ modern choreography, the traditional stances and techniques cast aside. The scene is extremely funny, but relies upon the audience instantly recognising Lau Gar Leung and their awareness of his work and kung fu lineage. As the battle continues, Hung picks up a pole, leading Leung to do the same, a grave mistake on Hung's part, since Lau Gar Leung's expertise in weapons is well established in his films. Leung wins the duel and tells his beaten opponent, 'Fatty, you're tops. I've fought with many men and you're the only one that has scared me.' It is a marvellous sequence in which Hung deconstructs the vital essence of the martial arts film – the fight scene – by drawing attention to the choreographers themselves, identifying himself and Lau Gar Leung on screen and highlighting their different styles. The sequence is postmodern in its approach to the staging of a fight, in the same manner as Leung's dismantling of Chang Cheh's penchant for disembowelment sequences in *Legendary Weapons of Kung Fu*. It is rather charming that Leung wins the duel, for Hung is not prepared to suggest that he is the superior martial artist to his senior.

Creatively, *Pedicab Driver* was the zenith of Hung's career. It displays his directorial skills in their most fully realised state, with a strong narrative binding the production together. The romance is certainly melodramatic, but this is deliberate and of Hung's films this is the most sympathetic to the female characters. When Tung and his fellows learn about Hsiao-Tsui's prostitution and turn against her, it is Ping who scolds them to be compassionate. Hung denies Hsiao-Tsui and Malted Candy a happy ending, for whilst a pure romantic melodrama might see the lovers united at the end, this is a kung fu hybrid and requires the impetus of tragedy and vengeance to drive the story towards the final showdown. The film contains other intertextual references including a *Star Wars* parody in the opening. The final battle between Tung and the thugs at Master Five's house is extraordinary, displaying Hung's talent for balancing comedy and drama side by side.

None of Hung's subsequent output was able to equal his accomplishments in *Pedicab Driver*. Several contemporary action/comedies followed, including *Pantyhose Hero* (1990) and *Slickers Vs Killers* (1991), but these were formulaic and followed the standard comedy–action–repeat blueprint. When the New Wave dominated the box office, Hung made films in that style, including *Moon Warriors* (1993) and *Blade of Fury* (1993), but he was following the pervading trends rather than creating or anticipating them. He continued to work regularly as a stunt choreographer and enjoyed commercial success directing Jackie Chan in *Mr. Nice Guy* (1997) and Jet Li in *Once Upon a Time in China and America* (1997), but neither film broke new ground artistically. Hung moved to Los Angeles and made two seasons of the television series *Martial Law*, about a Chinese cop in Hollywood. The action scenes were entertaining, even if the scripts were formulaic. Since the cancellation of *Martial Law*, Hung has appeared in several Hong Kong films, often doubling as fight choreographer. It remains to be seen if he can regain his potency as a director and continue to expand the limits of the martial arts genre as he did with such style in the 1980s. Alongside Lau Gar Leung and Yuen Wo Ping, Hung stands as one of the most innovative filmmakers Hong Kong has produced. His flexible approach to genre and his participation in creating the modern screenfighting style were essential to the continuing evolution of the martial arts film.

John Woo – Hong Kong Gangsters

John Woo is arguably the most successful of Hong Kong's directors to make the transition to working in the United States. Woo was born in Canton in 1946 and began his career at Shaw Brothers. He worked as an assistant director for Chang Cheh, whose influence can still be found in Woo's films. His movies are entirely male-centric, with female characters either absent or powerless, just as they were in Chang's films. Both directors favour isolated, lonely protagonists whose capacity for violence equals that of their opponents.

Woo started directing kung fu films for Golden Harvest, collaborating with Sammo Hung, who choreographed Woo's films *The Dragon Tamers* (1975) and *Hand of Death* (1975), also known as *Countdown in Kung Fu*. By 1978's *Last Hurrah for Chivalry*, many of Woo's signature themes were in place. This period story concerns the bond between two swordsmen, Chang (Wei Pai) and Tsing Yi (Damian Lau). It is akin to Chang Cheh's films, with an undisclosed homoerotic subtext. The two heroes are both loners until they meet and find that they are kindred spirits. Tsing Yi rejects the advances of a beautiful courtesan who throws herself at him, but in the final battle he sacrifices himself to save Chang. In the preceding fight scene, Tsing Yi is injured in the stomach, but covers his wound to continue fighting – a motif directly copied from Chang Cheh.

A Better Tomorrow (1986)

Woo's biggest hits in the late 1970s and early 1980s were comedies. He joined Mak Kar's company Cinema City and made two more comedies, but he was deeply unhappy with the direction his career had taken. His next project, *A Better Tomorrow*, written by Woo and produced by Tsui Hark, finally saw the director in his element. The film was a huge hit, leading to two sequels and marking the beginning of the contemporary Hong Kong gangster film.

The story tells of two brothers, Kit (Leslie Cheung) who has just graduated from the Hong Kong Police Academy, and his older brother Ho (Shaw Brothers veteran Ti Lung) who is a triad. Ho's dilemma is the choice between trying to go straight or to fall back in with his old triad pal Mark (Chow Yun Fat), until Mark is killed in a

12. Mark (Chow Yun Fat) from Woo's influential *A Better Tomorrow*. Gun play replaces displays of Chinese martial arts.

shoot-out with members of a rival gang, leaving Kit and Ho to exact revenge. The film is aggressively contemporary in both narrative and theme. The question of identity is expressed in the conflict Ho faces over whether or not he is still a gangster. This uncertainty is an allegory for Hong Kong's situation, caught between China and Great Britain; the motif of being trapped between opposing forces recurs constantly throughout Hong Kong cinema of this period. It is often expressed visually by having one character caught between two fighters. Other examples can be found in *A Chinese Ghost Story* (1987), where Leslie Cheung is caught between the blades of two swordsmen, and in the standoff at the end of *City on Fire* (1987).

The action choreography in *A Better Tomorrow* exchanges martial arts techniques for shoot-outs, declaring the film's contemporary character – kung fu would be anachronistic. The image of Chow Yun Fat blazing away with a pistol in each hand references Sydney Pollack's *The Yakuza* (1975) and became a staple of the Hong Kong gangster genre. These are male films about the importance of loyalty. In Woo's world the police and the triads are both capable of good and evil – it's all a question of brotherhood. Good cops and good triads are loyal to their fellows, whilst bad cops and bad triads are self-serving and greedy. Woo, more than any other filmmaker, glamorised the triad lifestyle, and his casting of Chow Yun Fat – a former soap opera actor – as the handsome and charming Mark, catapulted the actor to cinematic stardom and established Chow's screen persona as the suave tough guy who is quick with a gun.

A Better Tomorrow Part II (1987)

A Better Tomorrow Part II was more macho nonsense about loyalty. Kit is assigned to infiltrate the business operations of Si Lung (Dean Shek), a former triad trying to turn legitimate. Framed for murder by his ambitious second-in-command Ko, Lung heads to New York, where he meets Ken, the twin brother of Mark from the first movie. They return to Hong Kong, where Kit is slain by an assassin, leaving Lung, Ho and Ken to storm Ko's mansion, which they do in explosive fashion. All three are fatally wounded and sit waiting for the police as they bleed to death.

The issues of loyalty and identity are ever-present. Kit has to go undercover, seducing Lung's daughter Peggy, even though his wife is at home expecting a baby. He is caught between two personas, that of the husband and the undercover cop, just as Hong Kong was caught between China and the West. There is a lot of talk in the script about destiny and the inability to escape one's past, expressed by Lung, Ho and Ken. All three are ex-triads, trying to go straight, yet in the end they have to revert to their old selves, to act like gangsters, to destroy Ko. It is comparable to the Japanese notion of predeterminism, *shushigaku*, and Woo reinforces the Japanese reference, employing the principal icon of the *chambara* genre by having Ho use a Japanese *katana* sword in the final battle.

For all the violence, there is a powerful morality at work: the bad triads, including Ko, are destroyed, whereas whilst the good triads – Lung, Ho and Ken – also die, they do so having accomplished their goal. Yamamoto Tsunetomo would be proud. The three of them meet death sitting upright on chairs (like thrones) surrounded by the bodies of their vanquished enemies. What more could a nihilist wish for?

Typically for Woo, women remain powerless. The male characters make mighty sacrifices; their deaths are full of heroism and occur in slow motion. By contrast, the death of Lung's daughter Peggy is scarcely given a moment. The most overtly sentimental scene is Kit's death. The mortally wounded Kit calls his wife Jackie who is in labour. He lives long enough to learn of his baby's birth, before expiring, yet Woo never shows Jackie's reaction to Kit's death. Instead he focuses on Ho's reaction. Jackie is pushed out of the narrative by the male characters, making it clear that her emotions aren't as important as those of the men.

The two protagonists of *The Killer* (1989) are a cop (Danny Lee) and a triad hitman (Chow Yun Fat), but in Woo's view they are kindred spirits, two sides of the same coin. Identity is not defined by job title, but by morality. Typically, the female character Jennie (Sally Yeh) is powerless. She is blinded early in the story and spends the rest of the film wandering around helplessly. In the climax the cop and the assassin unite to take on the forces of the evil triad boss who wants them both dead. Set in a church, the final shoot-out is wildly over-the-top and deliriously melodramatic, as bullets fly, religious icons explode and doves fly in slow motion.

Both *Bullet in the Head* (1990) and *Hard Boiled* (1992) continue to explore loyalty and identity. *Bullet in the Head* is Woo's darkest film; three friends from Hong Kong go to Vietnam hoping to make their fortunes. Loyalty and brotherhood remain the principal issues, as Paul (Waise Lee) betrays his friends Ben (Leung Chiu Wai) and Frank (Cheung Hok Yau) when he is consumed by greed. In *Hard Boiled* Tony (Leung Chiu Wai) is an undercover cop posing as a triad. Tony's dilemma is that he makes an extremely successful triad and he wonders if he is a cop pretending to be a gangster, or vice versa. This ambiguity of identity is another example of the expression of the uncertain situation of Hong Kong in 1992 – is it a Chinese city pretending to be Western, or a Western city that is about to find itself forced to act Chinese?

After *Hard Boiled*, Woo made the transition to Hollywood, leading the Hong Kong filmmakers' diaspora. His output since the move has been mixed, but of all the Hong Kong directors to make the change Woo retained the stylistic and thematic elements that characterised his work more successfully than the rest of his fellow ex-patriots. *Face/Off* (1998) contains every trademark associated with Woo – it is a male-centred story about a cop and a terrorist trading places when their faces are surgically switched. *Mission Impossible II* (2000) saw Woo playing with identities as the characters assume a series of disguises and roles. This film is unusual for Woo as it features a strong female character, Nyah (Thandie Newton) but his usual trademarks, the extended gunplay, car chases and identity switches, are all in place.

It is perhaps because his most successful Hong Kong films combined the alienated heroes of the martial arts film with the iconography of the gangster genre that John Woo has made the smoothest transition from Hong Kong to Hollywood. Guns, unlike Chinese martial arts, fit easily into American stories.

Ringo Lam – Hong Kong on Fire

Lam Ling Tung, or Ringo Lam, was born in Hong Kong in 1955. He studied film at York University in Canada, but didn't finish the course and returned to Hong Kong. His first film was the hit romantic comedy, *Esprit d'Amour* (1983), produced for Mak Kar's Cinema City. He directed the fourth instalment in the 'Aces Go Places' series (*Aces Go Places IV*, 1986), before getting the chance to make *City on Fire* (1987), the movie that was the basis for Quentin Tarantino's *Reservoir Dogs* (1992). The film set the tone for all of Lam's subsequent work – it is a dark, cynical thriller in which the lines between hero and villain are extremely thin. Ko Chow (Chow Yun Fat) is an undercover cop, desperate to resign, who is convinced by his superior, Lau, to infiltrate a gang of jewel thieves. Ko succeeds in doing so, befriending career criminal Fu (Danny Lee) in the process. John Chan, a new, younger inspector who dislikes Lau, refuses to acknowledge that Ko is an undercover officer. Chan's men pursue Ko, arresting and beating him until Lau intervenes. Ko's fiancée, Hung (Carrie Ng), frustrated by his unreliability, leaves him and heads overseas. Ko and Fu join the rest of the gang for the robbery, which goes awry when an alarm is sounded. In the ensuing shoot-out with the police, Ko is shot in the stomach. At the warehouse where the survivors rendezvous, the leader of the gang, Lam, assumes that Ko is an informer and pulls a gun on him. Fu, convinced that his friend cannot be a traitor, points his gun at Lam, prompting Song, another thief, to point his gun at Fu. Ko is caught in the stand off, surrounded by their guns, but the arrival of the police interrupts them. As the police storm the warehouse, Ko confesses his identity to Fu before dying from his wound. Fu is taken in to custody as Ko is left on the floor of the warehouse.

Lam suggests that Hong Kong is a city without a future. Ko is a man trapped by fate, unable to decide his own identity. Lau wants him to be an undercover cop, but the other police treat him like a criminal, and when he is chased and beaten by the officers under Chan's command, he reacts like a criminal. When the raid on the jewellery store goes sour, Ko flees like a crook, and when a cop shoots him, he fires back. He sacrifices his life for the police, led by self-serving men who refused to accept him as one of their own. The rejection of authority figures is absolute – aside from the callousness of Chan, Ringo Lam finds no honour amongst thieves. In one scene Lam, the leader of the thieves, boasts to Ko that everyone in the gang will share equally in their good fortune and that they are all brothers, but in the climatic scene when Bony, one of the robbers, suggests that they surrender to the police, Lam kills him. Unlike Woo, whose characters have codes of honour, in Lam's world there is only chaos. The sole character to escape unscathed is Ko's girlfriend Hung, who leaves Hong Kong, fleeing the city without a future.

After *City on Fire*, Lam made the equally desperate *Prison on Fire* (1987). The movie seethes with hatred for authority, personified by Officer Hung (Roy Cheung), who runs the prison, and Madly (Shing Fui On), the triad boss who exploits his fellow inmates. Chow Yun Fat is outstanding as Ching, the prisoner who tries to protect Lo Ka Yiu (Leung Kar Fai), the newest inmate. A sense of hopelessness pervades the story, as the two protagonists are pressed from all sides, another metaphor for Hong Kong caught between China and the West. Lam continued to make his bleak visions with *School on Fire* (1988) and *Prison on Fire II* (1991), but took a rest from the relentless gloom to direct *Wild Search* (1989), a drama similar to Peter Weir's *Witness* (1985), that – uncharacteristically for the director – has a happy ending.

Lam's most overtly nihilistic work was *Full Contact* (1992). Chow Yun Fat stars as Jeff, an outlaw who agrees to help free his friend Sam from gambling debts by participating in a weapons heist organised by Judge (Simon Yam). Sam and Judge betray Jeff during the heist, but he survives and plans his revenge. Even more than *City on Fire*, *Full Contact* sees the world as completely lawless, where the forces of authority are powerless and both heroes and villains are wild and vicious. Jeff is ruthless in his quest for vengeance and his capacity for bloodshed is at least equal to that of his nemesis, Judge.

Lam's films are totally contemporary and his attempt to make a period New Wave film, *Burning Paradise* (1994), failed artistically. His work is unusual for a Hong Kong filmmaker because he rarely uses Cantopop in his soundtracks, preferring Western music. *City on Fire* features a bluesy saxophone score that would not be out of place in an American film noir, while *Full Contact* features American rock music. This may reflect Lam's time in Canada and his knowledge of

13. Ko (Chow Yun Fat) is the undercover cop struggling to define his own identity in *City on Fire*.

American culture, although it is easy to argue that he does not use Cantopop because it is too upbeat and vapid for his purposes. Despite his negative experience of making *Maximum Risk* in America, Lam has since made two more films with actor Jean-Claude Van Damme, *Replicant* (2001) and *In Hell* (2003), but none of his Hollywood projects contain the darkness or power of the best of his Hong Kong work.

Women Action Stars in Hong Kong Cinema

Since the original 'Wong Fey Hung' series, women have been portrayed with an unusual degree of strength and independence in Hong Kong cinema. King Hu showcased strong female characters in *Come Drink With Me* and *The Fate of Lee Khan* (1972). At Shaw Brothers, Chang Cheh discounted women, but Lau Gar Leung reintroduced them to the kung fu genre with Lily Li and Hui Ying Hung. When Hong Kong shifted to a contemporary action cinema, women were momentarily sidelined, particularly in the popular films of John Woo. Two of the key figures in the re-invention of the female heroine were Michelle Yeoh and Moon Lee.

Michelle Yeoh, who started her career as Michelle Khan, was a ballet dancer and former Miss Malaysia when she was cast in the Sammo Hung-produced, Corey Yuen-directed *Police Assassins* (1985) alongside American martial artist Cynthia Rothrock. The film is a standard Hong Kong action vehicle but Yeoh distinguished herself by performing her own stunts and fights despite having no previous martial arts training. Yeoh appeared in a number of action/comedy movies before retiring for a time after marrying producer Dickson Poon. After their divorce, she returned to her career with *Police Story III: Supercop* and enjoyed international success for her roles in the James Bond film *Tomorrow Never Dies* (1997) and Ang Lee's *Crouching Tiger, Hidden Dragon* (2000).

Moon Lee, like Yeoh, was a dancer by training, and began her acting career with non-action roles in *Zu: Warriors from the Magic Mountain* (1983) and *Mr. Vampire* (1985). She made her name in *Angel* (1987), directed by Teresa Woo, a low-budget action thriller that is basically a rip-off of the American television series *Charlie's Angels*. The film cast Japanese actress and martial artist Oshima Yukari as the villain and Moon Lee as one of the three Iron Angels on her trail. Throughout the film the action duties are performed by Oshima and the male leads, Alex Fong and Hwang Jang Lee (from *Drunken Master*). Moon seems to be another pretty starlet used as window dressing, until the film climaxes with a duel between Oshima and Lee, holding back the revelation of Lee's screenfighting abilities until the final reel. The battle between the two women was a furious affair and both actresses demonstrated excellent screenfighting skills and a high tolerance for pain in their performance of some very physical stunts.

Angel led to two sequels and a large number of imitators (as an aside, if you pick up the American release of the movie, *Midnight Angels*, there is an extra fight scene tacked on to the beginning, which spoils the surprise when Moon Lee bursts into action at the end). Oshima and Lee appeared together in several more films, including *Dreaming the Reality* (1991), *Kickboxer's Tears* (1992) and *Mission of Justice* (1992). *Angel* established what the fanzines at the time dubbed the 'Femme Fatale' subgenre, although this was a rather inappropriate term given that these women are action heroes, not the seductresses of American film noir. It is challenging to try to find parallel figures in American action movies, where women are not physically equal to their male counterparts. A defining characteristic of the Hong Kong action heroine is that she is usually more adept at martial arts than the men in the stories; for example in *Kickboxer's Tears*, Feng (Moon Lee) defeats the fighter who killed her brother. There is no loss of femininity accompanying the martial prowess of these heroines; rather the actresses are often pretty and petite. *Kickboxer's Tears* features an example of gender role reversal when Nan (Mark Cheng) is taken hostage in order to force Feng to accept a fight against Oshima's character. In an American film, it would be the girl taken hostage and the male hero who would have to fight for her freedom.

In *Kickboxer's Tears*, the female martial arts heroine appears fully formed, but in other works the figure may be used to parody the kung fu hero. In *Nocturnal Demon* (1990), Moon Lee plays Wawa, a girl from the mainland who goes to Hong Kong to stay with her grandfather. When the audience first sees Wawa, she is clearly the country bumpkin, dressed in a cheap plastic raincoat and preferring to use her roller-skates rather than pay for a taxicab to take her to her grandfather's place. On her way there, she witnesses a robbery and comes to the rescue of the cops, using her martial arts to defeat the leader of the thieves. The idea of hero from the countryside who is a kung fu master goes back to Bruce Lee's character in *Way of the Dragon*, but here the figure is diminished by taking the form of the dainty Moon Lee in her raincoat and roller-skates.

Nocturnal Demon is demonstrative of the postmodern nature of Hong Kong cinema in the early 1990s, offering a mixture of elements from the horror, martial arts and comedy genres. Director Ricky Lau, who made the successful *Mr. Vampire* series, does not always move smoothly from one mode to another, opening with a gruesome murder sequence that is promptly followed by some slapstick, but each distinct element is fairly well realised.

Lee made her last feature film, *Little Heroes Lost in China*, in 1997 and, after appearing in several Hong Kong television series, she retired from acting and has devoted her time to running a dance school. Whilst she is not as famous in the West as Michelle Yeoh, Lee was a physically gifted performer who helped to revive the fortunes of the female action heroine in Hong Kong cinema.

Chow Sing Chi – Parody and Deconstruction

Chow Sing Chi, sometimes credited as Stephen Chow, was born in 1962 and enrolled in the television station TVB's acting programme after high school. He spent four years hosting the children's show *Space Shuttle 430* before moving on to television drama in 1987. The following year he made his screen debut in *Final Justice* and appeared in the Jet Li vehicle *Dragon Fight* (1988), a role that offered a glimpse of his comic potential. He co-starred with Cheung Hok Yau in 1990's police thriller *Curry and Pepper*, and was matched for the first time with his frequent onscreen collaborator, Ng Man Tat, in the drama *Triad Story* the same year. Chow's contribution to developing the martial arts genre has been the 'nonsense' comedy,

14. Parodying the kung fu hero, Wawa (Moon Lee) in her raincoat and roller-skates from *Nocturnal Demon*.

known as *mo lei tau* in Cantonese, established with *All for the Winner* (1990), a parody of the massive Wong Jing/Chow Yun Fat hit *The God of Gamblers* (1989). Chow Sing Chi has remained in the nonsense genre ever since, becoming one of Hong Kong's biggest stars.

A frequent target for parody in Chow's work is Bruce Lee. Two pertinent examples are *Fist of Fury 1991* and *Legend of the Dragon*, both from 1991. *Fist of Fury 1991*, directed by Wong Jing, parodies the sequence from the original *Fist of Fury* when a group of Japanese present a placard reading 'Sick Man of Asia' to a Chinese kung fu school. The film mocks traditional notions of martial virtue in a tournament sequence that sees Chow's character Lau Ching take on a *karateka*. Chow's instructors distract the referee so Lau Ching can cheat, but to his surprise his opponent employs the exact same dirty tricks, trying to poke his eyes and grab his groin. When the referee turns his attention back to the competitors, they stop trying to attack each other's testicles and perform martial arts techniques, but with a complete lack of commitment, waiting until the referee turns his back again.

Legend of the Dragon, directed by Danny Lee, best known for his appearance in John Woo's *The Killer*, takes a traditional kung fu narrative structure and applies it to a story about snooker. Chow plays Chow Siu Lung, a young man from the rural Tai Oh district, who is the son of kung fu master Chow Fei Hung. The names are deliberate references to Bruce Lee – Lee Siu Lung in Cantonese – and Wong Fey Hung. Yuen Wah plays Chow Fei Hung and he frequently boasts about having been Bruce Lee's stunt double. This is funny in the narrative, but there is an intertextual level to the humour, for Yuen Wah really did double for Bruce Lee during the filming of *Enter the Dragon*. The story follows a similar path to *Way of the Dragon*, featuring a group of ruthless property developers who want to take Chow Fei Hung's land, like the Italian mobsters after Nora Miao's restaurant in Bruce Lee's film. Where matters in Lee's film were resolved through displays of martial arts prowess, in *Legend of the Dragon* the duels are replaced by games of snooker. Instead of taking on a foreign martial artist, like Chuck Norris, Chow takes on a foreign snooker champion hired by the villains – the British player Jimmy White. This pushes the film beyond the level of the parodies of Jackie Chan and Yuen Wo Ping and into deconstruction. All the motifs of the traditional kung fu film are present in the form of the student, his strict *sifu*, the foreign master hired to take on the hero, the series of confrontations leading to the final duel in which the hero has to surpass himself in order to triumph. Yet all these elements are broken apart by shifting the iconography from displays of fighting skill to games of snooker. All that remains are the empty forms of the genre, rendered hollow by Chow's particularly postmodern approach to his subject. Nothing is sacred and every tenet of the martial arts genre is considered fair game for parody.

Love on Delivery (1994), directed by Lee Lik Chi, further assaults the defining characteristics of the kung fu film. A restaurant delivery boy, Ho Kam An, comes into conflict first with a judo master, Black Bear, then a *karateka*, Tuen Shui Lau, all of whom are smitten with Lily (Christy Cheung). Kam An turns to kung fu master Tat (Ng Man Tat) to learn martial arts, leading to a final duel between Kam An and Tuen. The whole process is a series of gags that gleefully dismantle the iconography of the kung fu film. When Kam An fights Black Bear, Tat tells him that he'll be more powerful if he wears a mask, so Kam An fights disguised as Garfield, the cartoon cat. The ridiculous disguise robs the entire battle of any dignity or gravitas. No target is safe from belittlement. The scenes of Kam An training in martial arts parody countless films, including *The Chinese Boxer*, when Kam An is supposed to master Iron Fist techniques. Instead of thrusting his hands into a cauldron of gravel to toughen his fists, Kam An uses a bowl of rice, then a plate of spaghetti. The master–student relationship, so important in the traditional narrative, is belittled time and again and the final duel defies all expectation as Kam An and Tat employ a huge range of tricks to keep Kam An alive. This is an even more relentless assault on martial virtue than *Fist of Fury 1991*, as the pair do everything within their power to prevent Kam An from having to actually fight his opponent.

With the resurgence of period films after *Swordsman* and Tsui Hark's *Wong Fey Hung*, Chow turned his attention to the New Wave with *King of Beggars* (1992), directed by Gordon Chan. Chow plays So Chan, a young man who enters the imperial competition to appoint the scholar of martial arts, but So enters not out of a desire for self-improvement, but to impress the beautiful Yushang (Cheung Man, a regular leading lady in Chow's movies). So Chan wins the martial arts competition, but is disqualified when it is revealed that he cheated on the strategy exam because he is illiterate. As punishment So and his father are stripped of all their possessions and forced to become beggars. So learns the 'Sleeping Disciple's Fist' kung fu style and, along with the members of the Beggars' Association, thwarts a plot to assassinate the emperor, led by the ambitious Chiu (Tsui Siu Keung).

The movie makes fun of the outlandish kung fu styles so prevalent in the New Wave. When So Chan uses his 'Sleeping Disciple's Fist', he fights while asleep and in the climactic battle he has to master the 'Dragon Suppressing Palms' technique to defeat Chiu, who is incinerated by So's kung fu. The fantastic presentation of martial arts is easier to accept in a nonsense comedy, where the fight scenes are played for humour, than in the more straight-faced films by Tsui Hark and Ching Siu Tung.

Chow continued to satirise the New Wave with *Flirting Scholar* (1993), *Hail the Judge* (1994) and *Forbidden City Cop* (1996) and made a series of contemporary comedies until turning director with the 2001 project *Shaolin Soccer*. Chow stars as Sing, a Shaolin disciple who is convinced by former soccer player Fung (Ng Man Tat) that only through playing soccer can he spread his message about the value of Chinese kung fu. Like *Legend of the Dragon*, the film takes the motifs and icons of the kung fu film and transplants them to an alien setting. All of the players on Sing's team have a special kung fu skill that they employ on the soccer field and in the final match Sing and Mui (Vicky Zhao) have to combine their martial arts techniques, his Iron Leg and her Tai Chi, to score the winning goal. It is analogous to Hung Hey Kwun and Fong Sai Yuk combining their Tiger and Crane styles to defeat Che Kang in *Heroes Two*, except, of course, that Sing and Mui are playing soccer, not fighting the Manchus.

The movie uses computer-generated effects to render the superpowers of the kung fu soccer players and demonstrates the tendency of Hong Kong filmmakers to learn from Hollywood. Whilst the employment of new technologies invariably occurs later in Hong Kong that in the West, once mastered, Hong Kong filmmakers always embrace each new filmmaking tool with relish.

Kung Fu Hustle (2004) was Chow's first film to receive a major theatrical release in the West. It enjoyed an excellent critical reception and good box-office business, but it is not up to the standard of his earlier films. The script keeps Chow's character Sing, who is uncharacteristically unsympathetic, on the sidelines for most of the movie and the denouement, when he suddenly becomes a kung fu master, is unconvincing and contrived. Regardless, Chow has been a catalyst for the process of genre ever since finding success with *All for the Winner*. By constantly parodying and deconstructing whatever cinematic style is in vogue, he has kept Hong Kong cinema from becoming stale.

Tsui Hark and the New Wave

Tsui Hark was born in Canton in 1951 but lived in Vietnam until the age of fourteen when he went to high school in Hong Kong. He studied film at the University of Austin in Texas, before returning to Hong Kong and beginning his career directing television. His generation of filmmakers, including Ringo Lam and Ann Hui, were called the 'New Wave', although Tsui was uncertain as to the origins of the label: 'I never understood why they call us that. I asked Ann Hui one time. Because the French new wave, everybody got this philosophy, to make film more realistic, more verité. Our new wave never have this philosophy behind it' (Dannen and Long, 1997, p. 134).

Tsui is the aesthetic heir to King Hu's legacy and his return to the forms of the Mandarin-language cinema of the 1960s may explain the application of the 'New Wave' label to his work. Like King Hu, Tsui is not interested in using film to replicate history or to record Cantonese culture. This may be partially explained by his age and his upbringing, divided between Vietnam, Hong Kong and the USA, denying him any personal connection with Canton. Despite his revival of the older forms of Hong Kong and Chinese cinema, Tsui's style is modernist, even when dealing with classical characters. He makes extensive use of visual effects for the staging of action scenes, reflecting his interest in American filmmaking technology.

Tsui's first feature, *The Butterfly Murders* (1979) was a cross between a thriller and a martial arts fantasy. In 1983 Tsui experienced his first commercial success with *Zu: Warriors from the Magic*

Mountain. The film is pure fantasy, with wizards, magic swords and people flying through the air. An army scout, Chi (Yuen Biao) becomes caught up in a supernatural conflict and teams up with a young monk called Chen (Mang Hoi) to save the universe. The plot makes less and less sense as the film progresses, but there are several imaginative and spectacular set pieces. One particular sequence demonstrates the all-pervasive uncertainty about Hong Kong's situation prior to 1997: Chi reports to the two generals leading the army, they give him conflicting orders and each in turn threatens to execute him if he disobeys. Chi is in an impossible situation – to obey one general means defying the other and facing execution. It is an allegory for Hong Kong caught between the ideologies of China and the United Kingdom and Chi resolves his dilemma by fleeing for his life – rejecting the authority of both generals.

Peking Opera Blues was a big hit for Tsui Hark in 1986, the same year that he produced John Woo's influential *A Better Tomorrow*. *Peking Opera Blues* is not a martial arts film, but is a good example of Tsui's ability to use period stories to comment upon contemporary Hong Kong. The movie takes place during the republican era in China and concerns the pro-democracy movement, thereby directly addressing the issue of self-governance without mentioning Hong Kong by name.

In 1990 Tsui produced and co-directed *Swordsman* and the term 'New Wave' was redefined, because the film sparked a revival of the martial arts fantasy film. The original director on *Swordsman* was King Hu and the film owes a stylistic debt to both *Come Drink With Me* and *A Touch of Zen*. *Swordsman* takes place during the Ming dynasty but makes no attempt to recreate traditional Chinese martial arts. Instead, the fight scenes depend upon the use of wires and off-screen trampolines to enable the performers to leap across the screen. In place of authentic kung fu, the characters have superhuman abilities; they can bend steel and shatter objects with a gesture. It is precisely the same presentation of fantastical powers as found in *Come Drink With Me* and this particular approach pre-dates King Hu as Sek Kei notes in *A Study of the Hong Kong Martial Arts Film*:

> In the late 1940s Chinese films still lacked realistic and vigorous action scenes, and never featured fight scenes as such … Apart from employing cumbersome stage stylisations, martial arts films of the early days were apparently crude in cinematic style. Moreover, their martial

effects were placed in service of legendary feats, with little relation to physical realities. (Chan, Ng and Sek (eds), 1980, p. 27)

What all these films have in common is their source – they are adaptations of fantasy novels, rather than films about historical characters, like Chang Cheh's Shaolin films. They are not 'martial arts' films per se, for they contain few displays of authentic kung fu. When such films are approached as fantasy, they can be entertaining and the sequel, *Swordsman II*, starring Jet Li, was even more popular than the first film.

Wong Fey Hung/Once Upon a Time in China (1991)

As the New Wave of Hong Kong cinema gathered momentum, Tsui turned to the classical heroes for source material. His film that opened the floodgates for the return of the traditional kung fu heroes is known in the West as *Once Upon a Time in China*, although its Cantonese title is more straightforward – *Wong Fey Hung* (1991). Jet Li played the title character and his flagging career was revived when the movie was a smash hit, leading to five sequels and a frantic scramble to produce imitations. The film contains many contradictory aspects, simultaneously drawing upon the original series for ideas whilst featuring the fantastic elements that are part of Tsui's repertoire. The attention to detail in the period costumes and sets is reminiscent of King Hu's *The Fate of Lee Khan*, and the film contains many of the stock characters from the original Kwan Tak Hing series, including Buck-Teeth Soh (Cheung Hok Yau) and Lam Sai Wing (Kent Cheng). However, Tsui does not attempt a straightforward revival, he modernises the legend, adding a love interest in the form of Aunt Yee (Rosamund Kwan) and using the story to address the conflict between traditional Chinese culture and Western/foreign influence.

The story concerns Wong Fey Hung and the Black Flag Militia struggling to protect themselves and the local Chinese from the ever-expanding foreign influence in late nineteenth-century China. Fey Hung's life is complicated by the arrival of Aunt Yee, a Chinese woman who has spent time abroad and adopted Western manners. Fey Hung is drawn into conflict with a triad group, the Shaho Gang, who align themselves with Mr Jackson, an American who is tricking the local Chinese into signing themselves into slavery when he sends them to the USA. A down-on-his-luck kung fu master, Iron Robe Yim (Yan Yee Kwan), joins the Shaho Gang but his student Fu (Yuen Biao) is disgusted by the triads. The plot elements twist and turn and, whilst they never coalesce into a perfectly coherent whole, the film maintains sufficient narrative momentum to hold the viewer's attention.

The opening sequence sees Wong Fey Hung attending a Lion Dance with the Black Flag Militia and the central theme of the clash between cultures is immediately expressed when a group of French soldiers mistake the sound of firecrackers for gunshots and open fire on the Lion Dancers. The Lion Dance serves the second purpose of establishing the film's genre credentials as a kung fu movie and this claim is reiterated in the opening titles, which show Fey Hung leading the Black Flag Militia in practising kung fu. The music is the ubiquitous 'Under the General's Orders', the theme linked with Wong Fey Hung by the original series. Conversely, the choreography belies the movie's claim to kung fu authenticity. All the fight scenes rely upon extensive wirework and the characters possess superhuman levels of agility, like those in King Hu's films or Tsui Hark's fantasy work. In the climactic duel between Fey Hung and Iron Robe Yim, the combatants perform all manner of impossible acrobatics involving a series of ladders. The scene showcases a huge number of aerial flips, jumps and kicks, all performed with the aid of wires. There is little trace of traditional Chinese martial arts and none of the *Hung Kuen* style for which Wong Fey Hung was renowned. The choreography is more reminiscent of the hybrid kickboxing approach pioneered by Jackie Chan and Sammo Hung, with a handful of traditional kung fu gestures thrown in. Jet Li's background is in the high-kicking, acrobatic style of *Wu Shu*, which bears no resemblance to the *Hung Kuen* system, and both Wong Fey Hung and Iron Robe Yim perform many jumping and spinning kicks. These techniques are visually appealing but have no basis in traditional Southern Chinese martial arts. Lau Gar Wing is credited as martial arts director but Tsui Hark's influence is unmistakable. The film presents a paradox – it is a kung fu movie that contains no kung fu. This reflects the film's modernity, for whilst the story may take place in late nineteenth-century China, the film addresses itself

15. Jet Li as Hong Kong cinema's most revered icon, the folk hero Wong Fey Hung, in Tsui Hark's 1991 film.

to a contemporary audience and explores the question of Hong Kong's uncertain identity.

Identity is addressed through several means, the most obvious being Aunt Yee. She wears Western clothes, embraces foreign technology and speaks both English and Cantonese. When she offers to buy a Western-style suit for Fey Hung, he is confused;

> *Wong Fey Hung*:   Chinese shouldn't wear suits. Chinese are Chinese.
> *Aunt Yee*:   Soon, with railways, telephones … everything will change. China will change with the world.
> *Wong Fey Hung*:   You're right. Western guns and ships have arrived. Everything is changing. What will we become?

There it is, right there – 'What will we become?' – the question on the mind of every Hong Kong resident in 1991, the year the film was released. In an article written in the periodical *Index on Censorship*, Tony Rayns commented: '… the several Hong Kong movies which have dealt with the issue of emigration and/or the quest for a third-country passport have avoided going into the *reasons* for emigrating, clearly bending over backwards to avoid exacerbating a difficult situation' (Rayns, 1997, p. 94).

This may be refuted by arguing that it was completely unnecessary to articulate the reasons for seeking emigration; everyone in Hong Kong was concerned about their uncertain future under Communism. The Hong Kong newspapers and television were so consumed by this question that Chris Patten called them 'a one-issue media'. Tsui's film offers an excellent example of how Hong Kong filmmakers addressed this issue through allegory and metaphor. Hong Kong's unique position, caught between Communist China and the United Kingdom, but clearly being the product of neither government, is paralleled in *Wong Fey Hung* by showing the characters caught between the traditional (China) and the modern (the Western world). Aside from Aunt Yee, there is Buck-Teeth Soh, whose character was re-invented in Tsui Hark's version, wherein Soh has come to Po Chi Lam to learn Chinese medicine after studying in America. He stutters when he has to speak Cantonese, but enunciates perfectly in English.

The end of the nineteenth century, when China was forced to open up to the outside world by foreign military might, is an apposite setting for the story, marking the end of an era. This is both a reference to the changeover to Communist rule in 1997 and cinematically an idea borrowed from the Japanese *chambara* genre. Iron Robe Yim is every inch the *ronin*, the hungry stray dog familiar to the *chambara* film – an alienated, embittered warrior who moves from town to town challenging the local kung fu masters. When he allies himself with the Shaho Gang, he has no illusions about their repugnant nature. He is pragmatic, not idealistic, choosing financial security over immaterial questions about virtue. Yim is an excellent counterpoint to Wong Fey Hung, who remains a model of Confucian values. No matter how hard he is pressed by the Manchurian governor of Canton, Fey Hung abides by the rule of law. When the guards at the local jail offer to release Wong, he initially refuses, and only leaves the jail after learning that Aunt Yee is in mortal danger. Yim, on the other hand, is a desperate man, trapped by fate. His martial arts skills have been rendered irrelevant by the arrival of guns from the West and he ekes out a living as a street performer. Yim's very existence demonstrates the debasement of Chinese culture in the face of encroaching Western values. He is a tragic character and the inevitability of his fate is reminiscent of the alienated *ronin* in the works of Okamoto Kihachi and Kobayashi Masaki.

The final scene shows Fey Hung dressed in a Western-style suit as Aunt Yee takes his photograph. The personification of traditional Cantonese values and culture has been persuaded to wear foreign fashions. The message is clear: China must change with the outside world or, more exactly, Communist China must change to be able to accept Hong Kong.

Once Upon a Time in China and America (1997)

The film's success led to five sequels, three with Jet Li in the title role and two with Chiu Man Cheuk. The second film (*Once Upon a Time in China II*, 1992) continues to explore the relationship between China and the West as Fey Hung comes into conflict with the rabidly anti-foreign White Lotus Sect. The screenplay contains an indirect snub to the Chinese Communist Party by showing Wong Fey Hung meeting Sun Yat Sen, the founder of the Republic of China, whose party fought against the Communists. The third film added a new character to Wong Fey Hung's entourage in the form of Club Foot

Seven, played by Xiong Xin Xin, Li's stunt double in the first two films. By the fifth entry, the formula was running out of steam and the action scenes replaced martial arts with guns, staging the battles in a manner that owed much to the contemporary movies of John Woo. Jet Li made an unofficial sequel for director Wong Jing, titled *The Last Hero in China* (1993), but returned for the final instalment in the regular series, known in the West as *Once Upon a Time in China and America*, produced by Tsui Hark and directed by Sammo Hung. The script, which was written as the film was being shot, is unfocused, plot threads are left hanging and characters enter and disappear from the narrative without warning. Wong Fey Hung, Aunt Yee and Club Foot Seven travel to America, where Buck-Teeth Soh has opened a branch of Po Chi Lam. En route, their stagecoach is attacked by Native Americans and Fey Hung receives a blow to the head that leaves him with amnesia. He lives with a tribe of friendly Native Americans for a time, before running into Club Foot in the local town. Fey Hung recovers his memory, but the local Chinese are framed for robbery by the town's racist Mayor Brady. When bandits attack the town, it's up to Fey Hung, Club Foot and their American pal Billy to defeat the bad guys.

The most interesting scene occurs when Club Foot tries to restore Wong Fey Hung's memory by re-enacting fight scenes from the first two films in the series. Club Foot pads himself with clothes to impersonate Iron Robe Yim, then attacks with a pole, copying Lan Yuan Shu, the villain played by Donnie Yen in the second film. This sequence is purely intertextual, self-aware and postmodern. Club Foot's character was not introduced to the series until the third film, yet he is able to replay fight scenes that his character did not witness. As the fight progresses, the local Chinese grab musical instruments and play 'Under the General's Orders'. The only explanation is that they must all have seen the first two films, just as the audience must have seen them to understand the references. It reveals the postmodern approach to the cinema of Wong Fey Hung adopted by Sammo Hung. He does not use the film to forge a link with pre-Communist Canton, but uses it to form a connection with other films about the character. Hong Kong cinema has become self-referential.

Hung's approach is irreverent; when Fey Hung makes a long speech to the Chinese in America about the importance of presenting a positive image of China to the world, Hung shows the speech in a series of dissolves as Fey Hung's audience all fall asleep. This is a contrast to the Kwan Tak Hing films, where Fey Hung was apt to deliver sermons about Confucian values to an entranced audience. At the end of Sammo Hung's film, Fey Hung makes a second speech. It is much shorter than the first and when Fey Hung has finished, no one dares to move because no one believes that he is capable of such brevity. It is very funny, but only in reference to the established concept of Wong Fey Hung as virtuous windbag.

The Return of the Traditional Heroes

After Tsui's *Wong Fey Hung* there came a glut of movies featuring the classical kung fu characters as the New Wave gathered momentum. Jet Li added the characters of Fong Sai Yuk, Hung Hey Kwun, Chang San Feng and Chen Zen to his repertoire, with varying results. *The Legend of Fong Sai Yuk* (1992), directed by Corey Yuen (Yuen Kwai in Cantonese), is a delightful and wholly incorrect telling of the life of the Shaolin anti-Ch'ing fighter. Yuen's version does not even feature the Shaolin Temple. The story has two plot lines that join together in the final act. On the one hand, it concerns the Manchu emperor's attempts to have the anti-Ch'ing Red Lotus Society members killed. There is the classic kung fu plot device of a list of rebels that is being sought by a powerful Manchu kung fu master. This same plot device can be found in *Shaolin Mantis*, *Blood of the Dragon* and countless other films. The second narrative thread deals with Lei Lao Hu (Tiger Lu in the English language version). He was slain by Fong Sai Yuk in a duel to prove the superiority of Shaolin kung fu over the *Wu Tang* system, but Corey Yuen's film takes a modern and ridiculous approach to this story. Certain historical facts remain untouched – Fong Sai Yuk's father Fong Te is a silk merchant, and Sai Yuk has learnt kung fu from his mother, Miao Cui Hua, although this information merely serves as a jumping-off point for Corey Yuen to parody the mythology surrounding the character.

In this version Lei organises a kung fu competition to find a husband for his daughter Ting-Ting (Michelle Reis) and entrants do not face Lei in combat, but his wife Su Wan (Sibelle Hu). In Chang Cheh's *Men from the Monastery*, Lei and Sai Yuk fight on a series of wooden stakes with spikes below, so that anyone who falls is impaled. In Yuen's film, the fight is on a raised platform, but there are no sharpened stakes and the loser is the first person to touch the ground. Sai Yuk enters the contest and is about to triumph when he mistakes Lei's plain maid for the daughter, so he deliberately throws himself to the ground, losing the battle. When his mother, Miao Cui Hua (Josephine Siao) hears of this, she disguises herself as a man and enters the competition calling herself Fong Tai Yuk to save the family's reputation. She defeats Su Wan with such style and grace that the unfortunate woman falls in love with Fong Tai Yuk, oblivious to Cui Hua's deception. It is extremely funny and consciously iconoclastic, shifting the tone from the violence of Chang Cheh's film to one that is light and playful.

The prominence given to the women, Su Wan, Ting-Ting and Miao Cui Hua is another indicator of Yuen's modern approach. Chang Cheh kept women on the sidelines, but Corey Yuen gives them importance equal to the men. Josephine Siao came out of retirement to appear in the movie and enjoyed popular and critical acclaim for her performance as Sai Yuk's mother. A sequel followed the next year, reuniting the director with both Jet Li and Josephine Siao for more historically incorrect nonsense. The fight sequences use wirework to enhance the action and, like Tsui Hark's 'Wong Fey Hung' series, there is little in the way of authentic Chinese martial arts. What separates the two 'Fong Sai Yuk' films from those about Wong Fey Hung is that these are comedies. The humour makes the disregard for history and absence of authentic Southern Chinese kung fu more readily acceptable.

Considerably more inaccurate, and far less enjoyable, was *Hung Hey Kwun: The New Legend of Shaolin* (1994), directed by Wong Jing. Wong is Hong Kong's king of exploitation, churning out schlock with a speed that would make Roger Corman blush. His account of the life of Hung Hey Kwun displays a total lack of historical detail and the film is formulaic and derivative. Hung Hey Kwun was a student at the second Shaolin Temple, in Fukien, which was destroyed by the Ch'ing imperial troops aided by the renegade monk Bak Mei. In Wong Jing's film, Hung Hey Kwun's nemesis is Ma Ling Yee, but historically Ma Ling Yee was involved in the burning of the first Shaolin Temple in Songshan, which took place around 1662, long before Hung Hey Kwun was born. Where Corey Yuen plays with the history around Fong Sai Yuk for humorous effect, Wong Jing's story displays a flagrant lack of attention to detail.

The direction and story are insipid and Wong shamelessly copies a scene straight out of *Sword of Vengeance* from the Japanese 'Lone Wolf and Cub' series. The martial arts scenes in *Hung Hey Kwun: The New Legend of Shaolin* rely upon wire stunts and special effects and there is no trace of the *Hung Kuen* style of which Hung Hey Kwun was the founder. In the film Hey Kwun fights with a spear but the historical figure was famous for his skill with the pole. This is hard to excuse as artistic licence because, like much of Wong Jing's output, the film is poorly conceived and badly executed. It is not an attempt to create any sort of link with Cantonese history, but is film as lowest common denominator entertainment, made to capitalise on the popularity of period films.

Tai Chi Master (1993)

Far better are Jet Li's portrayals, in *Tai Chi Master* (1993), of Chang San Feng, the creator of Tai Chi Chuan, and, in *Fist of Legend* (1994), of Chen Zen, the Ching Wu fighter made famous by Bruce Lee. For these films Li worked with veteran choreographer Yuen Wo Ping, the director of *Drunken Master*. Wo Ping directed *Tai Chi Master*, a story about two monks, Junbao (Jet Li) and Chinbo (Chin Siu Ho), who have to leave Shaolin Temple after the impetuous Chinbo angers the monks. In the outside world, Junbao joins a group of anti-Ch'ing rebels that includes Siu Lin (Michelle Yeoh) and Reverend Ling (Yuen Cheung Yan), while Chinbo joins the Ch'ing army. Hungry for promotion, Chinbo leads the rebels into a trap where many of them are killed. Junbao escapes but is so distressed by his friend's betrayal that his mind snaps. He studies a scroll given to him by his master at Shaolin, 'The Book of Chi', from which he formulates the art of Tai Chi. The new system is tested in the climactic duel between Chinbo and Junbao, which Junbao wins. He adopts the name Chang San Feng and decides to spread his new style.

This is the plot of a classical kung fu movie, centred on the development of a new martial art, like *Heroes Two* or *Executioners from Shaolin*, although the choreography is in the New Wave style, with extensive use of wires for superhuman leaps and aerial attacks. There are techniques from traditional Chinese martial arts – when Junbao and Chinbo train at Shaolin they use the famous stance 'To Conquer the Centre with a Single Finger' from the *Hung Kuen* style, and the film opens and closes with Chang San Feng leading a large group in playing a Tai Chi form. Yet the traditional elements are countered by the wirework and superhuman acrobatics. In the final duel Junbao uses some Tai Chi techniques, but their potency is wildly exaggerated as he sends Chinbo flying with a flick of the wrist. This embodies the flexible approach of filmmakers in Hong Kong in the 1990s, willing to combine disparate elements in their efforts to keep the genre from becoming stale.

The story of *Tai Chi Master* is fictional, but balances the traditional with the modern. Chinbo is greedy and materialistic, faults that are always soundly condemned in Hong Kong movies, despite the 'get rich and get out' attitude so prevalent in Hong Kong prior to 1997. Junbao, on the other hand, is spiritually minded and free from desire. This is a throwback to the notion of martial virtue found in the original 'Wong Fey Hung' series. Junbao triumphs not only because he has superior technique, but because he is the more enlightened person – the two qualities are inextricable. This is an old-fashioned notion that was abandoned in the wake of Yuen Wo Ping's *Drunken Master* and this return to traditional ideas explains the application of the New Wave label to these films. The modern question of identity is expressed when Junbao loses his mind. He forgets himself and becomes a man with no identity. The motif of the helpless individual trapped between two powerful fighters is present in the sequence where Siu Lin is caught up in a battle between Junbao and Chinbo, the practically omnipresent metaphor for Hong Kong caught between China and the West.

Fist of Legend (1994)

The last classic character in Li's repertoire is Chen Zen, the character played by Bruce Lee in *Fist of Fury*. *Fist of Legend* was directed by

Gordon Chan with choreography by Yuen Wo Ping. The essential plot is the same as *Fist of Fury* – Chen returns to the Ching Wu School for the funeral of his master, who was poisoned by the Japanese. He decimates the Japanese fighters at their *dojo* and at the end duels their best fighter, in this case General Fujita (Billy Chow). The film displays none of the rabid anti-Japanese sentiment found in the original. Whilst Fujita is a monstrous villain, there are many positive Japanese characters. Chen falls in love with a Japanese girl, Mitsuko (Nakayama Shinobu), which would have been tantamount to heresy in the Lo Wei/Bruce Lee film. Furthermore Mitsuko's uncle, Funakochi (Kurata Yasuaki) helps Chen perfect his martial arts and the Japanese ambassador vociferously opposes General Fujita's brutal treatment of the local Chinese population. This is a contemporary approach to the story and reflects the decline in anti-Japanese feeling in Hong Kong on the part of a generation too young to remember the Japanese occupation during the Second World War. Perhaps more practically, the filmmakers were aware of Jet Li's popularity in Japan and felt reluctant to offend such a lucrative audience.

The film is a case study in intertextuality, referencing both *Fist of Fury* and Bruce Lee as a martial artist on- and off-screen. The fight choreography replicates Bruce Lee's fighting style, emphasising adaptability, flexibility and an open mind. Lee wrote:

> Combat is never fixed and is changing from moment to moment … *Jeet Kune Do* favours formlessness so that it can assume all forms and, since it has no style, *Jeet Kune Do* fits in with all styles. As a result *Jeet Kune Do* uses all ways and is bound by none and, likewise, uses any technique or means which serves its end. In this art, efficiency is anything that scores. (Lee, 1975, p. 24)

Fist of Legend conveys the same ideas of adaptability, putting Bruce Lee's philosophy into the mouth of Chen Zen, who, despite being played by Jet Li, acts as a cipher for Bruce Lee. Amongst Jet Li's films since 1991, *Fist of Legend* is the most restrained in the use of wires, concentrating on movements that resemble real fighting techniques. This is in keeping with Bruce Lee's approach to screen-fighting, since he disliked the trampolines and over-the-top acrobatics found in Hong Kong films in the 1960s and early 1970s.

When Chen returns to Ching Wu, he shares his ideas about martial arts with his fellow students, telling them to forget the limitations of traditional kung fu and to absorb techniques from other systems, one of Bruce Lee's principal ideas. When Jet Li's Chen fights with Ting An (Chin Siu Ho) to decide who is the best martial artist at the Ching Wu School, Chen begins using Chinese martial arts. After losing the initial exchanges, he abandons classical forms and dances on the balls of his feet in a direct imitation of Bruce Lee. He moves like a boxer, slipping punches and landing his own blows, mirroring Lee fighting Chuck Norris in *Way of the Dragon*. In a later fight with the Japanese master Funakochi, he uses this freeform style that Funakochi then copies – the fight becomes an exchange of ideas about martial arts. In the finale, when Fujita draws a sword, Chen uses his leather belt as a weapon. This is a perfect example of Bruce Lee's *Jeet Kune Do* – the flexible belt beats the unbending sword. The movie is not a slavish remake, but rather a tribute to Bruce Lee, performer and martial artist, although it possesses none of the nihilism of *Fist of Fury*. At the end of *Fist of Legend*, Chen does not die, but is smuggled out of Shanghai with the help of the Japanese ambassador, heading to Japan to be reunited with Mitsuko. The ending is far more hopeful than that of the original; perhaps Hong Kong filmgoers in 1994 were no longer willing to watch their heroes die. To do so might have been too unsettling in the face of 1997.

The New Wave movement, featuring period stories and greatly exaggerated martial arts, had the positive effect of raising the profile of Hong Kong cinema through the international art-house circuit. Many filmmakers contributed to the genre – Sammo Hung's *Blade of Fury* (1993), Jackie Chan's *Drunken Master II* (1994), Ringo Lam's *Burning Paradise* (1994), Yuen Biao's *Wong Fey Hung's Seven Invisible Kicks* (1993). Some of the films are good, some are dreadful, but all contributed to the progression of the genre. There were contemporary films that employed the same techniques in their fight scenes, including *The Dragon from Russia* (1990), *Saviour of the Soul* (1992) and *The Heroic Trio* (1992). These films feature the same imagery as the period swordsman films, with superhuman powers and characters flying through the air. Viewed as fantasy, they can be hugely entertaining, but it would be inaccurate to describe them as 'kung fu' films. *Burning Paradise* is a case in point. It was the first New Wave film to reunite on screen the historical figures of Fong Sai Yuk and Hung Hey Kwun, but the choreography contains only a handful of traditional stances scattered among all the special effects and wire stunts. The Tiger-Crane form of the *Hung Kuen* style, with which the two men are associated, is nowhere to be found. The story is nonsense, free from historical references beyond the identities of the two protagonists.

The Hong Kong film industry, which enjoyed a boom during the 1980s, began to struggle in the mid 1990s. Domestic films lost ground at the box office to American product and when the Asian economic bubble burst in 1997, filmmakers felt the effects. Where they had once financed their films based solely on pre-sales from the Asian markets, after the crash this was no longer possible. Combined with the looming handover to Communist China, many Hong Kong filmmakers looked for greener pastures. Tsui Hark's *The Blade* (1995) was a re-make of Chang Cheh's *The One-Armed Swordsman*, but the film's production values cannot compare to the 'Wong Fey Hung' movies as budgets shrank as local films lost ground to American imports. *The Blade* offers no authentic martial arts and sees the one-armed hero defeat his opponents by spinning around in a circle. The movie is delivered at fever pitch, from the dizzying handheld camerawork and jarring editing to the unrestrained hysteria of the performances. The end result is a disjointed mess indicative of a filmmaker in desperate search of a new aesthetic identity. Like many of his contemporaries, Tsui Hark pursued this via Hollywood.

The Hong Kong Diaspora

It is too simplistic to attribute the exodus of directors and stars from Hong Kong purely to the introduction of Communist rule, but many filmmakers made certain that if matters went badly in Hong Kong, they had secured residency abroad. The economic downturn throughout Asia contributed to the number of Hong Kong directors looking for production funds in the United States. Some filmmakers preferred to stay in Hong Kong where they retained greater creative control. Wong Kar Wai commented that he would rather work for a triad in Hong Kong than an accountant in America – at least the triads wouldn't question his creative judgement.

Of all the Hong Kong filmmakers who went to Hollywood, Tsui Hark fared the worst artistically. His two American productions, *Double Team* (1997) and *Knock Off* (1998) contain none of the trademarks or flair normally associated with Tsui. The scripts are terrible (*Knock Off* concerns tiny little bombs hidden in jeans and if you know what *Double Team* is about, you're a better person than I am) and Tsui seemed unable to connect with the material. The movies could have been directed by anyone and lack the scope and imagination of Tsui's Hong Kong productions. Tsui returned to making films in Hong Kong in 2000 with *Time and Tide* and has yet to attempt another American venture.

Ringo Lam was deeply unhappy with his American project, *Maximum Risk* (1996) after Columbia Pictures insisted he re-shoot several scenes to simplify Natasha Henstridge's character. The finished film does not compare favourably with his Hong Kong movies. As mentioned above, Sammo Hung made two seasons of the American television series *Martial Law*, which had entertaining action scenes but formulaic and repetitive scripts. He has returned to filmmaking in Hong Kong.

Jackie Chan has fared somewhat better, dividing his time between Hong Kong and American projects. The quality of his US films has been mixed and they rely upon teaming Chan with an American star – Chris Tucker in the *Rush Hour* (1998, 2001) films, Owen Wilson in *Shanghai Noon* (2000) and *Shanghai Knights* (2003), Jennifer Love Hewitt in *The Tuxedo* (2002). Chan's daredevil stuntwork has been severely curtailed by the restrictions imposed upon him by nervous producers and accountants in Hollywood. In *Shanghai Noon* Chan's character leaps between two train carriages, a stunt accomplished using special effects to impose Chan leaping over the gap and it is obviously faked. Compare this to the jaw-dropping stunts performed on a moving train in *Police Story III – Supercop* and the creative price of working in Hollywood is apparent. Chan's willingness to perform his own stunts is an integral part of his appeal and if Hollywood denies him the right to continue doing so, his popularity will likely suffer. *The Tuxedo* relies upon special effects for the action sequences and is very much a missed opportunity. Given free rein, Jackie Chan is the ultimate special effect without computer enhancement.

The most interesting part of the dispersal of Hong Kong film-makers has been the widespread use of Hong Kong martial arts choreographers throughout the world. Philip Kwok (Mad Dog in *Hard Boiled*) directed the fights in the French film *Brotherhood of the Wolf* (2001), Donnie Yen worked on the Japanese *Princess Blade* (2001), the German television series *Codename: Puma* and the American films *Highlander: Endgame* (2000) and *Blade II* (2002). Corey Yuen was action director on the massive American hit *X-men* (2000) and directed the French production *The Transporter* (2002). The most prolific ex-patriot choreographers are Yuen Wo Ping and Yuen Cheung Yan, whose work is discussed in more detail in the American section. The influence of Hong Kong martial arts cinema continues to grow. *Arahan* (2004), directed by Ryoo Seung-wan, is an excellent martial arts film from South Korea that draws heavily upon Hong Kong sources, featuring Chinese rather than Korean martial arts for the choreography and employing Hong Kong-style wirework to great effect. Meanwhile, it is worth considering the film that brought Hong Kong martial arts cinema into the American mainstream.

Crouching Tiger, Hidden Dragon (2000)

Ang Lee's international hit was a Chinese/American co-production and was distributed in the United States by Sony Pictures Classics, giving the film major studio backing. It received massive critical acclaim, won four Oscars, countless other awards and took over $128 million in North America, a remarkable achievement for a Mandarin-language film with an Asian cast.

The story concerns Li Mu Bai (Chow Yun Fat), a swordsman who wishes to retire from his life of violence, and Shu Lien (Michelle Yeoh), a swordswoman to whom Li has never confessed his love. Jen (Zhang Ziyi) is a spoilt aristocrat's daughter looking for freedom and pursuing a secret affair with Lo (Chang Chen), a bandit from the deserts. Jen's life is complicated by the presence of the outlaw Jade Fox (Cheng Pei Pei), posing as her governess, with a martial arts manual stolen from Li Mu Bai's *sifu*. When Jen steals Li's sword, called Green Destiny, she goes on the run and is pursued by Li, Shu Lien and Jade Fox. Li corners Jen and Jade Fox in a cave and he slays Jade Fox, but is poisoned and dies in Shu Lien's arms. Jen goes to see her lover Lo, who is waiting at Wu Tang Mountain. After spending the night with him, Jen throws herself off a precipice.

Western critics heaped praise upon the film. Roger Ebert in the *Chicago Sun-Times* wrote, '… like all ambitious movies, *Crouching Tiger, Hidden Dragon* transcends its origins and becomes one of a kind'. Kenneth Turan, in the *LA Times*, gushed, 'What we're not used to, what we haven't had much of at all, are films that transcend categorization, that remind us – simply, powerfully, indelibly – what we go to the movies for'. Bob Graham in the *San Francisco Chronicle* called it 'the movie of the year'. In the *Guardian* in the UK, Peter Bradshaw declared the film 'a masterpiece', before concluding '… if this film proves to be the father to a series of similar works, then it could almost be that a new popular genre of film-making has been born, or reborn: a new Asian western for the 21st century'. Xan Brooks, again writing for the *Guardian*, said, 'What we have here, then, is a sublime piece of work; a marriage of old and new so perfectly managed that it results in something altogether rich, strange and unusual. All hail the first great film of 2001.' Paul Tatara, reviewing the film for CNN, described it as, 'a unique cinematic experience'.

One of the few critics to break ranks was Amy Taubin in the *Village Voice*, who, unlike her contemporaries, came to the film well versed in Hong Kong cinema, and she found the movie wanting,

> A rare blend of low and high art, Wong Kar-Wai's *Ashes of Time* radicalises the genre's visual and narrative disjunction to the point of abstraction. Studiously middle-brow, *Crouching Tiger, Hidden Dragon* takes the opposite tack. Rather than leaping about in time, the story meanders along a linear route, plugging up gaps with character psychology and set decoration. But even on its own terms … the film is unsuccessful. *Crouching Tiger*'s dramatic line is so blurry that the central character is only a bystander to the climactic fight between forces of good and evil.

Much of the praise given to the film reflects the critics' unfamiliarity with Hong Kong cinema, for Lee's film is formulaic to the point of redundancy. The movie's relatively poor performance at the Hong Kong box office, where it was not in the top ten grossing films of the year, indicates that Hong Kong audiences found little in *Crouching Tiger, Hidden Dragon* to be excited about. They had seen it all before. Far from being 'one of a kind' as Roger Ebert claimed, the film follows the established pattern for any period New Wave production and owes much to King Hu's *Come Drink With Me*, made thirty-five years earlier.

The connection with *Come Drink With Me* is substantial, with the presence of Cheng Pei Pei, the heroine of King Hu's film, the most obvious link. Yuen Wo Ping's choreography is styled in the same manner as *Come Drink With Me*. The characters glide over rooftops and fly through the trees, presenting martial artists as superhumans, just as King Hu conceived them. The action scenes, particularly those with Chow Yun Fat, are speeded up, another technique reminiscent of *Come Drink With Me*. Like Han Ying Chieh's choreography, Yuen Wo Ping's work in *Crouching Tiger* combines authentic Chinese martial arts with a great deal of special effects and wirework. As fine an actor as he is, Chow Yun Fat is not a martial artist and his scenes rely heavily upon wirework and greatly speeded-up action for their execution. The scenes of characters leaping through the air and running up walls that entranced Western critics are so common in the fantasy films of Hong Kong as to be mundane to a Chinese audience. Some of the many films that employ this motif are Ching Siu Tung's *Duel to the Death* (1982) and *A Chinese Ghost Story* (1986), Yuen Wo Ping's *Iron Monkey* (1993) and the three films in the 'Swordsman' series.

The story contains many standard generic elements, including a stolen martial arts manual, a quest to avenge the murder of a *sifu*, a magical sword that renders the wielder nigh invincible, a fight in a teahouse and a noble, tragic hero who sacrifices himself, much like one of Chang Cheh's Shaolin heroes. To describe the film as transcending categorisation, as Kenneth Turan did in the *LA Times*, is nonsensical. It is generic in the pejorative sense. Far from being the 'father' of some new genre, as Peter Bradshaw suggested, the movie is another entry in an established form going back at least as far as 1965 and *Come Drink With Me*. To describe the film as 'a new Asian Western' reflects a cultural snobbery in which Asian films can only be assigned value in relation to Hollywood archetypes. *Crouching Tiger* is not a Western any more than *Shane* is a *chambara* without swords. To make either claim is to deny each genre's origins and their significance in the native cultures that spawned them.

Ang Lee is from Taiwan, a nation with an uncertain and perilous relationship with China, a country that, despite Taiwan's assertions of independence, continues to claim the island for itself. Parallels between Taiwan and Hong Kong are not difficult to fathom. Read as a metaphor for the quest for identity, the film suggests that subservience to tradition is the path to follow. The character that best illustrates this theme is Jen; she is young, self-centred, materialistic, yet yearning for independence. In a conversation with Shu Lien, Jen articulates this desire:

Jen: It must be exciting to be a fighter, to be totally free.
Shu Lien: Fighters have rules too. Friendship, trust, integrity, without rules we wouldn't survive for long.

Jen later remarks, 'I'm getting married soon. But I haven't lived the life I want.' Jen's arranged marriage can easily be construed as a metaphor for Hong Kong's reluctant handover to Communist rule. The issue of identity and freedom is further elaborated upon by Jade Fox, who tells Jen, 'Your parents will never accept you again. But why go home? We've come this far, we won't stop now … At last, we'll be our own masters.' It is easy to substitute China as the parent and Taiwan or Hong Kong as the child seeking control of their fate. Jade Fox is ruthless in her pursuit of self-enrichment and she is slain by Li Mu Bai, who is old-fashioned and a practical substitute for China, embodying ideals of self-sacrifice for the greater good, a desire to live by a strict set of rules.

If the movie has a message concerning Hong Kong and Taiwan's position with regard to China, it is best expressed when Jen throws herself off the mountain, following a legend that anyone who does so will have their wishes come true. She jumps to assuage her guilt for Li's death and a desire to bring him back to life. The errant child must sacrifice herself (her identity and desire for independence) to preserve the sanctity of China. This is surprising coming from Ang Lee, who might have been expected to offer a more humanistic, anti-totalitarian argument in light of Taiwan's continuing defiance of the Chinese Communist Party's claims of jurisdiction. Lee's choice to use Mandarin dialogue, not the Cantonese dialect prevalent in Hong Kong, and the narrative decision to have Li Bu Mai be a member of the pro-Manchu, anti-rebel Wu Tang group reinforces the underlying pro-authoritarianism tone. Had Li Bu Mai been a Shaolin fighter he would have been an anti-government malcontent and it is interesting to wonder why Lee chose to align the character and the film with the Wu Tang school. Perhaps he did not wish to make waves when working in China or faced pressure from the Film Bureau, or Lee may be expressing the Confucian notion of respect for authority and the rule of law, like Li Bu Mai in the movie.

Had *Crouching Tiger* been made ten years earlier, when the New Wave of period films was popular in Hong Kong, it may have seemed more innovative and original, but the New Wave had run its course by 2000, and the film offered the genre nothing that had not been seen before.

After the New Wave

When Hollywood productions began to dominate the Hong Kong box office, with *Independence Day* (1996) and *Jurassic Park* (1993) outgrossing local movies, Hong Kong producers began to copy American filmmaking techniques. This has meant the use of computer graphics and digital special effects, introduced to Hong Kong productions by Lau Wai Leung (Andrew Lau in English). Lau began his career as a cinematographer, his credits including Ringo Lam's *City on Fire* (1987) and *Wild Search* (1989). He directed the successful 'Young and Dangerous' series from 1996 to 1998, before he began adaptating stories from *manhua*, Hong Kong comic books, beginning with *The Stormriders* (1998). For those unfamiliar with Hong Kong kung fu comics, they are in the same vein as the films of King Hu and Tsui Hark, featuring martial artists with superhuman abilities and fantastic forms of kung fu that are pure invention. *A Man Called Hero* (1999), directed by Lau, was Hong Kong's highest grossing movie and is adapted from the popular comic series *The Blood Sword* by Ma Wing Shing. The film has trouble trying to squeeze the epic story of the original comics into one movie and the scope of the tale suffers in the process. It is interesting in the evolution of the genre, for *A Man Called Hero* contains no authentic martial arts at all. None.

The action scenes rely upon digital computer effects for their execution and feature characters with a range of superhuman abilities that would make Superman green with envy. In the final showdown between Hero and his nemesis Invincible, the two fighters bring the Statue of Liberty crashing down with the forces they unleash. This marks the completion of the second cycle of the process of genre in Hong Kong cinema, having returned to the same state as the films that preceded 1949's *The True Story of Wong Fey Hung*. The process has come full circle, back to a style of filmmaking relying upon special effects in place of displays of genuine Chinese martial arts.

It is ironic that the best of Hong Kong's choreographers, Corey Yuen, Yuen Wo Ping, Yuen Cheung Yan, are now working outside their native industry in the USA and Europe. The success of *A Man Called Hero* makes plain its appeal to Hong Kong audiences and Lau followed it with more of the same, *The Duel* (2000) and *The Avenging Fist* (2001). Perhaps with time Hong Kong filmgoers will desire a return to authentic Chinese martial arts on their screens. For the present, they must be content with the fantastic and perhaps in the wake of Hong Kong's handover to Communist China, it is fantasy and escapism that most satisfies the needs of its citizens.

A Chinese Odyssey (2002)

The nonsense comedy remains strong in the wake of the 'New Wave' and the handover. Jeffrey Lau, who worked on several Chow Sing Chi films as writer and director, made the period nonsense comedy *A Chinese Odyssey*. The film still speaks to the question of identity and, whilst it is set in Ming dynasty China, the movie always addresses itself to modern Hong Kong. The story concerns the emperor (Chang Chen) and his sister the princess (Faye Wong) who run away from the Forbidden City in search of adventure and independence from their domineering mother. The princess disguises herself as a man and meets Yilung (Leung Chiu Wai) and Phoenix (Vicky Zhao), siblings who own a restaurant. Both are attracted to the princess and matters are further complicated by the arrival of the emperor, posing as an out-of-work actor. In due course, true love conquers all when the emperor marries Phoenix and Yilung marries the Princess.

The film is highly intertextual, parodying martial arts movies, musicals and romantic melodramas. It contains many deliberately anachronistic elements that function both as jokes and reinforcements of the filmmaker's modern sensibility. When the emperor starts to enjoy his newfound freedom outside the Forbidden City, he adopts an enormous Afro hairstyle and designs platform boots for the Imperial Guards to wear. At one point when Phoenix calls out to him, he answers, 'Que pasa?' These are all indicators of an aggressively modern outlook. History is malleable, an idea played out in the film as the same event is often seen from different perspectives. Three different characters recount the first meeting of the princess and Yilung, and each time the story changes. There are three versions of how the princess escapes the Forbidden City; in the first she flies over the wall; in the second she breaks down the door with Iron Head kung fu; and in the third she simply strolls out. Lau plays with the notion of history and perception and at a stretch these scenes could be viewed as a criticism of the Chinese Communist Party's habit of revising history to serve its own ends (like airbrushing the Gang of Four out of photos of party rallies). When the emperor asserts his freewill against his mother the empress and declares that he will marry Phoenix with or without her blessing, this can be read as a metaphor for the importance of Hong Kong asserting the sanctity of its unique character in the face of pressure to fall in line with China. The emperor is the character who most effectively functions as a cipher for Hong Kong, as he reflects the multifarious nature of the city, combining a highly diverse range of Chinese and Western influences in his fashion and speech.

Identity is mutable in the story; the princess and the emperor try to abandon their old identities when they run away. The concept is further developed after the princess has gone mad with despair after Yilung fails the test set by the empress to allow the pair to marry. When Yilung finds the princess, she believes that she has become Yilung herself. In response, Yilung pretends to be the princess and having swapped identities, the lovers are united. The search for identity and meaning has evidently not been resolved after 1997, for Hong Kong's future remains uncertain.

The film makes great fun of the conventions of the kung fu genre. When Yilung returns home after two years' absence, he is confronted by Phoenix. They square off with great seriousness, until Phoenix rolls slowly and clumsily across the floor towards her brother. Instead of leaping high in to the air, he hesitantly hops over her. The execution of their 'duel' confounds the viewer's expectation and all the martial arts sequences are treated in a similarly ridiculous manner. It has become impossible to take the motifs of the martial arts genre seriously – the audience has seen it all before, so all that remains is to laugh.

With the advancing age of the Peking Opera School graduates, new stars have replaced them. None of the Peking Opera alumni could be described as conventionally handsome – Jackie Chan has a big nose, Sammo Hung is fat, and so on – but they rose to fame through their extraordinary physical skills. The young actors who have risen to prominence in the late 1990s are all good-looking but they lack the athletic skills of their predecessors. The cast of the box-office hit *Gen-X Cops* (1999) fit this mould, they look like models from a 'Gap' commercial, with their conspicuously stylish clothes and haircuts. The film suffers the usual maladies of any standard Hong Kong police thriller, with an incomprehensible plot, risible dialogue and underdeveloped characters. The cast, including Nicholas Tse, Stephen Fung and Sam Lee, may be handsome, but unlike their Peking Opera-trained predecessors, none of them can jump in the air and leave their footprints on the ceiling. The execution of their action scenes is reminiscent of an American production, relying upon special effects and stunt doubles and compares poorly with almost any Hong Kong production of the 1980s. It is a shame that physical attractiveness has replaced physical talent in the new generation of Hong Kong stars, but this was perhaps inevitable as Chan, Hung and their classmates were the last of their kind. If Jackie Chan, Sammo Hung and Yuen Biao have an heir, then it is Thailand's Tony Jaa (Panom Yeerum to use his Thai name). *Ong-Bak* (2003), starring Jaa and directed by Prachya Pinkaew, eschews wirework and computer effects in favour of the kind of extraordinary stuntwork and acrobatics found in Chan and Hung's best movies. The plot is over-familiar, about a country boy who happens to be a master fighter running into trouble in the big city, but Jaa is an exceptionally gifted screenfighter and the strongest contender to become the next global martial arts superstar.

Hero (2002)

The tremendous international success of *Crouching Tiger, Hidden Dragon* has prompted other filmmakers to attempt to duplicate its accomplishments. One of these is the mainland director Zhang Yimou, whose film *Hero* concerns Qin Shihuang, the warlord who unified China and built the Great Wall. Zhang is a highly respected filmmaker whose work has typically displayed a potent strain of humanism. Many of his films were banned when submitted for release in China and 1994's *To Live* has never been legally screened in the mainland. Nevertheless Zhang has received considerable critical acclaim outside China: *To Live* won the Grand Jury Prize at Cannes, *Shanghai Triad* (1995) won the Grand Technical Prize there in 1995 and *Not One Less* won the Golden Lion Award at the 1999 Venice Film Festival. What is so surprising about *Hero* is that it appears to run contrary to the humanism so prevalent in the rest of Zhang's work.

The story structure is akin to Kurosawa Akira's *Rashomon*, featuring contrasting accounts of the same events, all concerning the warrior Nameless (Jet Li), who is brought to see Qin Shihuang after having killed the three assassins most feared by Qin. The audience views different versions of the assassins' deaths until Qin realises that he has been deceived – Nameless convinced the three assassins to sacrifice themselves to allow him to get close enough to Qin to kill him. Nameless chooses not to slay Qin, having concluded that the warlord's ruthlessness serves the greater good; a unified country is more important than preserving the autonomy and identities of the individual kingdoms and races. Nameless surrenders to Qin, who sentences him to death.

The film is visually stunning, with wonderful design and breathtaking photography by Christopher Doyle. The action choreography by Ching Siu Tung makes constant use of wires and special effects and the characters all possess superhuman abilities. In one scene, Nameless battles the assassin Broken Sword (Leung Chiu Wai) while they fly over the surface of a lake. The sequence is beautiful to watch, but contains no trace of authentic Chinese martial arts. The use of swirling colours is reminiscent of the battles in Kurosawa's *Ran* (1985) and the fight scenes are expressionistic rather than naturalistic. Zhang's focus is on the relationships between the characters, rather than the act of fighting itself, so whilst the film features several lengthy action scenes it is not really about martial arts at all. The treatment of martial arts is so expressionistic and so overtly manipulated that the fights become deconstructed. They become exercises in visual style, wherein the talents of the filmmakers far outweigh the performance of the actors. This is a startling contrast to most martial arts cinema, where the performance, the physical act of staging a fight, is of primary importance.

> Hero received a warm reception from the Communist Party's film bureau, whose deputy director Zhang Pimu called it 'artistic, entertaining and thoughtful' (Joseph Khan, New York Times, 2 January 2003).

The film excuses Qin's ruthless authoritarianism, arguing that peace and prosperity can only be secured by the suppression of the individual to the state. Many Chinese historians have condemned Qin as a tyrant who perpetuated massacres, executed Confucian scholars and burned their books. Mao Tse Tung was an admirer of Qin and referenced the warlord as an inspiration and an example of how authoritarianism was necessary and desirable. It is remarkable that Zhang's film puts its support firmly behind this view of Qin, and even stranger that the cast features so many prominent Hong Kong stars, including Leung Chiu Wai, Maggie Cheung and Donnie Yen as the three assassins. Perhaps their presence reflects a desire on the behalf of Hong Kong's film community to find common ground with their counterparts on the mainland, and a reticence to cause friction with the Chinese Communist Party. This has not prevented many critics condemning Zhang's subservience in Hero: '"Commercial success? Yes! And think of all these hundreds of youngsters who have learned their lesson of 'worship the emperor' as they sit mesmerized by the fighting scenes," fretted film critic Wei Minglun in the Guangzhou-based Southern Weekend newspaper' (Antoaneta Bezlova, Asia Times, 23 January 2003).

Hero enjoyed considerable box-office success, which was fortunate for Zhang in light of the fact that it was China's most expensive production to date. The film won seven awards at the Hong Kong Film Awards, although they were all in technical categories. The story's pro-authoritarian message has not prevented it finding an audience, but it is possible to credit some of the box-office success to the high-profile cast. Zhang returned to the martial arts genre with *The House of Flying Daggers* (2004), which, like *Hero*, is visually dazzling although the script is melodramatic and shifts uneasily between political intrigue and romance.

It remains to be seen how Hong Kong filmmakers and audiences will address the question of their position under the 'one state, two systems' model granted by the Chinese Communist Party. The most salient point may be that to date Hong Kong's directors have avoided making films set in present-day China and until they begin to address their situation head-on, a clearly defined sense of identity may still elude them. Any filmmakers bold enough to tackle the issue will certainly face censure from the Chinese Communist Party, but China's own fifth generation of filmmakers, including Chen Kaige, Zhang Yimou and Tian Zhuangzhuang, all faced governmental condemnation at one time or another, but had the courage to criticise the Communist state. Hong Kong cinema is waiting for a director of similar verve to make their voice heard.

Hollywood and the USA

The Introduction of Martial Arts to America

The most obvious and important distinction between the United States and Japan and Hong Kong is that the USA has no indigenous martial arts. Where in Japan and Hong Kong martial arts are part of the native cultures, they have no equivalent in America. Boxing came with the British and Irish immigrants to the USA in the early nineteenth century and is far better established in the mainstream consciousness than any Eastern fighting art. Hollywood has made some classic boxing movies and whilst there is some common ground between boxing and martial arts films, a discussion of boxing in cinema is beyond the scope of this book.

Japanese martial arts came to the United States as a result of the American occupation of Japan after the Second World War. US servicemen who studied Japanese martial arts while stationed in the Far East brought the systems to the United States after their tours of duty. In the 1960s American karate practitioners began to organise tournaments, and karate's profile started to rise. Matters took a downturn in the 1970s following the popularity of Bruce Lee's films and the distribution of Hong Kong kung fu cinema in the West. Phoney kung fu schools run by men who claimed to be the grandmasters of their own personal systems sprang up overnight and the quality of instruction fell sharply. Every strip mall in America now seems to have at least one martial arts school and many of them claim to offer authentic instruction in every major discipline, despite being run by men who have never left the state they were born in, never mind travelled to the Far East.

With the popularity of kung fu, US film producers churned out plenty of low budget schlock featuring highly dubious displays of 'kung fu' and 'karate'. The television series *Kung Fu*, starring David Carradine, that ran from 1972 to 1975, contained very little that could be described as kung fu and an awful lot of silly posing and bad fortune-cookie philosophy. The underlying reason for the poor quality of these American productions was that they were invariably the work of second- or third-rate directors, whereas martial arts films made in Japan or Hong Kong could be the work of top-line filmmakers directing the biggest stars. Furthermore, the inherently alien nature of Eastern martial arts and their absence from the surrounding cultural landscape remain obstacles most filmmakers have been unable to overcome. Many American martial arts films cast their heroes as either ex-military servicemen or cops, as if involvement in either field made the study of Eastern fighting techniques obligatory. There is no overriding theme running through American martial arts films; they do not address a militaristic past like Japanese *chambara*, nor explore connections to a native culture or questions of identity like Hong Kong cinema. Where the Western is the quintessential American action genre, Hollywood martial arts films have never been able to forge a powerful connection with the surrounding culture.

Before Bruce Lee

Bad Day at Black Rock (1955)

Prior to the popularity of Bruce Lee and the international success of kung fu films like *Five Fingers of Death* (1972), only a handful of US productions featured displays of martial arts. An early example is *Bad Day at Black Rock* (1955), directed by John Sturges. The film has elements in common with the Western genre, but its portrayal of a stray dog hero would be equally at home in a Japanese *chambara*. John Macreedy (Spencer Tracy) travels to the isolated town of Black Rock searching for a Japanese farmer called Komoko, who has disappeared. Macreedy is met with naked hostility by many of the locals, led by Reno Smith (Robert Ryan), and finds himself taunted by the brutish Coley Trimble (Ernest Borgnine). Macreedy discovers the truth behind Komoko's disappearance, exposing the racist Smith and his accomplices, who murdered Komoko simply because he was Japanese.

Sturges started working in film while in the US airforce and his output reveals an abiding interest in Japan. He directed *The Magnificent Seven* (1960), the American remake of Kurosawa's *Seven Samurai*, and *A Girl Named Tamiko* (1962) about a Russian in post-war Tokyo torn between two women – one American, the other Japanese. *Bad Day at Black Rock* not only attacks the racism of Smith and his cohorts, but casts Macreedy as a stray dog and has a fight scene involving martial arts. Macreedy is a perfect example of the stray dog hero. He only has one good arm, a result of a combat injury, and his arrival in Black Rock immediately stirs up trouble. The villains do everything in their power to make Macreedy feel isolated and vulnerable – cutting the phone lines and refusing to send his telegrams – to break his spirit. They fail because Macreedy is already isolated. He's alienated from society, regarded as a cripple and treated with contempt, like the blind masseur Zatoichi. When Smith sends a telegram to a private detective in Los Angeles to investigate Macreedy's background, the detective reports that he was unable to find out anything at all, unable to even confirm his existence. Just like the protagonist in *Yojimbo*, Macreedy is a man without a past - a complete stray dog.

The fight between Macreedy and Coley Trimble sees the one-armed man defeat Trimble using what appears to be a Japanese martial art, perhaps *aikido* or jiu-jitsu. Trimble goes out of his way to provoke Macreedy, looking for an excuse to beat him up, until Macreedy has had enough. As Trimble bellows insults, Macreedy strikes him across the windpipe. Trimble, gasping for breath, swings at Macreedy who punches him in the gut, strikes him on the back of the neck, and knees him in the face. Trimble, furious, swings again, but Macreedy sidesteps the blow and counters with strikes to the back of the neck and kidneys. Off-balance, Trimble smashes through the saloon door, before staggering back to his feet. He charges at his antagonist and Macreedy catches his wrist, throwing Trimble using a wristlock and a trip. The massive brute slams into the floor, unconscious. It is a brilliant sequence, executed with style and precision by

16. Macreedy (Spencer Tracy) throws Trimble (Ernest Borgnine) in *Bad Day at Black Rock.*

the director and cast. The exultation that accompanies watching Macreedy dispatch Trimble is akin to watching Zatoichi dismantle a gang of *yakuza*, as the stray dog turns and bites his tormentor. There is a sense of poetic justice as the one-armed man uses Japanese fighting techniques against the virulently racist Trimble. The scene is the highlight of an excellent movie and the majority of subsequent American martial arts films pale next to this early effort. Given that the film pre-dates the 'Zatoichi' series and *Yojimbo*, it is open to question whether the similarities between the protagonists are the result of the universality of the concept of the stray dog or if Kurosawa and Misumi Kenji had seen *Bad Day at Black Rock*.

Another film to feature martial arts prior to Bruce Lee's international breakthrough was Tom Laughlin's *Billy Jack* (1971). The film seems very dated now, telling the story of a tough ex-Green Beret called Billy Jack (played by Laughlin) who watches out for the kids and staff of The Freedom School in small-town America. The local rednecks don't like Billy Jack or the hippies at the school and the standout moment comes when Billy Jack uses his *hapkido* skills to take on a gang of rednecks in the town park. Laughlin brought in Korean black belt Bong Soo Han to choreograph the sequence and Bong Soo Han doubles for Laughlin for much of the fight. The scene is well executed and Laughlin keeps the camera angles low and wide to capture the action, a technique that most American directors still seem unable to grasp. The film switches between slow motion and real time to control the pace of the fight and showcases Bong Soo Han's kicking skills. The entire sequence lasts for only a few minutes, but it was highly memorable. *Billy Jack* cost $800,000 to produce and took over $18 million at the box office. Laughlin followed it with two sequels, *The Trial of Billy Jack* (1974) and *Billy Jack Goes to Washington* (1977), that offered the same mix of action and earnest social comment.

The Yakuza (1975)

A rare example of an American production with a sincere interest in, and respect for, Japanese culture is *The Yakuza*, directed by Sydney Pollack. Harry Kilmer (Robert Mitchum) is an American ex-serviceman who was part of the American occupation of Japan. He returns to Tokyo for the first time in twenty years to rescue the daughter of his friend George Tanner (Brian Keith), who has been kidnapped by a *yakuza* clan led by Tono (Okada Eiji). Kilmer enlists the help of Tanaka Ken (Takakura Ken), whom he believes is the brother of his old flame Eiko (Kishi Keiko). As the two men are drawn further into conflict with Tono and his clan, it becomes clear that Tono and Tanner are business partners and have been manipulating Kilmer and Ken to their own ends. When Eiko's daughter and Kilmer's friend Dusty are killed in a *yakuza* attack, Kilmer and Ken exact a violent retribution.

17. Tanaka Ken (Takakura Ken) in Sydney Pollack's action-thriller *The Yakuza*.

Although an American production, the bulk of the movie was shot in Japan with a Japanese crew, including cinematographer Okazaki Kozo, whose work is excellent. The film addresses the concept of *giri*, translated as 'burden' or 'obligation' in the screenplay. The entire story is driven by *giri* – Kilmer goes to Japan because he is indebted to Tanner; Tanaka Ken is drawn back into the *yakuza* world because he cannot refuse Kilmer's request for help, as Ken is indebted to the American for saving Eiko's life during the post-war occupation. Kilmer and Ken are stray dogs and this quality binds the two. Ken's elder brother Goro describes him as 'something of a lone wolf', adding 'Ken is a relic, left over from another age and another country'. The film parallels Ken's situation with that of the *ronin* during the Tokugawa dynasty. He is a warrior whose skills have become obsolete, whose code of honour has lost its relevance. At the start, Ken has retired from the *yakuza* and makes a living teaching *kendo*, just as many samurai joined fencing schools when their services were no longer required on the battlefield. In the fight with Tono's men, Ken's jacket is torn off, exposing his *yakuza* tattoos. The true nature of the swordsman is revealed during combat; Ken sheds his veneer of respectability and reverts to his true self, the lethal *yakuza* swordsman. This reflects the Japanese notion of *shushigaku*, the inescapability of fate – Ken is unable to lay down his sword and live in peace.

Kilmer too is a stray dog, the script makes it clear that he has been unable to settle down since the end of his military service. He tells Ken that he has had numerous jobs since leaving the army, he has no family, has never married and it is apparent that Kilmer only found meaning in his life during the war. Like Ken, he is a wandering *ronin* at heart.

The action scenes are well handled, particularly the final battle when Kilmer and Ken storm Tono's household. Takakura Ken was a regular *chambara* actor, his work includes portraying Kojiro in Uchida's 'Miyamoto Musashi' series, and is a skilled screenfighter. Kilmer carries a pistol in one hand and a shotgun in the other. The climactic battle of John Woo's *A Better Tomorrow Part II* references *The Yakuza* and the image of the hero with a gun in each hand, much beloved by Woo in the form of Chow Yun Fat, has its genesis here in Robert Mitchum's character. Pollack's sequence is paced more slowly than any of Woo's films, but this serves to heighten the tension as Pollack alternates between sudden, explosive flurries and moments of stillness as opponents square off. At the close, Kilmer heads back to the USA, like the *ronin* moving on to the next town, still wandering, unable to overcome *shushigaku*.

Robert Clouse and Fred Weintraub

When *Enter the Dragon* was a huge hit in America in 1973, taking $25 million at the box office, director Robert Clouse and Fred Weintraub sought to repeat their success. With the death of Bruce Lee, they tried a series of martial artists, but their subsequent efforts were unsuccessful. They started with Jim Kelly, who played Williams in *Enter the Dragon*. *Black Belt Jones* (1974) tells the preposterous story of how Black Belt Jones saves a karate school in Harlem from being taken over by the mafia. The film is an example of the worst the 'Blaxploitation' genre was capable of producing, with a movie made by middle-aged white men, aimed at a young black audience. Clouse made a handful of thrillers before returning to the martial arts genre with *Game of Death* and *The Big Brawl*, discussed in the Hong Kong section. *Force Five* (1981) was another half-baked retread of *Enter the Dragon*, in which five martial artists have to rescue a pretty girl from the island of the evil Reverend Rhee. Aside from the painfully derivative script, *Force Five* lacks a star with the charisma and magnetism of Bruce Lee and Clouse's direction is as bad as ever. 1985 saw Clouse and Weintraub hit a new low with *Gymkata*. Having seen the acrobatic talents of the Hong Kong performers, Clouse and Weintraub cast American gymnast Kurt Thomas in the lead role as an American sent to enter a tournament imaginatively called 'The Game'. Unfortunately, unlike the Hong Kong stars, Thomas could not perform his gymnastics without proper equipment. In one absurd sequence, Thomas is pursued to a town square that just happens to contain a pommel horse, allowing him to use his gymnastics to dispatch his attackers. It's diabolical.

Next, Clouse hired Cynthia Rothrock, an American martial artist who began her acting career in Hong Kong. Never a particularly talented actress, Rothrock has some skill as a screenfighter but wasted her potential in low-budget, no-brain productions like the appalling *Triple Cross* (1993) or *Guardian Angel* (1994). Rothrock's collaborations with Clouse and Weintraub were the two 'China O'Brien' films, released in 1990 and 1991. The direction of the action scenes is hopeless as Clouse speeds up the film in an attempt to intensify the pacing. Sadly, this makes everything look comical, more slapstick than combat. Clouse finished his career with *Ironheart* (1992) and did not make another movie before his death in 1997.

In 1977 director John Landis made *The Kentucky Fried Movie*, a collection of comedy sketches that included *A Fistful of Yen*, a highly effective parody of *Enter the Dragon*. Bong Soo Han, from the 'Billy Jack' films, plays Dr Klahn, the film's version of Mr Han, and Evan Kim is excellent as Loo, the lead character modelled after Bruce Lee. The sequence shreds Clouse's film, exposing everything that is wrong with the original – the moronic plot, the terrible dialogue and the stereotypical presentation of Asians.

Chuck Norris, Cannon Films and Ninja

Chuck Norris was an American martial arts tournament champion in the 1960s and his movie break came when Bruce Lee cast him as Colt in *Way of the Dragon*. Norris had one line of dialogue in the entire movie but showed talent as a screenfighter and his duel with Lee is a classic. Sadly, his subsequent work has not been quite as memorable. Norris presents something of a contradiction – he is a devout Christian, softly spoken, whose career has been spent playing violent tough guys. If Norris appears uncomfortable playing the swaggering hero on screen, it is probably because his personality is unsuited for the role. After *Way of the Dragon*, Norris played the villain in *Yellow Faced Tiger* (1973), a Hong Kong production directed by Lo Wei, trying to cash in on Bruce Lee's legacy. Norris made his first American film with *Breaker Breaker* (1977), playing a karate-kicking trucker, before *Good Guys Wear Black* (1977), the first sincere attempt to launch him as an action star. The story concerns a secret deal between a sleazy diplomat, Conrad Morgan (James Franciscus), and the Vietnamese government at the end of the Vietnam War. In return for the release of American prisoners of war, Morgan promises to have the members of the elite Black Tiger unit killed, including their leader John T. Booker (Norris). Five years after the war, ex-Black Tigers start dropping like flies and a suspicious Booker tries to figure out why.

The problems with the film are many, but the worst is that this is an action movie with hardly any action. The opening titles play over footage of Booker fighting, setting up the expectation that a martial arts film is to follow. However, there are only three scenes in which Norris uses his martial arts and they are all short and executed with neither drama nor excitement. After the final fight sequence, in which Booker takes on three men, he jokes to his buddy, 'Enjoy the fight?' to which the guy replies 'Terrific'. I doubt anyone in the audience agreed.

More of the same followed. *A Force of One* (1979) casts Norris as a full-contact kickboxing champion taking on drug dealers. The acting and direction are mind-numbingly bad: in the scene when Matt Logan (Norris) learns of the death of his foster son, he displays all the intensity of someone who has found chewing gum on the seat of their pants. Despite casting real-life full-contact *karateka* Bill Wallace as his principal opponent, the film contains little action and the showdown between the two men is badly choreographed.

In *Lone Wolf McQuade* (1983), directed by Steve Carver, Norris is J. J. McQuade, a Texas ranger who takes on drug lord Rawley Wilkes (David Carradine), who just happens to be a martial arts champion. The attempt to cast McQuade in the mould of 'Lone Wolf' is badly misjudged. Where Ogami Itto is an alienated anti-hero whose only human relationship is with his son, McQuade has an ex-wife, a girlfriend, and a sidekick. He's far too integrated into society to claim to be a stray dog and when the sidekick dies halfway through the story, it makes McQuade seem incompetent rather than isolated. The action scenes are very weak, with fights frequently shot in medium close ups, preventing the audience from seeing the techniques, whilst Carradine is an unconvincing screenfighter.

Norris enjoyed his first hit with *Missing in Action* (1984), in which he played James Braddock, an American soldier who goes back to Vietnam to rescue prisoners of war. The film's success led to two follow-ups, *Missing in Action II: The Beginning* (1985) and *Braddock: Missing in Action III* (1988). The second film has a final duel between Braddock and the evil Colonel Yit (Soon-Teck Oh) but it is a far cry from the climactic duel in *Way of the Dragon*. Norris starred in second-rate action films throughout the 1980s, never achieving widespread fame beyond the home video market. He broke through to the mainstream on television with the series *Walker Texas Ranger* (1993–2001). The series featured regular action scenes in which Walker (Norris) and his buddies beat up the bad guys using their martial arts. The show was popular enough to last for nine seasons before Norris decided to move on. He has since filmed two made-for-TV movies, apparently intended to launch a new series, *The President's Man* (2000) and *The President's Man: A Line in the Sand* (2002), in which Norris plays a karate-kicking secret service agent.

The Cannon Group produced several of Norris's vehicles, including the 'Missing in Action' movies and the rabidly xenophobic *Invasion USA* (1985). Cannon was a struggling film production company when Menahem Golan and Yoram Globus bought it in 1979. Golan and Globus contributed to the martial arts genre with *Enter the Ninja* (1982), the film that launched a whole slew of American ninja movies. Historically, the ninja were Japanese warriors who did not abide by the rules of *bushido*. In warfare they were commonly used to sneak into enemy castles and start fires. They often entered hostile positions by dressing in the uniforms of the opposing army and carrying the enemy's standard – unthinkable behaviour for a samurai, but acceptable for the ninja. If one believes the American films about ninja, they are superhuman magicians and martial artists. *Enter the Ninja*, directed by Golan, starred Franco Nero as Cole, a Caucasian, who is a good ninja, and Sho Kosugi, who is Japanese, as Hasegawa, the evil ninja. Cole wears all white, Hasegawa all black. Subtle, eh? The plot concerns Cole defending his war buddy's property from an unscrupulous developer and culminates in a duel between the two ninja rivals. Nero had no martial arts training, so was doubled for his fight scenes by American *karateka* Mike Stone, but the action sequences are poorly executed. The film never overcomes the incongruity of two men dressed in full ninja uniforms in the twentieth century. Ninja may be acceptable in Japanese period films set during the Tokugawa dynasty, but they simply don't belong in contemporary stories.

Despite the formulaic plot, poor acting and weak fight direction, the film was something of a hit and led to countless imitations. Sho Kosugi built his career playing ninja, both in the television series *The Master* (1984) and in more films for Cannon, including the improbable *Ninja III – the Domination* (1984). This was a new low for American martial arts trash, telling the story of a beautiful female aerobics instructor called Christie who is possessed by an evil ninja. She begins to hunt down and kill the policemen who shot the evil ninja, using her newly acquired superpowers, requiring the timely intervention of a good ninja, Yamada, (Sho Kosugi), who must free her from the evil ninja's control.

It is a spectacularly bad film, although there is undeniably an audience for this kind of exploitation movie, featuring as it does plenty of action scenes (better executed than *Enter the Ninja* but a far cry from what was being accomplished in Hong Kong at the same time) and the sex appeal of the nubile Lucinda Dickey as Christie the aerobics instructor by day/ninja killing-machine by night.

On a roll, Cannon produced *American Ninja* (1985) the following year, starring Michael Dudikoff as Joe Armstrong, a US serviceman stationed in the Philippines who uses his ninja skills to fight evil drug dealers and lots of other ninjas (they sure do get around). Mike Stone was martial arts choreographer, but the ninja skills are still fantastically over-the-top and make no sense in the modern *mise-en-scène*. The film had a budget of around $1 million, but took over $35 million internationally, making it hugely profitable. Four more 'American Ninja' films followed in addition to countless imitations, including *American Samurai* (1993), *American Kickboxer* (1991) and *American Yakuza* (1994). These are cheaply produced, formulaic nonsense, made for the American video market and featuring a cast of B-list actors and martial artists, including, but not limited to, David Bradley, Mark Dacascos, Steve James and Michael Dudikoff.

Roger Corman's company New Horizon churns out straight-to-video martial arts films, often starring kickboxer Don Wilson. The films are made with little care and are the cinematic equivalent of fast food. The quality may be low, but they satisfy the expectations of their target audience of American teenage males and never deviate from the accepted formula. They bring nothing new to the genre and compare poorly with their Hong Kong counterparts. Hong Kong producer Ng See Yuen set up a division of Seasonal Films to make films for the US video market, including *American Shaolin* (1991) and *King of the Kickboxers* (1991). These films have competently executed action scenes, but suffer from terrible scripts and wooden acting.

A-list Action Heroes

Two martial arts stars in the United States were able to break out from the B-list, straight-to-video market to enjoy A-list status, albeit temporarily. They are Belgium-born Jean-Claude Van Damme and *aikido* black belt Steven Seagal.

Jean-Claude Van Damme

Van Damme started his career playing villains. He was the bad guy in *No Retreat, No Surrender* (1985), one of Ng See Yuen's American ventures, directed by Corey Yuen. Subsequently, Van Damme was one of the stuntmen who played the monster in the Arnold Schwarzeneggar vehicle *Predator* (1987). He played a villain opposite Sho Kosugi in *Black Eagle* before his first starring role in *Bloodsport* (1988), another opus from Cannon. The film claims to be based on a true story by Frank Dux, an American who purports to have won a secret martial arts tournament called the 'Kumite' in the Far East. Given the large number of martial arts events in the Far East, why Dux would have had to compete in secret is not a question he has ever been able to answer with any conviction. Regardless, Van Damme plays Dux, who runs away from the US army to go to Hong Kong to enter the Kumite to fulfil a promise made to his instructor. On the way he befriends another competitor, Jackson (Donald Gibb), and has time for a little romantic interest with a reporter (Leah Ayres) before facing off against the villainous Chong Li (Yeung Sze from *Enter the Dragon*) in the final match.

The action choreography set the pattern that all of Van Damme's subsequent films followed. He showcases his jumping, spinning kicks, all of which are performed with his right leg, never throws or complicated combinations, and he does the splits. The range of choreography in Van Damme's films has been extremely limited, with the same handful of movements repeated time and time again. In *Kickboxer* (1989), Van Damme plays Kurt Sloane, whose brother Eric is crippled during a fight in Thailand against champion Tong Po (played by Michael Qissi, who doesn't look even remotely Thai). Kurt finds an old master called Xian (Dennis Chow, who is clearly Chinese) to teach him *Muay Thai*.

Aside from all the interesting non-Thai people in Thai roles, the film professes to showcase the techniques of *Muay Thai*. The problem is that Van Damme doesn't employ *Muay Thai* in his fight scenes. When he performs the roundhouse kick, in both the training and fighting sequences, he uses the karate technique *Mawashi geri*, pulling his knee up to his chest before extending the leg, not the *Muay Thai* style *Te*, in which the kick is thrown from the ground without chambering the knee and force is generated by rotating the hips and feet. His jumping, spinning kicks have no place in Thai boxing and he carries his hands in a low posture, not like the high guard used by Thai fighters to protect their heads.

Van Damme did the same thing in *The Quest* (1996), an amalgamation of *Bloodsport* and *Kickboxer*, in which Christopher DuBois (Van Damme) goes to Muay Thai Island to learn martial arts before entering a secret tournament in the 'Lost City', which no one seems to have any great difficulty finding. Aside from the sheer stupidity of 'Muay Thai Island' (imagine going to 'Kung Fu City' or 'Karate Town'), Van Damme still doesn't employ Thai boxing techniques, carrying his hands down, using karate kicks and standing in a low, wide stance alien to *Muay Thai*. In the final Chris faces a massive Mongolian fighter (Abdel Qissi, the older brother of Michael Qissi from *Kickboxer*). Their duel highlights one of the major failings of Van Damme's films, in that his opponents do not have personalities. The importance of the nemesis in the martial arts film cannot be understated. The opponent pushes the hero to surpass himself and the best villains are doppelgangers – the dark reflection of the hero. Van Damme's onscreen opponents are punch bags with no human qualities. The Mongolian in *The Quest* does not have any dialogue; he is denied a voice, denied his humanity to ensure that the audience only cares about Van Damme's character. The same is true in *A.W.O.L.* (1990), also known as *Lionheart*, in which only one of Van Damme's opponents has a single line of dialogue. To give them a voice, to give them developed personalities, might allow the audience to identify with them and any such identification would make the fighting seem truly brutal and expose just how violent Van Damme's characters are. As long as his opponents remain voiceless and soulless, the audience can feel secure in their admiration for Van Damme, for how can his opponents be suffering when they never articulate any pain? The choreography in *A.W.O.L.* is amongst the stiffest in Van Damme's career, consisting of a series of single strike/ single counter/reaction exchanges. There are very few combinations, little interaction with the environment and certainly no Hong Kong-style acrobatics.

The most violent film in Van Damme's career is *Death Warrant* (1990), in which he plays Louis Burke, a cop sent undercover inside a prison to investigate a series of suspicious deaths. Inside, he meets Hawkins, played by Robert Guillaume from the American television series *Benson*. Burke instinctively trusts Hawkins from the moment they meet, although it is never clear why. Perhaps he has been watching *Benson*. The film has a disturbing internal morality based on earning respect through violence. When Burke is sent to prison, he is given the cover story that he was arrested for armed robbery because the crime has an implicit violence that the inmates will respect. When the prisoners learn that Burke is a cop, they want his blood, but after he kills the most dangerous man in the prison, the Sandman (Patrick Kilpatrick), the inmates treat him with respect and make no attempt to harm him. He is still an undercover cop, but he has demonstrated an enormous capacity for violence that earns him the admiration of the prisoners. Where in most Japanese *chambara* the protagonists are alienated from society by their violent natures, Van Damme's heroes are rewarded for their actions. In *Death Warrant*, Louis Burke gets the girl; in *A.W.O.L.*, Lyon is reunited with his family; in *Bloodsport* Frank Dux gets the girl, and so on. Admittedly, none of the other films are quite as nasty as *Death Warrant*, in which Burke dispatches the Sandman by driving his head onto a metal bolt, but there is no sense that violence has any negative human cost.

Van Damme's films occasionally veer into the territory of camp, although it is questionable whether this is intentional. There is a fight in *Sudden Death* (1995) that is one of the funniest ever staged, although the humour appears to have been unintended. Darren McCord (Van Damme) takes his two kids to a hockey game attended by the US vice-president. Terrorists take the vice-president hostage and it's up to McCord to rescue him, diffuse a bomb and generally save the day. At one point a female terrorist steals the costume from one of the ice hockey team's mascots, but is discovered by McCord, resulting in a bloody fight. The problem is that the terrorist performs the fight dressed as a cuddly penguin, so the audience is treated to the sight of Van Damme having a karate duel with a giant fluffy penguin. It's surreal, but absolutely hilarious, and the comic effect is only intensified by the desperately serious direction.

Van Damme enjoyed his biggest hit with *Timecop* (1994), which took over $44 million in the United States, but thereafter a string of poor films saw his star wane. *Streetfighter* (1994) was adapted from a video game, but the script was deliriously camp and the fight scenes poorly directed. Box-office revenues fell with every subsequent release, until 1998, when the ambitious *Legionnaire* did not receive a cinema release in the United States and went directly to video. This was particularly bad news for the star, since the project had a large budget for a Van Damme vehicle, $35 million. The main problem with *Legionnaire* was that it failed to deliver enough action. There are no martial arts displays and one unconvincing boxing sequence.

Van Damme attempted to recover some of his box-office clout with a sequel to *Universal Soldier* (1992), but *Universal Soldier: The Return* (1999) only took $10 million in North America. His next three films, *Replicant* (2001), *The Order* (2001) and *Derailed* (2002), went straight to video. There is still enough of an audience internationally and in the home rental market to keep Van Damme active, but his time as an A-list star appears to be over.

Steven Seagal

Steven Seagal is a highly ranked black belt in *aikido*, which he studied in Japan. He worked as martial arts instructor on *The Challenge* (1982) alongside Kuze Ryu, the Japanese fight coordinator who worked with Kurosawa. His break into movie stardom came after he taught *aikido* to Hollywood producer Michael Ovitz. Seagal's early films are action thrillers in which he invariably plays a tough cop who takes on gangsters or drug dealers. They are not martial arts films per se, but thrillers in which *aikido* supplants more conventional Hollywood screenfighting techniques. His characters defy the conventions of the stray dog anti-hero as they have familial and romantic relationships; in *Out for Justice* (1991), for example, Gino (Seagal) has a wife, a son and plenty of friends in the local community, hardly a stray dog. Seagal's breakthrough into the mainstream came in 1992, when *Under Siege* was an unexpected box-office hit. Directed by Andrew Davis with a budget of $12 million, the movie took over $150 million worldwide and suddenly Seagal was a major Hollywood player. The film is cut from the same cloth as the 'Die Hard' series and stars Seagal as Casey Ryback, a Navy Seal who is finishing his tour of duty as cook on a US navy battleship. When terrorists hijack the ship in pursuit of nuclear weapons, Ryback has to rescue his shipmates, stop the terrorists stealing the nuclear arsenal, and beat the hell out of the bad guys with his *aikido*. The film benefits from the casting of Gary Busey and Tommy Lee Jones as the lead villains and the two ham it up shamelessly from start to finish. The action scenes are handled with some imagination; unlike Chuck Norris or Jean-Claude Van Damme, Seagal has a fairly broad range of techniques and whilst he is not as athletic as his contemporaries, he makes up for this with the variety of ways in which he dispatches opponents.

After the success of *Under Siege*, Seagal assumed the director's mantle for *On Deadly Ground* (1994). The project was somewhat misjudged; Forrest Taft (Seagal) takes on the corrupt president of Aegis Oil, Michael Jennings (Michael Caine), who is building an oil refinery in Alaska. Injured in a trap set by Jennings, Taft is nursed back to health by the local Eskimos, including Masu (Joan Chen, who is Chinese), before returning to destroy the Aegis refinery. The film's eco-friendly message is well intentioned but the action scenes are too few and far between. As an epilogue, Taft delivers a lecture on the importance of preserving the natural environment and on the obsolescence of the internal combustion engine. Such sentiments are a welcome change from the macho posturing of Seagal's earlier films, but their treatment is heavy handed.

Under Siege 2: Dark Territory (1995) saw Seagal return to the role of Casey Ryback, this time foiling terrorists who take over a train. The film performed better at the box office than *On Deadly Ground*, taking $50 million domestically, but Seagal's next starring vehicle, *The Glimmer Man* (1996), only took $20 million. The good life was taking its toll on Seagal's physique and the lean, tall figure of *Out for Justice* was replaced by a more portly version. The fight scenes in *The Glimmer Man* rely more on frantic editing to create pace than on Seagal's martial arts skills and it was apparent that he was losing his edge. In *Fire Down Below* (1997), Seagal looked even more out of shape, despite the filmmakers' attempts to hide his girth under a collection of expensive leather jackets. The story reflected Seagal's environmentalism, concerning illegal chemical dumping in the Appalachian mountains of Kentucky, and Seagal plays Jack Taggert, a member of the Environmental Protection Agency sent to investigate the dumping of toxic chemicals and the death of the agency's man first assigned to the case.

The script never explains why a member of the Environmental Protection Agency would be a highly skilled *aikidoka*, relying upon Seagal's established screen persona to justify his martial arts prowess. The film contains plenty of action scenes and the eco-minded message is less heavy handed than in *On Deadly Ground*, but the film performed badly at the box office and Seagal's next film, *The Patriot* (1998), was released direct to video. *The Patriot* suffers from the same deficiencies as *On Deadly Ground*, containing very little action, without which there is nothing to attract Seagal's target audience.

Seagal did not make another film for two years until producer Joel Silver cast him in *Exit Wounds* (2001). The film paired Seagal with American rap star DMX and director Andrzej Bartkowiak, and was a success, taking over $50 million at the US box office. The plot is contrived, with Seagal playing another hard-nosed cop, this time teaming up with a dot.com millionaire, Leon Rollins (DMX), who is posing as a drug dealer to expose the corrupt cops who framed his brother. Hong Kong choreographer Dion Lam was hired for the fight sequences, which offer a combination of Seagal's hard-hitting style and the aerial wirework associated with the current generation of Hong Kong filmmakers. In the finale Seagal's character has a sword battle using the blades from a fabric cutter. The acrobatic style of the sword duel is inconsistent with the film's tone as a gritty action thriller and the fight seems out of place.

This temporary return to box-office form did not last and without producer Joel Silver, Seagal's subsequent projects failed to build on the success of *Exit Wounds*. *Half Past Dead* (2002) took only $15 million and *The Foreigner* (2003) went straight to video. In *Belly of the Beast* (2003), directed by Hong Kong veteran Ching Siu Tung, Seagal was showing his age. The director's Hong Kong-style choreography contains techniques from Tai Chi and *Pa Kua*, but Seagal's poor physical condition required the frequent use of stunt doubles. This is anathema to the very appeal of action heroes and helps explain the muted reception Seagal's later films have received and his inability to return to big-screen stardom.

American Martial Arts Films

The Karate Kid (1984)

A handful of American filmmakers have successfully adapted the motifs and icons of Hong Kong and Japanese martial arts films to Western settings. A straightforward attempt to transpose the essential elements of the martial arts film to an American background was John G. Avildsen's *The Karate Kid*. Avildsen won the Best Director Oscar for *Rocky* (1976) and *The Karate Kid* has much in common with the earlier work. Both feature working-class heroes and have similar structures, with the protagonist training hard for a final duel in which he has the opportunity to prove his worth both to himself and his immediate society. The story follows the most fundamental pattern of the martial arts genre, as the new kid in town Daniel LaRusso (Ralph Macchio) is targeted by the local bullies, led by Johnny Lawrence (William Zabka), who all attend the karate school run by John Kreese (Martin Kove), an unbalanced war veteran. Daniel befriends Mr Miyagi (Pat Morita), the Okinawan caretaker who lives in his building and when Miyagi saves Daniel from the gang and flattens them with his martial arts, Daniel convinces the old man to train him. A showdown is arranged between Daniel and Kreese's students at the All Valley Karate Tournament and Daniel fights his way through the preliminaries before facing Johnny in the finals. Despite an injured knee, Daniel uses Miyagi's Crane technique to win the match.

All the classic genre elements are present and correct – the master–pupil relationship, the importance of personal and spiritual growth, a series of confrontations leading to a climactic duel and the mastering of a new technique required to triumph. The roots of these motifs can be traced back all the way to *Sanshiro Sugata*, but director Avildsen and his cast inject them with sufficient energy that they do not seem stale. Macchio was chosen to play Daniel partly because he had absolutely no martial arts experience and Avildsen wanted someone who would look awkward and whose development on screen would be authentic. The link between physical and spiritual growth is played out as much of Daniel's training is boring, repetitive manual work. He has to overcome his own enormous impatience and self-absorption to learn from Miyagi, who recognises the need for Daniel to mature emotionally as he improves physically. The master–pupil relationship between Daniel and Miyagi is the focus of the narrative, more so than Daniel's romance with Ali (Elizabeth Shue), making clear that this is foremost a martial arts film, not a teen romance.

The presentation of martial arts in *The Karate Kid* is down-to-earth and lacks the exaggeration of movement and impact that are widespread throughout the genre. By the final duel, Daniel is still far from being a polished *karateka* and whilst the Crane technique is undeniably silly, the duel is carried off with conviction. The movie was a tremendous success and three sequels followed, each one following the established formula. In *The Karate Kid, Part Two* (1986) Daniel and Miyagi travel to Okinawa (where, conveniently for Daniel and the audience, everyone speaks English all the time), and Daniel has a duel in which he has to employ another new technique to defeat the

18. Miyagi (Pat Morita) and Daniel (Ralph Macchio) practise defence in *The Karate Kid*.

violent Chozen (Yuji Okumoto). *The Karate Kid, Part Three* (1989) is the weakest of the three, recycling the plot of the first movie as Daniel defends his title at the All Valley Karate Tournament whilst Terry Silver (Thomas Ian Griffith) messes with his head. The technique Daniel uses to win is unimpressive and the formula was running out of steam. In *The New Karate Kid* (1994), Daniel is absent and in his place Miyagi trains a wayward girl, Julie (Hilary Swank), so she can defend herself against the local thugs and develop some self-respect. By this point, the movies had become repetitive and the novelty that made the first entry successful had worn off. The movie only took $8 million at the American box office, compared to the first entry, which made over $90 million. The impact of the series was considerable and led to numerous imitations, like the inane *College Kickboxers* (1990), which is worse than the title suggests, and *Showdown* (1993), one of many low-budget efforts starring Billy Blanks, creator of the 'Tae-Bo' workout videos. Miyagi's Crane technique has become a popular target for parody, not least of all by Hong Kong star Chow Sing Chi in *Love on Delivery* (1994). *The Karate Kid* demonstrated that it was possible to make an entertaining American martial arts film, given a strong cast and a decent script, and it is a shame that most of the movies that followed had neither.

The Last Dragon (1985)

The Last Dragon, directed by Michael Schultz, performs the primary function of the kung fu comedy in demythologising the martial arts hero. Reflecting a Western sensibility, the subject for parody is not any of the traditional Cantonese heroes, but the most recognisable martial artist in the world – Bruce Lee. The story concerns 'Bruce' Leroy Green (played by Taimak), a young martial artist who runs a kung fu school in Harlem. Rather than avoid the cultural paradox presented by a black man teaching Chinese martial arts in Harlem, the film addresses them head-on, using the incongruity as a source of humour. Leroy is an urban black American who dresses like a rural Chinese man in a straw hat, Chinese jacket, trousers and slippers. He looks ridiculous, but this is deliberate. Leroy is obsessed with Bruce Lee's screen persona and the two men are visually linked throughout the film. In addition to the Chinese clothes, Leroy wears

19. 'Bruce' Leroy Green (Taimak) and his student Johnny (Glen Eaton) confront Sho'nuff (Julius Carry) and his gang in *The Last Dragon*.

a yellow-and-black tracksuit like one worn by Bruce Lee in *Game of Death*, and in the final fight scene a strobe effect is employed, replicating the sequence in *Fist of Fury* when Bruce Lee fights Bob Baker. Taimak's screenfighting style is modelled on that of Lee and he mimics Lee's animal screeches when he fights.

The screenplay parodies Lee's philosophical approach to martial arts through the character Johnny (Glen Eaton), one of Leroy's students. In *Enter the Dragon*, Lee described his style as 'The art of fighting without fighting'. In *The Last Dragon*, Johnny explains his unique approach to martial arts, 'You know how you're always teaching us to master the art of fighting without fighting? Well, you see, I did you one better. I mastered the art of fighting without knowing how to fight.'

All the essential genre motifs are present; Leroy is on a quest for enlightenment, trying to perfect himself and his martial arts. He is confronted by a rival martial artist, Sho'nuff (Julius Carry), the self-styled shogun of Harlem, who antagonises Leroy in the hope of drawing him into a duel. In the climactic battle Leroy experiences his epiphany and transcends himself, demonstrating the inextricability between defeating oneself and defeating one's opponent. The fight sequences are well choreographed and the performers are solid screenfighters, although there are moments when the kicks are filmed in medium shot – preventing the audience seeing the full range of motion – and the visual impact of the techniques suffers. Regardless, the film functions as a kung fu comedy, as it diminishes the icon of the kung fu hero and parodies Bruce Lee as martial artist and philosopher.

Big Trouble in Little China (1986)

Another film to reference Hong Kong cinema is *Big Trouble in Little China* (1986), directed by John Carpenter and starring Kurt Russell as Jack Burton, a truck driver who is drawn into an ancient Chinese conflict being played out in San Francisco's Chinatown. Jack ends up helping his friend Wang (Dennis Dun) rescue Wang's fiancée from the clutches of Lo Pan, an ancient demon who needs Wang's green-eyed fiancée to break a curse. Working for Lo Pan are the Three Storms, superpowered martial artists, and Wang and Jack join

20. Jack Burton (Kurt Russell) is the odd one out, surrounded by the members of the Chang Sing in John Carpenter's *Big Trouble in Little China*.

forces with the Chang Sing, led by wizard Egg Shen, to bring down
Lo Pan.

The film pays homage to the work of Tsui Hark and King Hu in
its presentation of martial arts and Chinese magic. There are monsters and demons and the kind of aerial combat found in *Zu:
Warriors of the Magic Mountain*. In the final battle Wang duels with
Rain (Peter Kwong), one of the Three Storms, and they exchange
sword blows whilst flying through the air. The Three Storms possess
superpowers common to the 'Swordsman' films of Hong Kong,
including the ability to project lightning bolts and the power to defy
gravity. The film treats the Chinese magical elements of the story
with respect and the humour comes from the treatment of the character of Jack Burton. Where *The Last Dragon* demythologised the
kung fu hero, *Big Trouble in Little China* parodies the American hero.
Burton is a macho trucker, but he is consistently diminished in the
narrative. When the Chang Sing let out their battle cry as they
charge, Jack shoots his gun into the air, bringing down a portion of
the ceiling that knocks him to the ground. Later, he passionately
kisses Gracie Law (Kim Cattrall) and spends the rest of the scene
running around with her lipstick all over his mouth. He is constantly
robbed of his dignity where the Chinese heroes are allowed to keep
theirs intact. This is unusual for an American production, where the
Caucasians are invariably the heroes and non-whites either sidekicks or villains, but illustrates that Carpenter's approach is based
on a respect for Chinese culture.

James Lew, an American martial artist, handled the fight choreo-
graphy, which is well executed and he includes the stance 'To
Conquer the Centre with a Single Finger', from the *Hung Kuen* style.
In the film the stance is employed by the heroic members of the
Chang Sing, but not by the villainous Wing Kong who work for Lo
Pan. This references the Shaw Brothers Shaolin films, where the
heroes could always be identified by their use of the *Hung Kuen* style
and the famous stance 'To Conquer the Centre' in particular. Chang
Cheh's *Heroes Two* (1973) is a typical example, in which Chen Kuan
Tai, playing Hung Hey Kwun, frequently adopts this stance, with
the palm of the hand facing forward and all the fingers bent bar the
forefinger which is extended. It is a subtle in-joke and demonstrates
the referential nature of Carpenter's film.

Blind Fury (1989)

In 1989 director Phillip Noyce made *Blind Fury*, an American adaptation of *Zatoichi Challenged* (1967), transposing the location from Tokugawa dynasty Japan to modern America. Nick Parker (Rutger Hauer) is an American soldier blinded in a battle in Vietnam, but rescued by villagers in the jungle and taught to use a sword by the local master. Having established Parker's background, the film puts the character in a typical Zatoichi situation as Nick comes to the rescue of a young boy whose mother has been killed and whose father, Frank (Terrance O'Quinn), is in trouble with mobsters. There are numerous parallels between *Blind Fury* and the *chambara* genre. Parker's old war buddy Frank Devereaux is in debt to MacCready, a mobster who runs a fixed gambling casino, like an *oyabun* running a *yakuza* gambling den. The thugs who work for MacCready are the American counterparts to the *yakuza* in *Yojimbo*, a collection of grotesque ugly brutes who are as ridiculous as they are dangerous. Noyce does not try to avoid the inherent cultural paradox presented by a blond-haired Caucasian man armed with a cane sword. Rather, he uses humour to diffuse this problem. When Parker uses his sword to kill a flying insect, an old woman watching him tells her husband, 'We should get one of those!'

Nick Parker is a stray dog hero, wandering from town to town, always finding trouble. The film establishes its *chambara* genre credentials right from the opening shot – a pan along a sword blade. Parker fights using a cane sword held with the same reverse grip used by Zatoichi. The choreography by Steven Lambert is excellent and the film contains the essential motif of the duel between rival masters. The opponent here is Sho Kosugi, star of the numerous ninja films produced by Cannon, playing a Japanese swordsman brought in to kill Parker. Their duel displays a wide range of techniques as Kosugi's assassin uses a conventional grip against Parker's reverse-grip style. In addition to the sword strokes, the fight is punctuated by punches, kicks and some acrobatics from Kosugi and their battle handsomely satisfies the *chambara* genre's requirement for the climactic duel.

The film has the same moral centre as the 'Zatoichi' series, as Parker takes the boy Billy (Brandon Call) under his wing and helps him grow from an unpleasant brat to a more developed human being. Furthermore, Parker's determination to find Frank – whom he's lost contact with since his return to the USA – springs from his need to forgive his old war comrade for abandoning him during the battle that cost Parker his sight. Like Zatoichi, Parker is a humanist with a powerful sense of compassion. At the close of the film, when Billy has been reunited with his father, Parker quietly slips away and the final shot shows him walking out of town, isolated in the frame, exactly like Zatoichi or Sanjuro. This final image confirms Parker's status as a *chambara* stray dog and *Blind Fury* is one of the most faithful and successful American adaptations of a martial arts film.

Road House (1989)

A less successful adaptation is *Road House*, directed by Rowdy Herrington. Dalton (Patrick Swayze) is the best bouncer in the business and is hired by Frank Tilghman to clean up his bar, the Double Deuce, in the small town of Jasper. Dalton comes into conflict with Brad Wesley (Ben Gazzara), the ruthless businessman who controls the town. Dalton's mentor Wade Garrett (Sam Elliott) comes to town to help Dalton, who begins a romance with Elizabeth Clay (Kelly Lynch), the doctor who patches him up after his altercations. Dalton kills Wesley's bodyguard Jimmy (Marshall Teague) in a fight and in return Wesley has Garrett murdered. Dalton tears into Wesley's house and kills his goons before the two men face off. Dalton batters Wesley but refuses to kill him. As Wesley pulls a gun the locals whose lives he has ruined appear, armed with shotguns, and execute their tormentor.

The film attempts to transpose the search for enlightenment through martial arts to an American setting. Dalton has a degree in philosophy and he lives a spartan lifestyle, renting a room in Jasper with few amenities – no television, no phone, no air conditioner. The script casts Dalton in the same light as Musashi Miyamoto or Sugata Sanshiro, as a hero on a quest for self-perfection through combat. However, the *mise-en-scène* of the southern United States in the 1980s does not readily lend itself to the concept of a search for enlightenment. Unlike *The Last Dragon* or *Blind Fury*, which use humour to mollify the cultural clash created by the application of Hong Kong and Japanese themes to US settings, *Road House* is determinedly serious. It is never clear what Dalton hopes to accomplish by pursuing a life devoted to self-discipline and the notion of Zen has no place in the American setting.

Other genre elements work better; Dalton is a functional translation of the *ronin*, the warrior for hire. He has no permanent home and his arrival stirs up trouble in the town. From the kung fu film, there is a *sifu* figure in the form of Wade Garrett, who trained Dalton, and the murder of the *sifu* and subsequent vengeance are common plot elements in kung fu cinema. The duel is present when Dalton and Jimmy square off in the movie's best action sequence, with a wide range of techniques and spirited performances from Swayze and Teague. The timing of the duel is misjudged, though, as the film climaxes before Dalton has confronted the man behind his misfortunes, Brad Wesley. The casting of Ben Gazzara as Wesley is not particularly effective. The character is the equivalent of an *oyabun* or triad boss, squeezing protection money from the local businesses, but as talented an actor as Gazzara is, he is not physically imposing enough to appear threatening. When Dalton and Wesley come to blows, their fight lacks the intensity of the earlier duel between Dalton and Jimmy and does not satisfy as a final confrontation. Furthermore, when Wesley is slain, not by Dalton, but by the local men driven to murder, this alleviates the burden of guilt from Dalton and prevents him from becoming alienated from society and fully adopting the role of the stray dog. Dalton's relationship with Elizabeth hits a bump when she sees him kill Jimmy, an act that horrifies her, yet in the epilogue the two lovers are together, with the implication that Dalton has stopped wandering and settled down. The end of Dalton's journey is not a spiritual awakening, but romantic fulfilment. This is in keeping with the ethos of the Hollywood action film – the hero gets the girl. It is in contrast to the protagonists of *chambara* cinema or the Shaolin heroes and reflects the filmmakers' American sensibilities. The Hollywood hero has a happy ending, quite unlike his Eastern counterparts, despite the fact that, although Dalton did not slay Wesley, he killed Jimmy and a fair number of Wesley's thugs. Dalton does not have to answer for the lives he has taken and the film suggests that violence and murder can lead to peace and happiness for the residents of the little town of Jasper.

Best of the Best (1989)

Directed by Bob Radler, *Best of the Best* contains some of the most effective action scenes staged in an American production and, whilst the story follows a typical kung fu narrative, the film rejects the notion of revenge so prevalent in martial arts movies. The plot concerns a *Tae Kwon Do* tournament between the American and Korean teams held at the World Games in Seoul, South Korea. The American team includes Tommy Lee (Phillip Rhee), whose older brother David was killed in a match against the leader of the Korean team, Dae Han (Simon Rhee). Tommy is consumed by a desire for vengeance, but frightened by his own hatred and anger. His teammate Alex Grady (Eric Roberts) breaks training to visit his son Walter in hospital, incurring the wrath of Coach Couzo (James Earl Jones). At the tournament the Americans are trailing on points when Alex narrows the gap in the penultimate match. His opponent lands an axe kick that dislocates Alex's shoulder, but Alex perseveres and wins his match. In the final, Tommy faces Dae Han and batters him savagely until the Korean is defenceless. Tommy can claim both victory and revenge, but he chooses not to strike, letting the Korean team win by a single point. At the medal presentation ceremony, Dae Han gives his medal to Tommy, asking his forgiveness for the death of Tommy's brother.

All of the leading characters, Alex, Tommy and Coach Couzo, grow as human beings during the story, expressing the genre theme of spiritual development being inseparable from physical advancement. Assistant Coach Wade (Sally Kirkland) highlights the importance of spiritual development alongside physical training:

> Coach, even with my help it will be difficult, if not nearly impossible, to defeat a team from Korea. As you know, their training is as much mental as it is physical and they've been doing it for most of their lives. We only have three months. Excuse me for saying so, Coach, but without my help all of your modern training techniques and hi-tech equipment won't mean shit.

Throughout training, Travis, the most unruly team member, refuses to participate in Wade's yoga and meditation sessions, and this costs him in the tournament. At the close of his match, his score is tied with that of his Korean opponent, so the victor is decided by a test of breaking – the winer is the competitor who smashes the most blocks. Having neglected to learn focus and relaxation, Travis loses to the Korean, whose concentration is total.

Alex has to defeat himself to win his match, a classic genre theme. When his shoulder is dislocated, Alex has to overcome his pain and self-doubt, for the injury exacerbates an old problem and Alex has questioned his ability to compete ever since. He succeeds in shutting out the pain and defeats his opponent Sae Jin Kwon (James Lew).

Tommy's confrontation with Dae Han is the emotional peak of the narrative, as Tommy confronts the man who slew his brother and his own desire for revenge. Their duel is an accomplished piece of choreography, showcasing the spinning and aerial kicking techniques for which *Tae Kwon Do* is renowned. Tommy leaves Dae Han bloodied and scarcely conscious. In a standard martial arts narrative at this point Tommy would kill his opponent and exact his revenge, fulfilling the duty of retribution placed upon him by his brother's death. Tommy refuses to strike, forfeiting the tournament and his chance for vengeance, in direct contravention of the genre formula. Tommy rejects death and chooses forgiveness. Dae Han is so humbled that he experiences a spiritual awakening of his own, demonstrated by his speech when he gives his medal to Tommy: 'To save a life in defeat is to earn victory and honour within. Your brother too was a great fighter. I deeply regret your loss and I offer myself as your brother.'

The message is that compassion is more valuable than revenge. This reflects the same humanism present in *Sanshiro Sugata* and is highly unusual for an American production. The film benefits from the excellent direction of the fight sequences, supervised by Simon Rhee, and a strong cast that includes Christopher Penn as Travis. The decision to defy genre expectations raises the film above the standard, formulaic action films produced in America and the quality of the demonstrations of martial arts is exceptional. Phillip Rhee holds a sixth degree black belt in *Tae Kwon Do*, whilst his real-life brother Simon, who plays Dae Han, holds a seventh degree black belt, so their presentation of the art is firmly rooted in authentic techniques.

Three sequels followed, but rather than continue to defy genre conventions, the later films are more formulaic. *Best of the Best II* (1993) sees Tommy, Alex and Travis involved with illegal martial arts tournaments, treading much the same ground as *Bloodsport* or any number of low-budget films about secret fighting competitions. The action scenes are handled with style, but the plot is hardly original and the sudden introduction of an adopted Native American family for Tommy makes no sense. For the third and fourth films, Phillip Rhee was the only remaining original cast member and he assumed the directorial role. The plots had become the stuff of standard action thrillers, with Tommy Lee taking on white supremacists in the third film and Russian mobsters in the fourth, but the fight scenes were still considerably better executed than in the bulk of American martial arts films. Bob Radler, who directed the first two films, moved to television, where he worked on *Mighty Morphin' Power Rangers*, *Police Academy: The Series* and *V.I.P.* Poor fellow.

Ghost Dog – The Way of the Samurai (1999)

The most interesting American exploration of the icons and motifs of the Japanese martial arts film is Jim Jarmusch's *Ghost Dog – The Way of the Samurai*, in which the director, best known for off-beat character studies, explores the *bushido* code in an urban American setting. Ghost Dog (Forest Whitaker) is an assassin in modern New York who works for the mafia through his contact Louie (John Tormey). When not on a mission, Ghost Dog studies Yamamoto Tsunetomo's *Hagakure*, the seminal book on the *bushido* code. Ghost Dog is hired to kill Handsome Frank, a mobster pursuing an illicit affair with the daughter of mafia boss Ray Vargo (Henry Silva). Ghost Dog completes the assignment, but kills Frank in front of Louise, Vargo's daughter (Tricia Vessey), and the mafia bosses decide Ghost Dog has to die. Ghost Dog begins eliminating the mobsters, but he steadfastly refuses to kill Louie, whom he regards as his lord. After disposing of all the gangsters, Ghost Dog allows Louie to kill him.

The film was released in 1999 and Jarmusch uses the end of the twentieth century to draw parallels with the demise of the samurai at the close of the Tokugawa dynasty and the dawning of the imperial restoration in Japan. The members of the mafia are all old men and they are three months behind with their rent on the building they use for meetings. They are relics, anachronisms, like Ghost Dog or the disenfranchised samurai who lost their stipends in the wake of the imperial restoration. This is articulated throughout the screenplay. Sonny, second in command to Vargo, tells Louie, 'A whole new century is coming ...', indicating that a new age is about to dawn, like the Meiji Restoration, whilst Ghost Dog later comments, 'Everything seems to be changing all around us, huh, Louie?' Vinny, one of the mafiosi, has the following exchange with Louie after being fatally wounded by Ghost Dog:

> *Vinny*: You know, Louie, there's one good thing about this Ghost Dog guy.
> *Louie*: What's that, Vin?
> *Vinny*: He's sending us out the old way. Like real fucking gangsters.

All these characters know they are the last of their kind, a dying breed, and Vinny appreciates the chance to die like a gangster. He is like the old samurai described in *Hagakure*:

> It is said that Tokunaga Kichizaemon repeatedly complained, 'I've grown so old that now, even if there were to be a battle, I wouldn't be able to do anything. Still, I would like to die galloping into the midst of the enemy and being struck down and killed. It would be a shame to do nothing more than to die in one's bed. (Yamamoto, 2000, p. 130)

Ghost Dog's lifestyle is based upon *Hagakure* and the film is punctuated by quotations from the book, beginning with the famous section 'The way of the samurai is found in death ...'. The readings from *Hagakure* comment upon the developments in the narrative and inform Ghost Dog's actions. Ghost Dog is aware that he is part of a dying breed, but refuses to give up the *bushido* code that gives meaning and structure to his life. His fate is predetermined, reflecting the concept of *shushigaku*, and Ghost Dog approaches death resolutely and without question, just as *Hagakure* exhorts a samurai to do. When he confronts Louie, the scene is staged like a duel, but Ghost Dog has emptied his gun and does not defend himself, allowing Louie to shoot him. His death is a form of ritual suicide, his personal version of *seppoku*, dying rather than turning against his *daimyo*. Ghost Dog refers to himself as Louie's 'retainer', a direct translation of the word 'samurai', and he is bound by a powerful sense of duty, of *giri*. He has several opportunities to kill Louie, but refuses each one, rigorously following his code of fealty.

The film makes numerous references to the *chambara* genre and Jarmusch includes all of the essential visual motifs. On two separate occasions, Ghost Dog is visually linked with a stray dog, asserting his claim to the status of *chambara* hero. Ghost Dog uses a gun, not a sword, for assassinations but after shooting someone, prior to returning the handgun to its holster, he performs the *iaido* motion *chiburi*. This movement is intended to shake the blood from a sword blade before it is returned to the scabbard, to prevent the metal rusting. There is no practical reason for Ghost Dog to perform this movement with his gun, but it further confirms his genre status, visually linking him with the sword-wielding samurai. Jarmusch includes a scene in which the character practises martial arts and swordplay on the rooftop where he lives, ensuring that the *chambara*'s principal icon, the sword itself, is present and accounted for. In another reference to Japanese cinema, Jarmusch uses gang member colours to draw a comparison between the urban gang members and the samurai clans. The gang members pronounce their membership by the colours of their clothes, like the samurai carrying banners into battle to distinguish between friend and foe, examples of which can be found in Kurosawa's *Ran* (1985) and Inagaki's *Samurai Banners* (1969).

A copy of the book *Rashomon* passes between the characters, another reference to ancient Japan. The presence of the book suggests that all may not be what it seems, since the title story deals with the subjectivity of truth. This is confirmed in the aftermath of Ghost Dog's death, when Louie reports to Louise Vargo, the daughter of the dead mob boss. She has taken control of her father's clan, raising the possibility that she orchestrated the entire affair to her own ends. It is Louise who gives Ghost Dog the copy of *Rashomon* when he kills Handsome Frank and when Ghost Dog passes it along to Louie, who then returns it to Louise, the book has come full circle. Parallel with this, before his suicide, Ghost Dog gives his copy of *Hagakure* to Pearline, a little girl he has befriended and one of the characters through whose hands *Rashomon* passes. The final shot shows Pearline engrossed in *Hagakure* and the audience hears her voice reading the final extract from the book. The *bushido* code is passed on to another generation and Jarmusch leaves open the question of whether the code will serve Pearline better than it did Ghost Dog.

21. Ghost Dog (Forest Whitaker) practises martial arts in *Ghost Dog – The Way of the Samurai*, Jim Jarmusch's exploration of the *bushido* code.

Like all of Jarmusch's movies, *Ghost Dog – The Way of the Samurai* has a slow, meditative pace, but it is a meticulously constructed work and an excellent exploration of the *bushido* code, certainly the best such analysis performed by any American filmmaker.

Enter The Matrix

If one film can be said to be responsible for introducing American audiences to Hong Kong choreography, it is Larry and Andy Wachowski's *The Matrix* (1999). The film had a budget of $63 million, but took over $374 million worldwide. It was a monster hit and radically changed the way American films present martial arts.

Thomas Anderson (Keanu Reeves), a computer hacker who uses the pseudonym Neo, is pursued by both a group of rebels led by Morpheus (Laurence Fishburne) and the agents of an unnamed organisation led by Agent Smith (Hugo Weaving). Through Morpheus, Neo learns that the world he believes in is a virtual reality called the Matrix, created by a race of hostile machines that use human beings held in stasis as their energy source. Morpheus believes Neo is 'The One', destined to fulfil a prophecy whereby he will be able to manipulate the Matrix and bring about the downfall of the machines. Neo battles Agent Smith within the Matrix, but is shot and killed. He is reborn within the Matrix as 'The One', able to manipulate the virtual reality at will and he defeats Agent Smith.

The script contains biblical elements (Neo as Christ, Cypher as Judas, Morpheus as John the Baptist, Neo's death and resurrection) and concepts from the hacker community. More relevant here is the fact that *The Matrix* functions as a deconstruction of the kung fu film in its presentation of martial arts within a virtual environment. The Wachowski brothers were familiar with Hong Kong cinema and hired Yuen Wo Ping to handle the fight scenes. In an interview in *American Cinematographer* magazine in 1999, Larry Wachowski commented upon the different approaches of Hollywood and Hong Kong filmmakers to the execution of fight sequences:

> Andy and I love Hong Kong action films, and we both feel that they're miles ahead of American action films in terms of the kind of excite-

ment that the action brings to the story. American filmmakers have gotten to the point where they create their fights in the editing room. Those types of sequences are just designed for a visceral, flash-cut impact, and the audience's brains are never really engaged ... Hong Kong action directors actually bring narrative arcs into the fights, and tell a little story within the fighting. (Probst, 1999, p. 34)

The Wachowskis gave the principal cast to Yuen Wo Ping and his team for four months to train in martial arts. Rather than stunt doubles performing the action, Keanu Reeves, Carrie-Anne Moss, Laurence Fishburne and Hugo Weaving executed their own elaborate fight sequences. Cinematographer Bill Pope noted:

These fights were not shot as Americans shoot fight scenes, in which the camera is usually set over one character's shoulder as another throws a punch, missing the person's face by a mile. Instead, the brothers and Wo Ping insisted that if a character were to hit someone in the face, they had to *really* hit them in the face! You can see every blow, and you can even see the dust coming off the actors' clothes as they're hit! (Probst, 1999, p. 35)

The results were fight scenes unlike any previously staged by American filmmakers and, indeed, unlike anything accomplished by any Hong Kong production when Wo Ping's choreography was combined with the visual effects created by John Gaeta. The sum total of these endeavours has been copied by numerous action filmmakers and inspired many Western directors to hire Hong Kong choreographers and stuntmen. The choreography contains a huge range of techniques, in particular a large number of stances and movements from Chinese martial arts that American audiences would not have previously encountered. The actors perform their scenes with total commitment and the climactic duel between Neo and Agent Smith is superbly executed.

The film contains the essential ingredients of the kung fu narrative. There is the master–pupil relationship between Neo and Morpheus, and the requirement for the student to exceed the *sifu* and go beyond the limits of their instruction. Morpheus is unable to defeat Agent Smith, but Neo overcomes Smith following his epiphany and resurrection. Neo's search for truth, for identity (is he 'The One' or not?) parallels the exploration of identity found in Hong Kong cinema post-1981. Neo has two selves, a physical one and a virtual counterpart. It is the virtual element to the story that

provides the basis for deconstruction. Training in martial arts techniques is an essential part of the kung fu genre, but in *The Matrix*
Neo does not have to endure the physical hardships of training.
Martial arts techniques are uploaded into his brain, bypassing the
arduous physical process, and the movements are only performed
in the virtual world. Neo himself never physically performs martial
arts. All his demonstrations of fighting skills, against Morpheus in

22. Trinity (Carrie-Ann Moss) combines grace and power in *The Matrix*.

the training hall or against Agent Smith in the Matrix, are virtual representations carried out by a projection of Neo's consciousness, not by Neo himself. The fights are therefore virtual projections of conflict, taking the notion that displays of martial arts on screen are the externalisation of the hero's inner conflict to its extreme. Neo and Agent Smith do not ever physically come into contact with one another; Agent Smith has no physical self, he exists as a program within the Matrix. They fight as abstract figures, devoid of physical substance. The fights are thereby robbed of their physical dimension and all that remains are the movements, the visual images of fighting. Neo's moment of self-realisation, when he becomes 'The One' and thus defeats both himself (his idea of his limitations) and his opponent, is purely metaphysical. There is no progression of martial arts skill, for Neo does not fight on the physical plane. When he defeats Smith, it is not through fighting, but by willing Smith out of existence, negating him by his control over the Matrix. The notion of combat is rendered abstract, deconstructing the defining element of the martial arts film – the fight itself.

The tremendous success of the film led to two sequels, although neither of them continued to explore the martial arts genre in the same manner as the first. *The Matrix Reloaded* (2003) does not continue to deconstruct the kung fu film, but rather is an exploration of the conflict between duty and desire, much like a Japanese samurai film with the concepts of *giri* and *ninjo*. This tension arises as Neo is torn between his love for Trinity (Carrie-Ann Moss) and his mission to save Zion and destroy the Matrix. The final instalment, *The Matrix Revolutions* (2003), is the least interesting of the trilogy and of no consequence to the martial arts genre.

Hong Kong Imports

After *The Matrix* came a flood of American films that employed Hong Kong choreographers to direct their fight sequences. Of all these, the film that most closely resembles a Hong Kong action film is *Charlie's Angels* (2000), directed by Joseph 'McG' Nichol with martial arts direction by Yuen Cheung Yan. The movie follows the

23. Natalie (Cameron Diaz) strikes a pose in *Charlie's Angels*, choreographed by Yuen Cheung Yan.

model of the contemporary Hong Kong action film in that the script is a collection of set pieces, switching freely between action, comedy and musical numbers. The plot is secondary and makes little sense, but the narrative is not the primary text – the visuals are of main importance. Following in the path of the Wachowski brothers, the principal cast trained with Yuen Cheung Yan prior to shooting and performed their fight scenes themselves. The sequel, *Charlie's Angels: Full Throttle* (2003) was cut from the same cloth, but placed greater emphasis on stunts than martial arts techniques, despite the continued presence of Yuen Cheung Yan.

The Hong Kong style of choreography, combining martial arts techniques with wirework, has become so widespread in Hollywood that it has become the new standard. Yuen Cheung Yan was action director on the comic-book adaptation *Daredevil* (2003) whilst Yuen Wo Ping worked on Quentin Tarantino's *Kill Bill* (2003, 2004) films. Jet Li and Corey Yuen continued their partnership outside Hong Kong, starting with *Lethal Weapon 4* (1998), a lacklustre entry in the Mel Gibson/Danny Glover series in which Li was introduced to the American mainstream playing a villain. His first leading role came in *Romeo Must Die* (2000), directed by Andrzej Bartkowiak, in which Li plays Han Sing, a Chinese cop out to avenge the death of his brother. Despite the title bringing to mind *Romeo and Juliet*, the film has nothing in common with Shakespeare's play and there is no romance between Li's character and Trish, the female lead played by Aaliyah. The acting and direction are dreadful and the plot formulaic. The action scenes make excessive use of wire stunts, lacking realism and any potential visceral impact is consistently undercut by the frantic and obtrusive editing. There are even three X-ray shots showing bones being crushed, reminiscent of the Japanese film *The Street Fighter* (1974), indicative of the exploitative nature of the movie.

The most interesting aspect of the film is the extent to which it reveals the implicit racism against Asian men so prevalent in American cinema. Han Sing and Trish never kiss or display any mutual attraction. There is a taboo regarding Asian men in Hollywood that counterbalances the Western fetish for Asian women. There are countless American films in which white men are romantically or sexually involved with women of Asian origin. A handful of examples include *The World of Suzy Wong* (1960), *You Only Live Twice* (1967), *The Karate Kid Part II*, *Salute of the Jugger* (1988), *Kickboxer* (1989), *Showdown in Little Tokyo* (1991), *Wayne's World* (1992), *The Transporter* (2002), and the American TV series *Shogun*. It is considerably more challenging to compile a list of films in which Asian men are sexually or romantically involved with non-Asian women. The absence of any sexuality in Jet Li's character in *Romeo Must Die* follows a long tradition of films in which Asian men are sexually neutral or undesirable. In *Showdown in Little Tokyo* it is the white character played by Dolph Lundgren who gets the Asian girl played by Tia Carrere, not the Asian-American character played by Brandon Lee. Chow Yun Fat's first American vehicle, *The Replacement Killers*, pairs him with actress Mira Sorvino, but the pair never share an onscreen kiss, which would be unthinkable if the male lead was white.

Jet Li's second film as a Hollywood leading man broke this taboo and allowed his character to have a relationship with a non-Asian woman. *The One* (2001) was directed by James Wong and had Corey Yuen as choreographer. The film is an improvement on *Romeo Must Die*, despite a silly script. Yulaw (Jet Li) is a renegade who travels between parallel universes killing different versions of himself. As he eliminates his alternate selves, their life force is divided amongst the remaining versions, all of whom grow in strength and speed as a result. The final alternate is Gabe Law, a member of the Los Angeles Police S.W.A.T. unit, married to T.K. (Carla Gugino). Yulaw kills T.K. before he faces off against Gabe, who defeats him. Gabe is sent to an alternate universe where T.K. is still alive, whilst Yulaw is sent to the Hades Universe, a prison dimension, where he is attacked by the other inmates and forced to fight a seemingly endless stream of assailants.

Corey Yuen's choreography in *The One* is far superior to his work in *Romeo Must Die* and the fight sequences employ a range of visual effects styled after *The Matrix* to enhance the action. Most unusual for an American production is the emphasis on Chinese martial arts and the performance of techniques from the *Pa Kua* style. The villainous Yulaw employs a linear, aggressive style and in one sequence the film cuts back and forth between Yulaw playing a fast, direct kung fu form and Gabe practising the soft, circular move-

24. Jet Li takes flight in *The One* as Gabe and Yulaw exchange kung fu techniques.

ments of *Pa Kua*. Yulaw comments 'the shortest distance between two points is a straight line', while Gabe talks of his grandfather telling him that life is a circle and he must find his centre. In the final duel, Yulaw attacks Gabe with hard, straight techniques, overpowering him, until Gabe switches to *Pa Kua* and uses the circular movements to deflect Yulaw's strikes and outmanoeuvre him. This is an excellent example of the kung fu duel, showcasing Chinese martial arts and emphasising the link between personal development and the improvement of martial arts technique. The movie marks the increasing influence of Hong Kong choreographers upon American action filmmakers. No American choreographer would have employed an obscure Chinese style like *Pa Kua*, but the presence of Corey Yuen makes this possible.

Li's third starring role outside Hong Kong was *Kiss of the Dragon* (2001), directed by Chris Nahon, and produced by French filmmaker Luc Besson, director of *Leon* (1994) and *The Fifth Element* (1997). The story concerns a Chinese policeman, Liu Jian (played by Li), who is sent to Paris to help the French police, led by Richard (Tcheky Karyo), arrest a Chinese drug smuggler. Richard murders the drug dealer and frames Liu; it seems Richard is heavily involved in the drug trade and prostitution. Liu eludes the French police and comes to the assistance of Jessica (Bridget Fonda), an American forced into prostitution by Richard, who holds her young daughter. After Jessica is shot, Liu takes her to a hospital, then storms the police headquarters, wiping out Richard's gang of corrupt cops. He confronts Richard and kills him using an acupuncture technique, the 'Kiss of the Dragon' of the title, before reuniting Jessica with her daughter.

Corey Yuen's choreography is his most naturalistic work in years. There is very little obtrusive wirework and the fight scenes look like an approximation of hand-to-hand combat. The performers use the hybrid screenfighting style common to Hong Kong cinema during the 1980s, relying upon fast combinations of kicks and strikes. There is a visual reference to Bruce Lee's *Fist of Fury* when Liu storms the police building. He accidentally intrudes on a police combat training class and finds himself surrounded by officers wearing karate uniforms, and the staging of the scene immediately brings to mind Bruce Lee attacking the Japanese in their *dojo* in *Fist of Fury*.

The film casts Li's character as the hero and Tcheky Karyo's character as pure evil. The script contains no ambivalence about the fact that Liu is a policeman from Communist China – he is the good guy who saves Jessica and her daughter from Richard's clutches. The Chinese characters are portrayed positively whilst the French authorities are corrupt and morally bankrupt. This attitude is more in keeping with a Hong Kong production, aside from the fact that Li's character is from Communist China, not Hong Kong itself. Unfortunately Li's character is sexually neutral. When Jessica offers to have sex with Liu and he refuses, she asks if she is not his type. He replies 'I don't have a type', marking a step backwards from *The One*, which allowed Li to have a sexual identity that is denied him here.

Kill Bill (2003, 2004)

Arguably the worst attempt to transpose the elements of Hong Kong and Japanese martial arts films to an American movie are the two parts of Quentin Tarantino's *Kill Bill*. The first movie is a collection of disparate ideas taken from other films. Once again an American director treats Chinese, Hong Kong and Japanese concepts and icons as all being part of one amorphous idea of 'Asia'. The film's biggest failing, aside from a poor script and weak performances, is that whilst Tarantino throws together countless different genre elements, he fails to respect the integrity of each ingredient. There is no attempt at parody, pastiche or deconstruction. It is simply a poorly conceived homage that, despite the huge number of intertextual references, fails to reveal anything new about the genre in the process.

The film opens with the Shaw Brothers logo, but bears no resemblance to a Shaw Brothers kung fu film. There is no internal morality at work, all the characters are equally violent and there is no sense of any human price for the violence. In this regard, the film is comparable to the Japanese 'Lone Wolf and Cub' series, devoid of any social agenda and presenting acts of extraordinary brutality as entertainment. Despite the presence of the Shaw Brothers logo, the film has far more common with the 1970s *chambara* movies made by Toho Studios than with any Hong Kong production. The central character is an alienated sociopath whose principal means of interaction with other human beings is combat, like Ogami Itto or Lady Snowblood.

The incoherent use of genre motifs pervades the film. Uma Thurman's character wears a yellow-and-black tracksuit, an obvious reference to Bruce Lee, but her fighting style contains no references to Lee's at all. Instead, she fights with a Japanese samurai sword. The character Gogo (Chiaki Kuriyama) is Japanese and is dressed as a schoolgirl, again fetishising an Asian female. When she fights using a ball and chain she performs Chinese rope-dart forms and the film never addresses why a Japanese fighter is using Chinese martial arts. Veteran Shaw Brothers kung fu actor Lau Gar Fei appears as a Japanese *yakuza*, conveniently ignoring the fact that he is Chinese. In the final battle the image switches from colour to black and white, a reference to the work of Chang Cheh in *Heroes Two* and *Men from the Monastery*, but there is no underlying aesthetic reason for the switch in *Kill Bill – Volume One*. Tarantino has claimed that the shift to monochrome was to assuage nervous film censors, but this is as unconvincing as the similar claim for Chang Cheh's use of monochrome in *Men from the Monastery*. In Tarantino's film, it is unmotivated by anything happening on screen and is another intertextual reference included in the movie without consideration for the reasons the technique was originally employed in the source material.

There is no attempt at deconstruction, merely duplication. In the sequence rendered in the style of a Japanese *animé*, the body of a slain *yakuza* is seen with a tattoo of a spider on his head, referencing Sydney Pollack's *The Yakuza*, but Tarantino does not expand upon this image. Uma Thurman's character tears out someone's eyeball in a manner akin to Sonny Chiba in *The Street Fighter*, while Chiba himself appears as a swordsmith, not as Terry Surugi. O-Ren Ishii (Lucy Liu) wears a white kimono and her appearance and fighting style are modelled on Yuki from 'Lady Snowblood'. The duel between Uma Thurman's vengeful assassin and O-Ren Ishii takes place in the snow, reinforcing the allusion, but again there is no attempt to comment upon the work being referenced.

Kill Bill – Volume Two offered more of the same incoherence. Lau Gar Fei reappears, this time in the role of Pai Mei, complete with white hair and long beard, a reference to the master of White Eyebrow kung fu played on numerous occasions by Lo Lieh at Shaw Brothers (in the section on Hong Kong cinema above, I use the spelling Bak Mei, but Tarantino uses Pai Mei, so I use that here). Tarantino does not have his version of the character use the White Eyebrow style, but sees him performing the *Hung Kuen* form of the Tiger-Crane fist. A cursory review of the Shaolin films of Chang Cheh and Lau Gar Leung makes it clear that Pai Mei was the villain and thus never employed the *Hung Kuen* system that was the style used by the heroes. For all his claims to be a Hong Kong cinephile, Tarantino does not appear to have been paying attention.

The presence of a Chinese monk teaching martial arts in a contemporary setting is a paradox that Tarantino simply ignores. Likewise, he chooses not to address the incongruity of a white woman wielding a samurai sword. All the period elements – the swords, Pai Mei, the Tiger-Crane form – do not fit in with the modern setting, but the film never attempts to reconcile this problem.

An unsettling element running through both films is the prevalence of violence against women. The male characters in the story die fairly swiftly – Budd is poisoned and expires quickly, whereas Bill dies in a fashion that appears to be both painless and instantaneous. By comparison, the female characters endure considerable and prolonged suffering. O-Ren Ishii has the top of her head sliced off; Elle has her eyes torn out; Gogo's death is bloody and violent; Sofie Fatale has her arm cut off; Beatrice (Uma Thurman's character) is shot, drugged, buried alive and almost raped. In a scene in a Mexican brothel, the camera picks out a disfigured prostitute who has been mutilated by her pimp. The script is a tirade of gender-specific insults that do not bear repetition. Far from offering a vision of female empowerment by casting a woman as the protagonist, Tarantino objectifies and brutalises all the women in the narrative, displaying a disturbing and virulent misogyny.

Kill Bill is a perfect example of the problems and failings of American filmmakers trying to emulate Hong Kong and Japanese martial arts cinema. The plot is formulaic, based on a simplistic quest for vengeance that has become redundant and the jumbled mixture of genre icons and motifs is testament to the American habit of lumping the cultures of the Far East into one convenient category that overlooks the unique properties of each country and region.

Aftermath

American filmmakers have faced a unique set of problems in their presentation of martial arts in cinema. The inherently foreign nature of the martial arts themselves has proved an obstacle many filmmakers have been unable to overcome or are oblivious to. Recently, the influx of directors, stars and choreographers from Hong Kong has had a profound impact upon the quality and character of American action films. Whether Western audiences will grow tired of wire stunts and Chinese martial arts after they have lost their novelty, only time will tell.

Glossary

Abbreviations:
    Can – Cantonese
    Jpn – Japanese
    Kor – Korean
    Man – Mandarin
    Th – Thai

Aikido (Jpn) – The way of harmony. Founded by Morehei Ueshiba, this art emphasises using an opponent's energy against them. It employs strikes, joint locks and throws.

Bakufu (Jpn) – The shogunate government in Togukawa Japan.

Budo (Jpn) – *Bu* relates to matters of war and the military, *budo* means military way or warrior way. It is often used to refer to the collected arts of the many weapons originally from Okinawa, including the nunchaku, the tonfa, the sai.

Bushido (Jpn) – The warrior code of the samurai class.

Chambara (Jpn) – A swordplay film.

Chi (Man) – Internal energy, known as *Ki* in Japanese.

Chinese Boxing – See kung fu.

Choy Li Fut (Cant) – A kung fu system combining elements of both Northern and Southern styles, mixing long- and short-range techniques.

Daimyo (Jpn) – A regional governor in feudal Japan.

Dojo (Jpn) – A martial arts school.

Dogi/Gi (Jpn) – A martial arts uniform.

Eagle Claw – *Ying Jow Pai* in Cantonese, a style inspired by the movements of an eagle, employing an eagle claw form with the thumb and first two fingers used to attack vulnerable targets.

Escrima – a Filipino martial art that includes empty-handed techniques but is best known for the use of sticks and knives; also known as *Arnis* or *Kali*.

Giri (Jpn) – Duty or obligation; the loyalty owed to one's lord or clan.

Hapkido (Kor) – The Korean form of *aikido*, with joint locks and throws, although *hapkido* features more kicking techniques than its Japanese predecessor.

Hara-kiri (Jpn) – Ritual suicide, performed by cutting one's belly open before being beheaded.

Hung Kuen (Cant) – The kung fu style made famous by anti-Ch'ing revolutionary Hung Hey Kwun. Principal forms include the Five Animals/Five Elements form, the Tiger-Crane fist and the stance 'To Conquer the Centre With a Single Finger'. Known as *Hung Gar* in Mandarin.

Iaido (Jpn) – The art of drawing the sword and striking in the same motion.

Jeet Kune Do (Can) – Bruce Lee's philosophy of martial arts, emphasising an open mind and an adaptable approach to combat, not limited by traditional forms.

Jidai-geki (Jpn) – A period drama.

Jiu-jitsu (Jpn) – The original unarmed martial art of Japan, developed to be used by samurai as a last resort on the battlefield should they lose their sword.

Judo (Jpn) – translates as 'The Gentle Way'. Developed from jiu-jitsu by Jigaro Kano, this is a form of grappling, emphasising throwing techniques.

–ka (Jpn) – The suffix ka added to the name of a Japanese martial art denotes a practitioner of said art, e.g. a *judoka* practises judo.

Katana (Jpn) – The long sword of the samurai class.

Karate (Jpn) – Originally codified by Gichin Funakoshi, this is a martial art that was developed in Okinawa from Chinese White Crane kung fu. There are several main styles of karate, including *Shotokan*, *Kyokushinkai* and *Wado Ryu*.

Kempo (Jpn) –The Japanese translation of kung fu, a term used in Japan to denote martial arts of Chinese origin. There are several distinct schools of kempo, including *Shorinji* kempo and *Kosho Ryu* kempo.

Kendo (Jpn) – The way of the sword – Japanese sword fighting

Ki (Jpn) – Internal energy.

Kodachi (Jpn) – The short sword of the samurai.

Kung fu (Can) – A general term for Chinese martial arts.

Lion Dance – A traditional part of the curriculum at kung fu schools.

Manga (Jpn) – Japanese comic books.

Mantis kung fu – A style based on the movements of the praying mantis, with the hands bent at the wrists, mimicking the insect.

Muay Thai (Th) – Also known as Thai boxing, this is the national sport and martial art of Thailand. A very powerful and effective style that combines punches, kicks, elbow and knee strikes with a limited form of wrestling allowed whilst standing.

Ninja (Jpn) – Non-samurai warriors and spies from the Tokugawa dynasty, famous for their stealth.

Ninjo (Jpn) – Personal desire.

Ninjutsu (Jpn) – The art of the ninja.

Nunchaku (Jpn) – A weapon originally from Okinawa, composed of two pieces of wood linked by a chain or cord.

Oyabun (Jpn) – Boss of a *yakuza* gang.

Pa Kua (Can) – Known as *Baguazhang* in Mandarin. This is another of the internal Chinese martial arts, like Tai Chi. *Pa Kua* can be recognised by its circular movements, performed with the palms facing outwards.

Ronin (Jpn) – A masterless samurai, one with no steady position or clan membership. Literally translates as 'man on the wave'.

Sai (Jpn) – A three-pronged weapon from Okinawa, used to break the blade of a sword.

Savate – The French form of kickboxing.

Sensei (Jpn) – Martial arts master and instructor.

Seppoku (Jpn) – Another term for *hara-kiri*.

Shogun (Jpn) – Japan's military ruler.

Shorinji kempo (Jpn) – The Japanese translation of Shaolin kung fu. Founded by Doshin Soh, who placed great importance on the cultivation of a moral character through martial arts and Buddhism.

Shuriken (Jpn) – A throwing weapon.

Shushigaku (Jpn) – The concept of predeterminism.

Sifu (Can) – Martial arts master and instructor.

Snake fist – A kung fu style in which the hand is held with the fingers pointing rigidly forwards imitating a snake's head. The fingers are used to thrust into vulnerable spots, like the eyes and throat.

Tae Kwon Do (Kor) – Literally meaning 'hand and foot way', *Tae Kwon Do* was formally established in 1955 by Choi Hong Hi. The art was inspired by Japanese karate, but has become famous for the heavy emphasis on kicking techniques.

Tai Chi Chuan (Man) – The Cantonese name for this martial art is *Tai Geek Kuen*, but Tai Chi is commonly used in the West. The style was invented by Chang San Feng and emphasises suppleness, pliability and balance. Tai Chi Chuan forms are practised slowly and fluidly and the focus is on the generation of internal energy, not muscular strength.

Tang Soo Do (Kor) – A Korean form of karate.

Tiger and Crane form – One of the principal forms of the *Hung Kuen* style, imitating the movements of the two animals. The Tiger style uses the hand as a claw, whilst the Crane style involves bringing the tips of the fingers and thumb together in a beak shape that is used to attack vulnerable targets.

Tiger style – *Fu Jow Pai* in Cantonese, this kung fu style is based on the movements of a tiger, using the hands as claws.

Tonfa (Jpn) – A weapon of Okinawan origin and the model for the modern nightstick or baton used by US police officers.

White Eyebrow – A kung fu style named after Bak Mei, known for his bushy eyebrows. Recognisable by the use of the fist with the fore-knuckle extended.

Wing Chun (Can) – One of the southern Chinese martial arts, making use of close range techniques, such as trapping hands, intended to tie up an opponent's limbs creating an opportunity to strike.

Wu Shu (Man) – The official martial art of Communist China; very acrobatic in nature.

Yakuza (Jpn) – Gangster.

Bibliography

Beasley, W. G., *The Japanese Experience: A Short History of Japan* (Weidenfeld & Nicolson, London, 1999)

Berry, Chris (ed), *Perspectives on Chinese Cinema* (British Film Institute, London, 1991)

Bradshaw, Peter, 'Crouching Tiger, Hidden Dragon', *Guardian*, at http://film.guardian.co.uk/News_Story/Critic_Review/Guardian_Film_of_the_week/0,4267,417897,00.html; downloaded 12 August 2003

Brooks, Xan, 'Crouching Tiger, Hidden Dragon', *Guardian*, at http://film.guardian.co.uk/News_Story/Critic_Review/Guardian_review/0,4267,418205,00.html; downloaded 12 August 2003

Carey, Peter, 'Travels in the Floating World', *Guardian*, 27 November 2004

Chan, Jackie, and Yang, Jeff, *I Am Jackie Chan* (Pan, London, 1999)

Chan Ting-ching, Ng Ho and Sek Kei (eds), *A Study of the Hong Kong Martial Arts Film* (The Fourth Hong Kong International Film Festival, Hong Kong, 1980)

Clouse, Robert, *The Making of Enter the Dragon* (Unique Publications, California, 1987)

Dannen, Fredric, and Long, Barry, *Hong Kong Babylon* (Faber & Faber, London, 1997)

Ebert, Roger, 'Crouching Tiger, Hidden Dragon', *Chicago Sun-Times*, at http://www.suntimes.com/ebert/ebert_reviews/2000/12/122211.html; downloaded 12 August 2003

Galbraith IV, Stuart, *The Emperor and the Wolf* (Faber & Faber, London, 2001)

Graham, Bob, 'Great Leap Forward', *San Francisco Chronicle*, at http://www.sfgate.com/cgi-bin/article.cgi?f=/c/a/2000/12/22/DD54467.DTL; downloaded 12 August 2003

Henshall, Kenneth G. *A History of Japan: From Stone Age to Superpower* (Macmillan, London, 1999)

Hunter, Jack (ed), *Intercepting Fist: The Films of Bruce Lee* (Glitter, London, 1999)

Kazuzo Kudo, *Dynamic Judo* (Japan Publications Trading Company, Tokyo, 1967)

Kerr, Alex, *Dogs and Demons: The Fall of Modern Japan* (Penguin, London, 2001)

Kurosawa Akira, *Something Like an Autobiography* (Vintage, New York, 1983)

Lawrance, Alan, *China Under Communism* (Routledge, London, 1998)

Lee, Bruce, *Tao of Jeet Kune Do* (Ohara, California, 1975)

Lee, Linda, *The Bruce Lee Story* (Ohara, California, 1993)

Meyers, Richard, Harlib, Amy, Palmer, Bill, and Palmer, Karen, *Martial Arts Movies: From Bruce Lee to the Ninjas* (Citadel, New Jersey, 1985)

Mishima Yukio, translated by Sparling, Kathryn, *Yukio Mishima on Hagakure: The Samurai Ethic and Modern Japan* (Basic Books, New York, 1977)

Mitchell, David, *The Official Martial Arts Handbook* (Sphere, London, 1984)

Miyamoto Musashi, translated by Harris, Victor, *A Book of Five Rings* (Flamingo, London, 1989)

Patten, Chris, *East and West* (Macmillan, London, 1998)

Phillips, Peter (ed), 'Project Censored', in *Censored 2004* (Seven Stories Press, New York, 2003)

Probst, Christopher, 'Welcome to the Machine', *American Cinematographer*, April 1999

Rayns, Tony, 'The Well Dries Up', *Index on Censorship*, Vol. 26, No. 1, January/February 1997

Rechtshaffen, Michael, 'Crouching Tiger, Hidden Dragon', *Hollywood Reporter*, at http://www.hollywoodreporter.com/thr/reviews/review_display.jsp?vnu_content_id=890776; downloaded 12 August 2003

Richie, Donald, *The Films of Akira Kurosawa* (University of California Press, London, 1984)

Richie, Donald, *A Hundred Years of Japanese Film* (Kodansha, London, 2001)

Silver, Alain, *The Samurai Film* (Columbus, Kent, 1983)

Tatara, Paul, '"Crouching Tiger, Hidden Dragon" A Gripping, Poetic Tale', CNN.com, at http://www.cnn.com/2000/SHOWBIZ/Movies/12/11/review.crouching.tiger/; downloaded 12 August 2003

Taubin, Amy, 'Fear of Flying', *Village Voice*, at http://www.villagevoice.com/issues/0049/taubin.php; downloaded 12 August 2003

Turan, Kenneth, 'Crouching Tiger, Hidden Dragon', *Los Angeles Times*, at http://www.calendarlive.com/movies/reviews/cl-movie001214-6.story; downloaded 12 August 2003

Turnbull, Stephen, *Samurai Warlords: The Book of the Daimyo* (Guild, London, 1989)

Turnbull, Stephen, *Ninja: The True Story of Japan's Secret Warrior Cult* (Firebird, Dorset, 1991)

Yamamoto Tsunetomo, translated by Wilson, William, *Hagakure: The Book of the Samurai* (Kodansha, Tokyo, 2000)

Yao, Xinzhong, *An Introduction to Confucianism* (Cambridge University Press, Cambridge, 2000)

Select Filmography

Not sure where to start with martial arts cinema? The following titles are some of the author's personal favourites.

Japan

Seven Samurai (1954), director: Kurosawa Akira, cast: Mifune Toshiro, Shimura Takashi

Yojimbo (1961), director: Kurosawa Akira, cast: Mifune Toshiro, Nakadai Tatsuya

Harakiri (1962), director: Kobayashi Masaki, cast: Nakadai Tatsuya, Ishihama Akira

The Tale of Zatoichi (1962), director: Misume Kenji, cast: Katsu Shintaro, Shimada Ryuzo

Sanjuro (1962), director: Kurosawa Akira, cast: Mifune Toshiro, Nakadai Tatsuya

Samurai Assassin (1965), director: Okamoto Kihachi, cast: Mifune Toshiro, Aratama Michiyo

Samurai Rebellion (1967), director: Kobayashi Masaki, cast: Mifune Toshiro, Nakadai Tatsuya

Red Lion (1969), director: Okamoto Kihachi, cast: Mifune Toshiro, Iwashita Shima

Roningai (1990), director: Kuroki Kazuo, cast: Katsu Shintaro, Tanaka Kunie

Aiki (2002), director: Daisuke Tengan, cast: Haruhiko Kato, Ishibashi Ryo

The Twilight Samurai (2002), director: Yamada Yoji, cast: Sanada Hiroyuki, Miyazawa Rie

Hong Kong

The Fate of Lee Khan (1972), director: King Hu, cast: Roy Chiao, Mao Ying
Way of the Dragon (1972), director: Bruce Lee, cast: Bruce Lee, Nora Miao
The Chinatown Kid (1977), director: Chang Cheh, cast: Fu Sheng, Sun Chien
Drunken Master (1978), director: Yuen Wo Ping, cast: Jackie Chan, Yuen Siu Tien
Shaolin Challenges Ninja (1978), director: Lau Gar Leung, cast: Lau Gar Fei, Yuka Mizuno
Warriors Two (1978), director: Sammo Hung, cast: Casanova Wong, Sammo Hung
Prodigal Son (1981), director: Sammo Hung, cast: Yuen Biao, Lam Ching Ying
Project A (1983), director: Jackie Chan, cast: Jackie Chan, Sammo Hung
Pedicab Driver (1989), director: Sammo Hung, cast: Sammo Hung, Mok Sui Chung
The Legend of Fong Sai Yuk (1992), director: Corey Yuen, cast: Jet Li, Josephine Siao
Love on Delivery (1994), director: Lee Lik Chi, cast: Chow Sing Chi, Ng Man Tat
Shaolin Soccer (2001), director: Chow Sing Chi, cast: Chow Sing Chi, Ng Man Tat

Hollywood

Bad Day at Black Rock (1955), director: John Sturges, cast: Spencer Tracy, Ernest Borgnine
The Yakuza (1975), director Sydney Pollack, cast: Robert Mitchum, Takakura Ken
The Last Dragon (1985), director: Michael Schultz, cast: Taimak, Julius Carry
Big Trouble in Little China (1986), director: John Carpenter, cast: Kurt Russell, Dennis Dun
Ghost Dog – The Way of the Samurai (1999), director: Jim Jarmusch, cast: Forest Whitaker, John Tormey

Picture Credits

1, 2: Toho Company Ltd / Ronald Grant Archive
3: Shochiku Films Ltd / Ronald Grant Archive
4: Copyright Momentum Asia
5. 6, 7, 11, 15: Copyright Hong Kong Legends
8, 9, 10: Golden Harvest Company Ltd / Ronald Grant Archive
12: Copyright MIA
13: Hong Kong Legends / Ronald Grant Archive
14: Gold Double Productions Ltd, Lau Kun Wai Productions Ltd
16: MGM / Ronald Grant Archive
17, 22: Warner Bros / Ronald Grant Archive
18: © 1984 Columbia Pictures Industries, Inc
19: Golpix / Ronald Grant Archive
20: Ronald Grant Archive
21: Photo by Abbot Genser (c) 1999 Plywood Productions Inc
23: © 2000 Global Entertainment Productions GmbH & Co. Movie KG
24: © 2001 Revolution Studios Distribution Company, LLC

Index